DEREGULATING
FINANCIAL SERVICES

A Mid America Institute for Public Policy Research Book

DEREGULATING FINANCIAL SERVICES
Public Policy in Flux

Editors
GEORGE G. KAUFMAN
ROGER C. KORMENDI

WITHDRAWN

BALLINGER PUBLISHING COMPANY
Cambridge, Massachusetts
A Subsidiary of Harper & Row, Publishers, Inc.

International Standard Book Number: 0-88730-111-8

Library of Congress Catalog Card Number: 86-3355

Printed in the United States of America

Library of Congress Cataloging-in-Publication Data

Deregulating financial services.

   Bibliography: p.
   Includes index.
   1. Banks and banking—United States. 2. Banks and banking—United States—State supervision. I. Kaufman, George G. II. Kormendi, Roger C.
HG2491.R42   1986   332.1'0973   86-3355
ISBN 0-88730-111-8

CONTENTS

v

LIST OF FIGURES AND TABLES

PREFACE

This volume contains seven essays that analyze the responses required in public policy to deal adequately with the dramatic and far-reaching changes in the financial services industry that have occurred over recent years in order to provide for an efficient and safe financial system. Six of the essays are original papers presented at a symposium by the Mid America Institute for Public Policy Research on June 25 and 26, 1985, in Chicago, Illinois. The seventh paper, which has previously been published in much the same form in the *Journal of Bank Research*, presents a historical overview of government regulation of financial services. It served as the basis for the opening remarks at the symposium.

The symposium was designed to bring together leading officials of a broad range of financial institutions, federal and state regulators, and academic experts to jointly review, analyze, and discuss the implications of ongoing changes in the financial services industry and to construct an agenda for public policy responses. There were some seventy participants in the symposium, representing a wide range of the financial services industry by both activity and size. (A listing of the participants and the affiliations appears at the end of this volume.)

Summaries of the papers in this volume, which had been previously circulated among the participants, were presented at two general sessions, one on each day of the conference. The papers were prepared by leading academic experts and were designed to review the issues in a number of important areas of public policy concern, to identify and assess the options, and to make recommendations. Three papers were presented at each session, and each set was discussed by a panel of three respondents selected from industry, regulatory agencies, and academe. These sessions were each followed by concurrent discussion sessions of a smaller number of participants in which the analyses and options were discussed and recommendations developed by each group.

The final session of the symposium was a plenary session in which the recommendations of the break-out discussion groups were used as a basis for constructing both a final set of recommendations for public policy initiatives and an agenda for further research by the group as a whole. These recommendations were adopted by majority vote and are published at the end of the volume. Because of the wide range of interests represented, all participants were provided with a chance to review the recommendations after the symposium and to record their disagreement and/or dissent with any of them. The recommendations were distributed widely in order to serve as a basis for developing and assessing legislative and regulatory changes on a timely basis.

As noted, the first paper by Professor George Benston reviews the historical development of financial regulation in the United States through the enactment of the Depository Institutions Deregulation and Monetary Control Act (DIDMCA) of 1980 and the Depository Institutions (Garn-St Germain) Act of 1982. He argues that the reasons for the regulations varied according to the problems of the day. These included prevention of centralized power; concern over institution solvency; provision of financial services as a social goal; attempts to allocate credit socially, particularly to housing; and prevention of discrimination and unfair practices in the provision of these services. Benston concludes that most if not all of these reasons are no longer valid.

The next paper by Professors Benston and George Kaufman identifies and evaluates the sources of risk in financial intermediation, analyzes the causes and consequences of bank runs and failures, and reviews the importance of bank failures in U.S. history. They conclude that, although individual banks have become riskier, bank runs and failures are generally not more important or contagious than the failures of most other firms. Thus, individual bank instability is unlikely to destabilize the financial system or economy as a whole. Our fears of bank failures stem primarily from the financial holocaust of the 1930s, which was not representative of bank crises either before or after. Thus, as long as there is credible minimum federal deposit insurance, less public policy concern need be paid to bank safety.

Professor Allan Meltzer examines the effects regulatory agencies have had on bank efficiency. He argues that federal and state regulators have not always acted effectively to prevent bank crisis. Their inconsistent policies have generated uncertainty in the industry. They have also tended to confuse individual bank failures with the failure of the banking system. Moreover, they have increased individual bank risk by not pricing deposit insurance on the basis of risk and have not punished management and shareholders of larger banks that have failed in economic terms. The paper recommends that (1) banks record assets at market value and recognize losses when they occur; (2) the regulatory agencies establish guidelines for periods in which lender-of-last-resort assistance is provided to banks. and (3) deposit insurance be priced with respect to the riskiness of the bank.

Professor Edward Kane analyzes the implications of the current structure of federal deposit insurance on the performance of the financial services industry in greater detail. He argues that a large number of savings institutions had technically failed but remained in business with the implicit help of federal funds. This encouraged additional risk taking by other institutions, as well as the institutions in question, and has threatened viability of the insurance funds. The paper recommends (1) market-value accounting for banks; (2) increasing FDIC authority to close failed institutions; (3) scaling deposit insurance premiums to bank risk; (4) reducing the maximum deposit insurance coverage per account; (5) opening up deposit insurance to competition with private insurance supplementing federal insurance; and (6) limiting the ability of the FDIC and the Federal Reserve to bail out economically failed banks.

Professor Michael Mussa considers the implications of deregulation for competition and fairness among different segments of the financial services industry. He points out that when alternative suppliers compete on the same footing, without benefit of government support, competition promotes the survival and prosperity of the most efficient suppliers. On the other hand, the willingness and ability of depository institutions to accept artificially low rates of return on business activities outside the scope of their main function implies that these institutions have an unfair competitive advantage over other participants in these businesses. Further, the exploitation of this artificial and unfair advantage can reduce economic efficiency. Mussa concludes that all change should not be presumed for the better simply because it is consistent with the general policy of "deregulation" and with a belief in the benefits of "increased competition." He believes that there are good reasons that some activities of depository institutions should be regulated and that these institutions should not be allowed to compete on an unrestricted basis with suppliers of other types of financial services.

Professor Franklin Edwards examines the implications of deregulation on the concentration of financial activity. Two of the most frequently expressed concerns about increased concentration are that (1) it may result in greater economic power and (2) it could cause inefficient institutions to fail because of their size. Edwards argues that there is little evidence to support the first concern. An increase in size can be said to reduce the risk of failure through diversification as much as it can increase the risk. Deregulation of geographical barriers to branch banking is likely to increase concentration on the national and state levels but to lower it in local markets. Deregulating bank powers is likely to reduce concentration. He concludes that the likely net result of deregulation is increased concentration, but without increased risk or excessive political power.

Professor Robert Eisenbeis focuses on the relationship between an institution's risk exposure and expanding the powers of federally insured depository institutions. He reviews the reasons for restricting the powers of insured institutions and concludes that traditional concerns over excessive concentration, conflicts of interest, and safety remain valid. However, pursuit of these objectives has at times produced incentives that have resulted in inefficient operations and reduced competition. The current list of permissible powers to different financial institutions is difficult to rationalize. In addition, the failure to scale deposit insurance premiums to an institution's risk exposure has increased the risk exposure of the deposit insurance agencies. New powers should be evaluated primarily on the basis of their impact on the riskiness of the overall institution and thus on the insurance fund rather than on their own riskiness per se. This will vary, depending on the nature of the institution's other activities and on the ability of the insurance agency to monitor the risk. Eisenbeis prefers this criterion to the current general prohibitions of certain activities to different types of institutions.

The public policy recommendations adopted by the symposium participants after their two-day immersion in the pros and cons of the issues are well considered and reflect the consensus of an important cross-section of industry practitioners, regulators, and analysts. They should provide readers with an understanding of the interrelationship of the rapid and dramatic changes in the financial services and public policy and serve as a basis for reshaping public policy to improve the efficiency and safety of this important industry. In part, the symposium and its recommendations led to the recognition of a need for ongoing independent analyses of emerging problems and policy changes affecting the financial services industry from the viewpoint of their implications for the financial system as a whole and the public interest. As a result, the Shadow Financial Regulatory Committee was organized in early 1986. The Committee consists of some twelve respected experts on financial institutions and markets, including academics, practitioners, and former regulators. Six of the seven authors of the papers presented at the symposium are members of the Committee.

DEREGULATING
FINANCIAL SERVICES

1 FEDERAL REGULATION OF BANKING
Historical Overview

George J. Benston

Banking is and has been one of the most regulated of industries. In almost all countries and at all times since the establishment of banking, governments have imposed controls on the institutions, even when most other businesses were free to operate subject only to the statutes and other general rules of law. In the United States, the extent of regulation has ranged from the free entry banking period of the 1800s, when banks still were supervised and required to maintain specified reserves against the notes they issued, to the extensive controls imposed in the 1930s. The Depository Institutions Deregulation and Monetary Control Act of 1980 removed some regulatory restrictions (such as allowing thrift institutions to make consumer and business loans) while imposing others (such as requiring non-interest bearing reserves for all chartered institutions' demand and similar deposits). But as increased nominal interest rates raised the opportunity cost of holding money as deposits at the regulated, chartered financial institutions and as the cost of electronic and telephonic fund transfers declined, the development of products and services designed to avoid the regulations and competition by unregulated providers of financial services increased. It is imperative, therefore, to determine whether the present regulatory structure best serves the public interest and should be extended to all providers of financial services (the level playing field simile), whether regulations

Updated version of paper initially printed in *Journal of Bank Research* 13 (Winter 1983): 216–44. Reprinted with permission.

should be removed from all providers (perhaps a free-for-all would be a parallel simile), or whether some other restructuring and/or consolidation of the regulations and regulators would be desirable.

However, before changes in the existing order are recommended, the reasons for the past and present regulatory situation should be delineated and analyzed. In this regard, two considerations are likely to be important. First, there were reasons for regulating financial intermediaries more than almost any other industry; should some regulations be removed, the conditions that gave rise to them might re-occur, to the detriment of some people. It is best if the lessons of history are not relearned. Second, the present situation in the United States may make previously relevant regulations no longer applicable or useful. These vestigial regulations impose burdens on society without any compensating benefits. This chapter identifies the antecedents and contemporary relevance of the present set of regulations and regulatory agencies.

The analysis presented in the next section leads to the conclusion that most of the historical reasons for regulating financial institutions are no longer relevant (if they ever were) to our society. These reasons (which are discussed below) include taxation of banks as monopoly suppliers of money, the prevention of centralized power, bank solvency and the effects of failures on the economy, the provision of banking services as a social goal, support of housing and other attempts to allocate credit as social goals, and the prevention of invidious discrimination and unfair dealing against persons. What is needed, therefore, is abolition of most federal regulation. Indeed, with the exception of deposit insurance, the only currently meaningful reason for regulating financial institutions is to control the money supply and protect some suppliers of financial services from competition. Assuming that the last reason is not considered to be desirable and can be overcome politically, almost all restrictions on entry (including intra- and interstate branching and the offering of all financial products), prices and the restructuring of organizations should be removed. With the exception noted below, financial intermediaries should be treated the same as other corporations.[1]

Consequently, almost all of the *raison d'être* of the federal regulatory agencies would be obviated. In particular the Office of the Comptroller of the Currency (OCC), the Federal Home Loan Bank Board (FHLBB) and the National Credit Union Administration (NCUA) would serve simply as chartering agencies for depository institutions. Because mutuals are not owned by investors who put their resources at risk, the FHLBB and the NCUA would have to act as the ultimate authority that could remove incompetent or dishonest managers. Stockholder-owned institutions, though, would be regulated no differently than other corporations. Charters would be granted to depository institutions if they had deposit insurance provided by an insurer that was approved by the OCC, the FHLBB or the NCUA. The existing deposit insurance agencies — the FDIC, FSLIC, and FCUSIF — would be authorized to provide insurance to any depository institutions so that there would be some competition among insurors. (Therefore, it is important that they not be merged into a single agency as has been proposed). In addition, non-government insurers (such as major insurance companies) and banks could be recognized by the chartering agencies and could offer their services to the depository institutions. Because they bear the risk of failures, the insurers would impose whatever restrictions on the activities of the depository institutions that they felt useful, subject to the same sort of mutual agreement that insurance companies exercise with their other clients.

The Federal Reserve Board would cease to have any responsibilities for bank supervision. The payments facilities would be divested and set up as a separate corporation with shares held privately. Reserves probably would continue to be required of depository institutions, although reserves need not be required if the Federal Reserve can predict changes in the money supply as well. And the Fed would lend reserves and provide currency at market rates that were consistent with its mandate to conduct monetary policy.[2] In the further interest of equity and efficiency, the taxes imposed on depository institutions would be the same as those imposed on other corporations. This would require the Fed paying interest on the required reserves and the Congress removing tax subsidies.

In short, it is time that we recognized that financial institutions are simply businesses with only a few special features that require regulation. The following analysis provides the reasoning and evidence on which this conclusion and the recommendations are based.

BASIC REASONS FOR REGULATING BANKING

Taxation

The Historical Record. Perhaps the oldest reason for regulating banking was to enhance the ability of those who had political power, whether monarchs or legislatures, to raise revenues (tax). Before the advent of central banking taxation took two forms: Seigniorage from the production of money and loans at lower than risk-adjusted market rates.

Seigniorage is the difference between the accepted and the commodity value of money. When the government could maintain a monopoly over the money supply, it could require people to use the designated money at its token value by declaring it to be legal tender. Since money costs considerably less to produce than its accepted or token value, the producer (the government) benefits. Even when people could substitute among other forms of money, the convenience over commodities (such as gold) of money that was backed by the power of the government to punish forgers enabled governments to obtain seigniorage from the production of money. However, because governments often abused their power to produce legal tender by debasing the currency and printing paper money with apparent abandon, people tended to prefer bank notes produced by private banks. Hence, governments tended to regulate banks for two reasons. One was to restrain the banks' interference with the government's gains from seigniorage. The second was to permit banks to produce money but tax them by requiring them to lend money to the government at favorable rates and/or to give an ownership share to those who controlled the government—such as the monarch and his associates.

Government regulation therefore took the form of restricting people from the money creation aspects of banking by requiring governmentally granted charters. Needless to say, relatively few charters were granted, since competition among money suppliers would reduce the profits from money creation, profits that could be garnered by government directly, through seigniorage, or indirectly, via loans from and ownership shares in the chartered banks that would be subsidized by the monopoly profits earned with the aid of regulations that restricted their competition.

Loans at less than market rates (net of an allowance for risk) were a favored means by which monarchs and other governmental officials taxed banks. (More accurately, the tax was imposed on the users of bank money, who were prevented from benefiting from competition among banks.) Unfortunately, but predictably, the governments tended to use this form of taxation for revenue to finance extravagances and wars, which led them to enhance further the possibility of the banks achieving monopoly profits that could be taxed additionally (fattening the calf). Sometimes the governments overdid it; loans were defaulted and banks failed (killing the golden goose). Thus a cause of major banking failures was overtaxation by government.

Central banking grew out of the use of banks as a source of governmental revenue (Smith 1936). As the bank that served as a revenue source for the government was given more complete monopoly powers and served as the government's primary source of loans, it became an instrument of government—the central bank (such as the Bank of England). The existence of a central bank permitted the government to enhance its revenue from seigniorage since the notes of the bank tended to become the only legal tender (they were the only notes accepted in payment of taxes). Occasionally this led to extreme excesses, as in the case of the monopoly given to John Law in 1716 for his Banque Generale, which issued notes with such abandon that the bank failed within five years, bringing the economy of France down with it. But most often, the central bank used its monopoly powers effectively, which included restraining excess production of notes and using the power of government to prohibit or control the issue of notes and deposit services by competitors.

Probably because of their experiences with the near-monopoly powers of the Bank of England,[3] the U.S. founding fathers generally were against the establishment of a central bank, whether privately or governmentally controlled. For this reason, together with the preeminence of states' rights and the desire of existing banks to avoid the dominance of a strong national bank, banking was regulated by the states until 1863, with the exception of the First and Second Banks of the United States, whose twenty-year charters were not renewed when they expired. Prior to the National Currency Act of 1863 and National Banking Act 1864 (which established federal chartering), state chartered banks often were required to hold state bond issues as backing for their notes (Rockoff 1974: 141-67). National banks (the notes of which supplanted the state banks' notes when the National Banking Act of 1864 imposed a prohibitory tax on them) were required to keep U.S. obligations as collateral. While concern for the note holders was an important reason for this requirement, it also benefited the governments involved. State and federal reserve requirements on demand deposits similarly reflected the governments' interests.

The creation of the Federal Reserve in 1913 gave the United States its first central bank. By requiring member banks to hold reserves with the Federal Reserve or (since 1960) in vault cash, neither of which bears interest, the federal government imposed a tax on these banks and on their customers. When the reserve requirements were extended to all suppliers of third party transfers (checking accounts and equivalents) by the Depository Institutions Deregulation and Monetary Control Act of 1980, this tax was imposed generally (though still not evenly) (Benston 1978: ch. 3). Since the Federal Reserve remits 90 percent of earnings on its investments in U.S. government obligations to the U.S. Treasury, in effect the tax is collected by the Treasury.

The Present Situation. Though regulation of and limitations on bank charters were instituted as a means of maximizing the amount of tax (direct and indirect) that could be imposed on banks and users of bank money, this type of regulation is no longer meaningful in the United States. Neither state nor federally chartered banks are required to invest in state or federal obligations or lend to the governments at favorable rates. But by imposing reserve requirements on all providers of this party transfers, the Federal Reserve can and does impose a tax on users of bank money. However, the amount of this tax and the efficiency with which it is collected is reduced by regulations other than reserve requirements that might be imposed on financial institutions. Limitations on charters or any other restrictions that impose costs on users of bank money reduce the value of this asset to users and therefore reduce the amount of tax that can be imposed. Therefore, assuming that a tax on users of bank money is desirable (an assumption that is questioned below), banking regulations other than reserve requirements on all money providers should be repealed.

Prevention of Centralized Power

The Historical Record. As noted above, the United States has a history of concern for and aversion toward centralized power. This concern was reflected in part by the refusal of Congress to renew the charter of the First Bank of the United States in 1811 and President Jackson's veto of the charter of the Second Bank of the United States in 1836. One argument against these banks was that they were too powerful (although many scholars believe that the discipline imposed by the banks on their state-chartered rivals was a more important reason for their demise.)[4]

The prohibitions against intrastate branch banking enacted by several of the states also may be considered to be a reflection of a basic bias against bigness. But the record does not support this as a general interpretation of branch banking legislation. While the branching activities of the Second Bank of the United States, in particular, were objected to by the state bankers with whom the Bank competed, by the end of the nineteenth century twenty states permitted branch banking. However, though the number of branches had increased somewhat from 1834 to 1900 (from 100 to 119), the increase in the number of banks over this period was so great (from 406 to 12,423) that the percentage of branches to banks declined from 24.5 percent to 0.0 (Carson and Cootner 1963: 65). As the automobile increased mobility in the 1920s, branching increased steadily to 785 branches operated by 397 banks in 1915 to 3,005 branches operated by 724 banks in 1934 (Carson and Cootner 1963: 73).

The increasing technological desirability of branching gave rise to two developments. One was the adoption of the McFadden-Pepper Act of 1927, which conceded to national banks limited power to branch in their home cities, subject to state legislation. (The home city restriction was removed in 1934.) The second was increased attempts by local bankers to have laws enacted that would restrain competition from larger banks. This often successful attempt linked branching with the underlying popular fear of centralized power. In this regard, an early observation by H. Parker Willis, the most influential U.S. banking academic of his time (or perhaps any time) is instructive and still pertinent. He states (Willis 1902: 23–24) that the owners of small banks assert that branching

> would result in building up a money power which would crush the small banks out of existence. A more absurd reversal of the actual facts in the case could scarcely be imagined. What the establishment of branches would actually do would be to destroy the local money power which now practically stifles many forms of legitimate industry by a pressure of excessive interest rates, and by other even less justifiable means.

Perhaps because the validity of Parker's remarks was recognized or possibly because the bankers in some states saw the advantages of branching, only a third of the states in the later 1920s prohibited banks from operating branches, a third permitted limited branching, and a third allowed statewide branching. Presently, only twelve states prohibit branching, fifteen allow limited branching, and twenty-three allow statewide branching. Thus, a prohibition against branching neither was nor is the rule in the United States, and it is difficult to view the restrictions placed on this type of banking organization as a manifestation of a general fear of centralized power. Though the fact that interstate branching and nationwide banking has been prohibited argues in favor of the hypothesis that fear of large banks is a continuing feature of U.S. banking regulation, an alternative, or perhaps supplementary, explanation is that the restrictions have been based more on the local bankers' desire to protect themselves from competition. This is discussed below.

It also is important to distinguish the particular aspects of banking toward which the concern about centralized power was directed. Principally, centralization of the power to grant loans and make investments was the object of the founding fathers' fear. The centralization of note issuance also was important when bank notes were the most important circulating medium. Once demand deposit banking developed, there appeared to be relatively little concern about the centralization of this banking product. Nor was the centralized offering of collateral banking services ever considered much of an issue.

The Present Situation.   Fear of centralized note issue is meaningful but irrelevant for bank regulation; the Federal Reserve now controls or can control the money supply.[5]

Fear of the provision of centralized depository services has been stated as an important issue by bankers who oppose intra- and interstate branching. They claim that without these restrictions large branch banks would come to dominate the country and local communities. In large measure, their concern is based on the assumption that there are considerable economies of scale in banking operations, such that banking is akin to a natural monopoly. However, empirical studies have not found this to be the situation. Earlier studies (using data from the 1960s) found some economies of scale with respect to operating costs (with output defined as the number of accounts processed and average dollar size of accounts), but higher costs of branching. These effects were offsetting for larger branch banks (see Benston 1972; Benston, Hanweck, and Humphrey 1982a). A recent study that uses nationwide data for 1975 through 1978 found diseconomies of scale and very similar average costs for branch and unit banks when all variables were held constant (including the average size of accounts), except the numbers of accounts and branches. Most important for the present question, a small unit bank had slightly lower operating costs than a similar branch of a branch bank, all other things held constant (Benston, 1982b). Therefore, there is no reason to believe that smaller unit banks and small banks generally have a cost-disadvantage, such that they could not compete with large banks. Consistent with this conclusion is the experience in New York state when statewide branching was permitted and several New York City banks opened offices in out-of-city locations. They were unable to take much business away from the existing banks.

Because banking does not appear to be subject to economies of scale, the removal of restrictions on entry can only serve to decrease the centralization of banking services, particularly in local communities that are served by few banks.[6]

Loans to large and to many middle-sized borrowers, at the present time, are made nationwide, indeed worldwide, by banks. Loans and other sources of capital, such as direct and publicly placed bonds and equity shares, also are available from a very large number of non-banking services. Thus most business borrowers can look to commercial banks in all states and in other countries, to insurance companies, to pension funds, to venture capital companies, and to underwriters for short- and long-term capital. Trade credit is another source of funds for businesses. Government agencies also supply loans. Consumers can borrow from and through commercial banks, thrift institutions, mortgage bankers, consumer finance companies, sales finance companies, life insurance companies and retailers, among others.

Since enactment of the "Garn-St Germain Depository Institutions Act of 1982," which removed most of the restrictions in thrift institutions' lending to business, the principal constraint on peoples' opportunities for obtaining financing from banks is the Glass-Steagall Act provisions. These prohibit commercial banks from underwriting and dealing in corporate bonds and equity securities and from investing in equities. Similarly, underwriters are forbidden from offering depository services. This prohibition presently is supported by reference to fears of banks controlling loan and equity sources of funds. But were banks allowed to offer customers funds packaged as securities as well as loans, this would hardly result in a concentration of power, as long as the customers have the alternative of obtaining funds and services from insurance companies, pension funds, investment companies, underwriters, and others. Another frequently expressed fear concerns the possibility of banks abusing their fiduciary responsibilities. In particular, they might use information gathered in the course of lending to trade in a corporation's equities. Or they might attempt to "bail out" of a bad loan by selling equities to the public, the proceeds of which would be used to repay the bank. If these fears were valid, though, they apply equally to underwriters, since they hold, buy, and sell the corporate obligations. It also is important to note that though these fears presently are expressed, they were not given as arguments for the Glass-Steagall Act. Rather, Senator Glass (who, prior to the bank failures that triggered the Act, had attempted to legislate the separation of investment from commercial banking) believed as a matter of banking theory that the loans and investments of depository institutions should be limited to self-liquidating obligations (the real-bills doctrine.)

Restrictions on interstate banking and branching also limit, somewhat, the numbers of potential sources for loans for people living in less populated states and communities and in communities that straddle state borders. At the least, these restrictions tend to raise the price of loans to borrowers. Again, considering the multitude of sources for loans that are now available, there seems no reason to believe that any fear of centralized power can justify continuing these restrictions.

Avoidance of Competition

The Historical Record.   Bankers are not unique in wanting to foreclose or limit competitors. As is discussed above, such limitations served the interests of monarchs and other governmental authorities and were the source of such regulations as restrictive chartering. In the United States, where, compared to Europe, many more banks were chartered, such restrictions on competition also took (and still take) the form of limiting or prohibiting branching. While these prohibitions often were (and still are) justified as a means of limiting centralized power, the reasoning and evidence given above is contrary to this rationale.

Limitations on the right of nonbanks to offer banking services also were used to restrain competition. Until recently, thrift associations were prohibited from offering checking accounts to their customers.

In most states they also were prohibited from offering consumer loans other than those related to real estate and a few types of specialty loans (such as education loans.) Nor could they offer checking accounts and loans to businesses. The prohibition against dealings with business were justified on the grounds of potential self-dealing by the officers of mutual associations and their charge to look to the needs of individual consumers. But these restrictions were maintained long after the thrift associations had changed from small, charitable institutions to large-scale lenders to real estate-related enterprises as well as individuals.

Since banking was a regulated industry, the power of government also was used by the banks' competitors to constrain competition by banks (such as the Glass-Steagall Act, which prohibits banks from offering securities underwriting services). Direct investments in companies not considered by the regulations to offer bank-like (congeneric) services also were prohibited. The argument for these constraints were couched in terms of concern for the safety and soundness of the banks or fear of centralized power by the banks. But the Glass-Steagall Act prohibitions were not based on empirical findings demonstrating that the provision of securities services by banks contributed to failures or to cheating of customers.[7] Rather, the evidence supports the belief that the investment bankers and underwriters were concerned about severe competition from banks and bank affiliates and sought (successfully in 1933) to eliminate these competitors.[8] Similarly, such businesses as travel agencies and computer service companies have sought to keep banks from providing services on the grounds that this would exceed the banks' legally granted powers. Thus regulation has worked both ways with respect to banks, though in either instance the cost was borne by consumers.

The Present Situation. The desire and possibly the power of business people to restrain their competition is still with us. Commercial bankers do not want to face competition for business loans and deposits from thrift associations. Bankers who run small unit banks fear having to compete with the branch managers of large banks. Bankers in some states do not want to compete with bankers in neighboring or any other states. Brokers want to offer checking accounts but do not want bankers to offer brokerage services. And so forth.

But the ability of people in and at the periphery of the financial services industry to prevent others from competing for their customers is increasingly being eroded by technological change fueled by the opportunity cost of high nominal interest rates and the advantages of avoiding restrictive regulations. Three (of many) specific examples illustrate this situation:

1. The transfer of funds by check first was offered by thrift institutions by means of negotiable orders of withdrawal and by credit unions with share drafts. Both forms of transfers look like checks, can be used as checks, but are legally not called checks. Better yet (for the consumer), interest is paid at the savings rate, which, while constrained by Regulation Q, is still greater than the rate of zero permitted on regular demand deposits.

2. Stockbrokers offer their customers de facto checking accounts on which interest is paid at market rates. Furthermore, they are not constrained by geographic limitations but can operate nationwide. And they simultaneously can offer clients a wide range of investment alternatives, including direct ownership of stocks and bonds and participation in funds.

3. Offices that solicit and service business and consumer loans are operated by major banks directly and as holding company affiliates in major cities throughout the country. Unregulated mortgage bankers and sales finance companies offer consumer loans throughout the country.

Thus the present set of regulations serve bankers who want to constrain competition primarily with respect to services provided on the local level, particularly deposit services where the depositor wants personally to deposit and withdraw funds. On the other hand, the regulations prevent bankers from organizing their operations in whatever way is most efficient for a given market and set of products and also prohibit them from directly offering a full range of services to their customers.

Bank Solvency and the Effects of Failures
the Economy

The Historical Record.   Bank failures were not always considered to be horrendous occurrences to be avoided at all costs. All enterprises that involve risk may be sufficiently unsuccessful, poorly managed, fraudulently run, or the victims of bad luck. Banks are no exception;

the record shows that banks regularly failed throughout history. Many of the more spectacular bank failures were due to overly rapacious taxation by monarchs and other government officials. In these cases, regulation served to increase the ability of the rulers to overuse their power to the detriment of the banks' other customers, owners, employees and often of the state. While it is true that many banks failed because their operators acted incompetently or fraudulently, it appears that failures were more often the consequence of governmental interference or incompetence.

The experience of the United States, which (together with Scotland) was one of the few countries that permitted competitive banking, is particularly instructive.[9] Prior to 1837 bank charters had to be obtained by special acts of the state legislatures. In part to avoid the corruption that tended to accompany the granting of these quasi-monopolies, and in part because of the public demand for more banking facilities and a sentiment toward unrestricted enterprise (and possibly because the rents obtainable from issuing bank charts were largely exhausted), Michigan in 1837 and New York and Georgia in 1838 enacted free bank chartering laws. These laws permitted anyone to open a bank who provided a minimum amount of capital and deposited with a state agent a specified amount of bonds that could be sold to repay the holders of bank notes (which served as hand-to-hand currency) should the bank fail to redeem the notes as promised. By 1860, eighteen of the thirty-two states had passed such laws (Michigan twice) (Rockoff 1974).

Because some of the state laws were drawn so as to permit the bankers to issue notes with face value in excess of the market values of the bonds, and because the public was led to believe that the bonds provided adequate security for the notes, "wildcat" banking was profitable in some of the states. Wildcat banking occurs when bankers issue many more notes than they can redeem and, if the notes stay in circulation long enough (the term *wildcat banking* refers to establishing redemption offices in areas populated primarily by wildcats), the issuers can profit even if they later become bankrupt. In these states, there were many bank failures. Michigan, in particular, suffered such a rash of failures (the typical life span of a free bank was no more than six months) that the legislature suspended the law after about a year, in April 1838. The reason for this bad experience was that the notes issued by the Michigan banks did not have to be redeemed in specie and could be backed by mortgages.

Consequently, Rockoff explains (1974: 146), people would "create a mortgage on a worthless piece of property, have it certified as being valuable by some friends, and then transfer it to a wildcat bank in exchange for a mass of bank notes. . . . Other [currency issues] were simply frauds which operated in violation of the free banking laws."

Nevertheless, the losses suffered by the public as a consequence of holding worthless or depreciated bank notes were not great. Including the $1 million lost by holders of Michigan bank notes and $394,700 lost in the first years of New York free banking (after which losses were negligible), estimated losses in the eighteen states through 1860 totaled only $1,852,900, or less than 2 percent of the money stock (Rockoff 1974: 150–51). Indeed, despite its bad experience, Michigan reinstated free banking in 1857. On the other side of the ledger, free banking resulted in increased banking services and lower profits to banks (and, hence, lower costs to consumers). Furthermore, private regulatory arrangements, such as the Suffolk system in Boston and the New York Clearing House, virtually eliminated the member banks' failures to redeem their notes for specie.

The national banking system, created in 1863, represented a continuation of free banking, since entrepreneurs were able to obtain bank charters without having to get special bills passed by state legislatures. However, they did have to put up more capital than was generally required for state charters, maintain specified reserves against their deposits, and could issue bank notes only in amounts that did not exceed the lesser of 90 percent of the market value or 100 percent of the par value of registered U.S. bonds, which had to be deposited with the U.S. Treasurer. Even then there were many bank failures for reasons that included actions by the U.S. Treasury that reduced the amount of bonds available for backing note issues, and a prohibition of branch banking that was not relaxed somewhat until 1927.

Even after 1927 (indeed, to this day) banks are restricted from branching within many states and across state lines by state-enacted laws. These laws restrain banks from efficiently diversifying their operations geographically. Hence, they are more liable to local and area economic failures and depressions. This is borne out by the data, which show that from 1921 through 1931, when 8,916 banks were suspended, only seven were banks with more than ten branches; of these, only three operated branches outside the city of the head office (Benston 1973: table 2). It should be noted, however, that permission to branch intrastate is unlikely to have benefited most of the banks that failed. As is described further below, the largest group of failures was among small banks in agricultural states. Had interstate branching been permitted, these banks could have diversified sufficiently, as did the Canadian banks, where nationwide banking was permitted and only one bank (in 1923) failed.

The data on bank suspensions since about the turn of the century might, by contemporary standards, seem to describe a total banking collapse. Between 1890 and 1899, 1,084 banks were suspended, 1,789 were suspended between 1900 and 1920, and 5,712 between 1921 and 1929 (Benston 1973: table 2). Expressed as annual percentages of active banks, the suspensions in each of the periods are 1.50 percent, .34 percent, and 2.30 percent. As annual percentages of the deposits of active banks the deposits of the suspended banks are .10 percent for the 1900–20 period and .42 percent for the 1921–29 period. And in the period of the largest number of suspensions, 1921–29, the average annual losses borne by depositors as a percentage of deposits are only .15 percent. Thus, in the decade before the debacle of the Great Depression, the losses to depositors were not very great. Perhaps this is the reason that, despite the large number of suspensions, there were no successful moves to "reform" the system. Nor did the bank suspensions adversely affect the economy in general. In fact the overall growth of the economy was particularly great in the 1920s, the period of the greatest number of suspensions. To the contrary, the principal cause of the suspensions appears to have been adverse local economic conditions, particularly those in the agricultural regions of the western grain states (where 47 percent of the suspensions during 1921–29 occurred) and of the southeastern and southwestern states (with 18 percent and 11 percent of the suspensions).

The Great Depression saw 9,096 bank suspensions between 1930 and 1933. These are 11.29 percent per year of the active banks; they held 4.14 percent of the deposits. Between 1930 and 1933 the average annual losses borne by depositors as a percentage of deposits averaged .81 percent, 5.4 times the loss rate of .15 percent experienced in the 1920s. While the great number of bank failures undoubtedly affected the economy negatively, most scholars agree that the banks were primarily the victims rather than the cause of the Great Depression.[10]

However, it should be noted that bank runs exacerbated by government actions and inaction, played an important role in the Great Depression and in previous financial collapses. "Black Thursday" 1873 saw the failure of Jay Cooke's banking house and the first closing of the New York Stock Exchange. In 1874 the Treasury reduced the money supply by retiring greenbacks. These events were followed by six years of depression. The failure in 1884 of former President Grant's firm, Grant & Ward, and of the Marine National Bank sparked runs and the consequent failure of numerous banks and brokerage houses. The panic situation, which was confined to New York banks, also were due to an outflow of gold resulting from the sale of foreign owned securities. The Panic of 1893 was touched off by the 1890 failure of the London banking firm of Baring Brothers, which specialized in financing U.S. enterprises. Baring's European creditors demanded that Americans pay their debts in gold. As a consequence, the base money supply was depleted, a multiple contraction resulted, and 1891 saw a mini-panic. In 1892, fears that the federal government would abandon the gold standard resulted in gold hoarding, which further exacerbated the situation. During the following 1893 panic over 600 banks and thirteen of every 1,000 businesses failed in perhaps the second-deepest depression (after the depression of 1837) in the nation's history before 1930. The New York Clearing House suspended convertibility to specie, which ended the run. The situation also was helped by J.P. Morgan's negotiation of a sale in Europe of a $100 million U.S. bond issue. Panic struck again in 1907 when New York City and several corporations were unable to sell high-yielding bond issues. The Knickerbocker Trust Company failed (largely as a consequence of speculation with depositors' funds), and several major banks experienced severe runs. Again, the panic situation was set up by an outflow of gold (basic money) when the Bank of England raised its discount rate in retaliation for the U.S. Treasury having subsidized gold imports in the prior year.

The creation of the Federal Reserve in 1913 was supposed to rid the country of these recurring collapses. As the lender of last resort, with great resources and the power of the printing press, it should have been able to better the New York Clearing House's and J.P. Morgan's record. But when the Bank of the United States collapsed in 1930, runs were made on other banks. And the Fed did not prevent the collapse of a third of the banks during the next several years. Though the losses to depositors and others as a consequence of the panics that preceded the Federal Reserve were considerable, the costs absorbed by the public after the creation of the central bank appear to be greater. The sharp and relatively short depressions of 1837, 1873, 1893, and 1907 should be compared with the Great Depression of the 1930s. The recession of 1920–21 should be contrasted with the sharper recession of 1937–38 (when the Fed doubled the required reserves ratios), and the relatively small post-World War II recessions, and the present recession. And the cost of losses in purchasing power absorbed by depositors because of the non-wartime inflations of 1916–17 and the 1970s to the present should be compared to the losses depositors took because of bank failures at all times, including the 1930s. The record may not give one faith in regulation by a central bank as a means of protecting depositors and maintaining the solvency of the banking system and the economic well-being of the nation.

The creation of the Federal Deposit Insurance Corporation in 1933 was a salutatory innovation. Since most depositors no longer need fear that their funds will be lost should a bank fail, runs have largely become a relic of the past. The word "largely" is used because uninsured depositors (those with over $100,000 in an account) have reason to fear loss of their funds, particularly if the FDIC closes the bank rather than arranges for its assumption by another bank. Furthermore, the event of a bank failure gives large depositors reason to question the safety of their funds in other banks where the assets held and operating procedures appear to be similar to those of the failed bank. For example, when the Penn Square and Abilene National banks failed in 1982, other banks faced the problem of convincing depositors that their funds were safe. However, the snowballing effect of pre-FDIC runs did not occur. Nor did banks that were unconnected to the failed banks experience difficulties.[11] Nevertheless, the banking authorities panicked in 1984 when Continental Illinois appeared close to collapse. The FDIC guaranteed all the bank's and its holding company's liabilities, and then, in effect, federalized it.

The question to be considered, then, is whether bank failures or even the possibility of limited bank runs are presently a matter for concern more than the failure of any non-regulated enterprise.

The Present Situation. With the possibility of a bank failure causing runs on other banks largely a concern of the past, and with protection of bank note holders no longer meaningful since the currency is provided and guaranteed by the Federal Reserve, what reasons can be adduced for governmental concern about the solvency of banks? This question can be answered by considering the costs to the principal persons who would be affected by a bank failure: owners, employees, borrowers, depositors, and users of other banking services.

The owners (stock and bondholders) clearly are hurt by failures. But their position is no different than that of the owners of other enterprises. In fact, because banks use little if any specialized assets, the owners tend to lose less than had they owned the shares of most other types of businesses. Mutual banking organizations—mutual savings banks, savings and loan associations, and credit unions—are an important exception. The mutual form was adopted for these institutions because they began as charitable or fraternal, nonprofit organizations. Most of them are constrained by competition in the market place to operate as efficiently as do stockholder-owned institutions. But unlike the situation for stockholder-owned enterprises, monitoring by stockholders and the securities market is not present. Consequently, should a mutual institution be operated inefficiently or fraudulently, there is a need for a supervisory government agency to step in to protect the equity in the assets that, in effect, belong to the community.

Employees of banks also would be adversely affected by the failure of their employers. Because so many banks operate similarly, however, bank employees have skills that are readily transferable, unlike the employees of most other enterprises. In addition, a failed bank is likely to be absorbed into another bank rather than dissolved. Hence bank employees are less in need of governmental concern than are other workers.

Borrowers would lose the value of their contacts with the officers of a failed bank and the officers' knowledge of them. But if the failed bank is taken over by another organization, the cost is likely to be small. Depositors whose accounts are fully insured suffer, at most, a short delay and some inconvenience until their accounts are paid off or transferred to another bank. Uninsured depositors might lose. But since they are holders of large accounts (currently over $100,000), it seems likely that they are capable of assessing the risks and obtaining sufficient compensation, *ex ante*, for the risks. In any event, the historical record suggests that the expected losses are relatively small. Nor are the users of other bank services likely to be seriously inconvenienced, since if entry were not restrained by regulation, there are likely to be many competing sources of services available.

This leaves only the owners and others associated with banks that might experience runs because an apparently similar bank failed. To the extent that these banks are misperceived as offering greater risks to uninsured depositors, they will bear unfairly imposed costs. But the possibility of runs also gives banks a salutary incentive to conduct their affairs such as to engender confidence among their large depositors. The complete removal of this concern by depositors and of the banks about depositors' fears is likely to lead to greater than optimal risk-taking by banks. In the following section, some changes in the present institutional arrangements are suggested that should lead to a better balance between these conflicting concerns.

To summarize, in today's environment with FDIC insurance, the effect of a failure of a bank on employees and customers (and hence on communities) and even on owners is likely to be less than for most other types of enterprises. With bank runs virtually not a problem, the possibility of failure is no longer a valid reason to subject banks to special regulations other than deposit insurance requirements. (The interests of the deposit insurance agency and of the banks with respect to deposit insurance are considered next.) Indeed, there is reason to believe that many of the regulations imposed on banking increase the possibility of failure. In particular, regulations restricting branching reduce the banks' ability to diversify their deposits geographically. Restrictions on the types and maturities of the products that they can offer their customers similarly restrict their ability to diversify their portfolios. (Witness the current situation of thrift institutions because of past regulations.) Hence, they are more vulnerable to unexpected changes in local economies, the fortunes of specific industries (such as housing), and interest rates. The regulations also reduce the alternatives available to customers should a bank fail. Therefore, if concern for bank failures is an important issue, these restrictive regulations should be removed. The only supervising function that might be justified from a concern with failures is the ultimate supervision of mutual institutions.

Deposit Insurance

The Historical Record.   Federal deposit insurance, established 1933, came about as a consequence of the very large number of bank failures of the early 1930s. These were primarily the consequence of the joint effect of a major sustained decline in the money supply and the fractionalized U.S. banking system, where interstate branching was not allowed and many states prohibited or restricted branching.[12] Consequently, the portfolios of a large number of banks were not diversified geographically or across many types of businesses. Hence, they were inordinately subject to the effects of local economic collapses and to a rapid decline in the money supply. The banks in other countries did not suffer similar failures because they were able to meet deposit drains with funds drawn from other areas. While the U.S. banks had established relationships with other banks from whom, presumably, they could borrow funds, these express or implied contracts apparently did not hold up in the generally adverse conditions of the early 1930s.[13]

Following the collapse between 1930 and 1933 of 9,096 commercial banks (36.4 percent of those operating in 1929), 526 savings and loan associations (4.4 percent of the total in 1930), and 10 mutual savings banks (1.7 percent of the number in 1930), some reform was politically, if not economically, necessary. The smaller unit banks opposed branch banking and, considering that in 1930–31 93 percent of the suspended banks had total loans and investments of under $2,000,000 (70 percent were under $500,000), they reasonably feared both gradually lost deposits and runs as depositors sought the safety of larger banks. The large banks wanted to eliminate the payment of interest on demand deposits, since they had been unable to sustain repeated agreements to limit competition among themselves for the deposits of correspondent banks and large nonbank depositors (Golembe 1975). The apparently politically acceptable compromise was a liberalization of the branch-limiting McFadden Act to permit national banks to branch to the extent that state banks could branch (but not permission to branch regardless of state law either within states or nationally), the legal prohibition of interest payments on demand deposits, and the establishment of the Federal Deposit Insurance Corporation. Although the FDIC insured individual deposit accounts only to a maximum of $2,500 (raised the next year to $5,000), assessments were imposed on a bank's total deposits. Thus the larger banks, that held largely uninsured deposit accounts, subsidized the small banks. But as Carter Golembe estimated (1975: 7), this cost was almost exactly offset by their savings of interest payments on demand deposits.

Federal deposit insurance not only has benefited smaller and particularly unit banks, it has made bank runs no longer a serious problem. Banks are unlike all other enterprises in being subject to the externality of runs. For example, if someone is a bondholder of General Motors Corp. and believes that the company has or is about to absorb large losses, the best that person can do is sell the bond to someone else before the buyer learns of the bad news. The bondholder cannot successfully get General Motors to repay the bond until it is legally due. But if someone is a demand depositor in a bank and believes that the bank is in financial difficulties, funds can be removed by the person simply by writing a check or personally making a withdrawal. Since a rapid withdrawal of funds by depositors may force the bank to sell assets at distress prices or borrow at high rates, this may result in losses that exceed the stockholders' investment, losses that will have to be absorbed by the remaining depositors. Therefore, even if the bank is paying depositors interest that compensates them for the risk they take, the depositors are well advised to remove their funds if the probability of a failure times the deposit balance exceeds the cost of making another banking arrangement plus any interest that might be foregone if it were credited on a delayed basis. With deposit insurance, those depositors whose balances do not exceed the insured amount need not fear a bank failure. While depositors with uninsured balances face potential losses should the bank fail, they need not fear a panic by the presumably uninformed holders of smaller accounts. Furthermore, depositors' experience with the FDIC gives them reason to believe that the deposit liabilities of most banks (especially very large ones) will be assumed by other banks without loss to the depositors. Hence, while they are not completely shielded from loss, the risk is very small and the incentive for panic withdrawals is concomitantly small.

But because federal deposit insurance saves insured depositors (and, to a large extent, uninsured depositors, as well) the cost of learning about the operation of banks, it also serves to free the banks from the discipline of those depositors' concerns. In this situation, the banker has an incentive to put the depositors' funds into risky assets. Should the events turn out well, the banks' stockholders reap the benefits. Should events turn out badly, the FDIC pays off the depositors. While the stockholders also are likely to lose their investments, in the absence of a sufficient risk premium or other costs imposed by the FDIC, the expected gains from risk-taking exceed the expected losses.[14]

Previous (prior to the FDIC) U.S. history bears out this expectation and also provides lessons that should be useful today. Prior to the National Banking Act of 1863, deposit guarantee systems were established in New York (1828), Vermont (1831), Indiana (1834), Ohio (1845), and Iowa (1858) (Benston 1973: 50–52). The New York and Vermont systems were state run and the others were based on mutual agreements among the participating banks. Their systems operated successfully, largely because they included the authority of the plan officials to monitor operations of the participating banks and control excessive risk-taking.[15] A second wave of deposit guarantee plans for state banks occurred after 1908. With one exception (Mississippi), the plans did not include effective supervision and they failed. These included the compulsory plans of Oklahoma (1908), Nebraska (1909), and South Dakota (1916) and the voluntary plans of Kansas (1909), Texas (1910), and Washington (1917). Since depositors were told that their money was safe, there was a great incentive for unscrupulous operators to take excessive risks. Indeed, the record shows greater failure rates of guaranteed banks than among similar non-guaranteed banks operating in the same areas. The Mississippi plan (1915), which included supervision and bank examinations, continued until 1930.

Thus a cost of deposit guarantee represents effective supervision by the insurance company or other authorities and/or the charging of risk-adjusted rates. While fees that reflect the risk could be charged by the FDIC, Federal Savings and Loan Insurance Corporation (FSLIC), and National Credit Union Share Insurance Fund (NCUSIF), they have opted instead to impose costs in the form of on-site examinations on the insured institutions. When the operations of the institutions are considered to be unsafe, the institutions are subjected to more frequent and more extensive examinations. The cost of these examinations include per diem fees (levied by some agencies) and the cost of disruption. Restrictions on the institution's right to expand and required infusions of capital also are imposed. More severe penalties include cease and desist orders, the removal of the institution's officers, and its closing or merger with another institution. The extent to which these costs exceed the benefits from deposit guarantees and alternatives to the present system are considered next.

The Present Situation.   The necessity for mandatory deposit insurance could be obviated if the Federal Reserve could be counted on to provide the reserves required to offset runs and if the removal of regulations made it possible for banks to offer depositors an acceptable mix of interest payments, diversified portfolios, and private insurance. But considering the almost universal expectation by depositors with smaller account balances that they need not acquire information about the riskiness and management of bank assets, continuation of deposit insurance appears to be unavoidable. Also, considering the cost to these borrowers of assessing risks, an insurance system would seem to be cost effective.

The present system though suffers from three important defects. One is that the procedure of charging depository institutions a flat fee against their total deposit liabilities gives the institutions an incentive to hold riskier assets and have less equity. At the same time, the insurance agencies (FDIC, FSLIC, and NCUSIF) have a complementary incentive to overregulate the institutions, since the agencies lose should a failure occur but do not garner the gains from a risk taken. There is no reason to believe that the outcome is reasonably close to optimal, particularly with the respect to the efficient allocation of capital. Second, bank runs still can be a problem, since uninsured depositors have a considerable incentive to remove their funds if they believe a bank will fail and not be assumed. Probably because of this expectation, very large banks (which hold relatively large amounts of uninsured deposits) have been loaned large sums of money by the Federal Reserve to keep them from failing and, when they failed, assumptions rather than payments were arranged by the FDIC. Consequently, depositors in such banks are de facto, 100 percent insured, and they no longer serve as monitors of the banks' activities. Collaterally, banks that are thought to be subjected to the payout procedure are placed at a competitive disadvantage. Third, the methods of examination and supervision employed by the agencies are unlikely to be efficient, since each is in a monopoly position with respect to its institutions—for example, national banks cannot elect to be examined by the FDIC rather than by the Comptroller of the Currency. Although the agencies have made some attempts to improve their supervisory methods in recent years, Flannery and Guttentag (1980: II, 218) (among others) find the techniques used to "fall well short of the state of art. As long as the agencies have a clientele that has no alternatives, they need not be too concerned with the costs of inefficient examinations and over-supervision.

The flat fee compared to variable-risk-fee defect could be corrected by requiring the insurance agencies to charge risk-related fees. One might ask, though, why they have failed to adopt this procedure, even though it has been suggested by most writers on the subject and is used by most private companies. The answers might be that the assessment of banking risk is too difficult, would engage the agencies in too great an involvement in banking activities (since risk-related fees have the effect of directing a banks' allocation of resources), or that there presently is no incentive for the agencies to change established procedures. While there is some validity in each explanation, I prefer the last, which implies that unless the present legal arrangements are altered, the flat-fee system will remain.

The remaining possibility of bank runs could be eliminated and the monitoring by depositors enhanced by the following change. All deposits transferable on demand (including savings deposits for which the thirty-day waiting period is almost never invoked) would be completely insured. But all time deposits over, say, $10,000, would not be insured at all unless a bank wished to purchase the insurance. Under this regime, runs could not occur because the time deposits could not be withdrawn until maturity. But if a bank was thought to be operated in a manner that might result in a failure, the expectation would be reflected in the interest rates it would have to offer on its time deposits and certificates.

Finally, the defects of inefficient examination and supervision and the charging of inappropriate insurance fees can be cured, or at least reduced, by introducing competition among insurers for the business of financial institutions. Competition can be introduced first by permitting any depository institution to be insured by any of the three federal agencies. The agencies would be permitted to levy the types (such as variable rates) and levels of charges and monitoring mechanisms (such as examinations) that they felt desirable, and the institutions could switch among the agencies much as any person can choose insurance companies. Then, to introduce even more competition into the market for deposit insurance, depository institutions should be permitted to purchase insurance from private companies or from other banks, as long as these companies and banks were approved by the chartering agency (about which more is said below). The private insurance can be in place of or supplementary to government agency insurance. So that the public is not misinformed, the depository institutions would have to prominently state the insurer they use, much as they now must state "Member Federal Deposit Insurance Corporation."

One should consider the concern that competition among insurers might lead to "agency shopping" by badly or fraudulently run banks wanting to escape regulation. Two factors argue against this possibility. One is the evidence of switches in bank charters. During the years 1960 to 1966, when Comptroller of the Currency James Saxon liberalized regulations, state banks had an incentive to convert to national charters. In the years since the late 1960s, when the opportunity cost of required reserves increased considerably, banks had an incentive to switch to non-member bank status. But the number of state banks adopting national charters from 1960 through 1977 relative to the number at year end 1977 was only 5.9 percent. In the same eighteen-year period, 6.3 percent of the national banks became nonmembers (Miller 1980: II, 495–96). A detailed study of these (and other) changes revealed that "some, but not many, bankers abuse the forum shopping principle of choice (Miller 1980: II, 492). The second, more important factor, is that a depository institution cannot change to another insurer unless that insurer accepts the institution. Since the insurer bears the cost of a failure, it has a strong incentive to refuse to accept institutions that are badly or fraudulently run.

Control of the Money Supply

Even those economists who do not declare that control of the supply of money is essential believe it to be desirable. The Federal Reserve can effect this control in several ways. As is the procedure in many countries, the central bank could issue and withdraw legal tender by buying and selling securities (open-market operations) and by printing currency. The demand deposits (which hereafter includes such close substitutes as NOW accounts) portion of the money supply then could be controlled via the substitution by money users of currency for deposits and vice versa. The principal problems with this procedure are that demand deposits comprise the bulk of the money supply, the link between deposits and currency is inexact, and there are real resource costs in not permitting the public to have the amount of currency required for day-to-day transactions. Most of these problems can be avoided by using required reserves against demand deposits to control the money supply. The central bank can determine the amount of reserves that banks (hereafter denoting all suppliers of demand deposits) hold with one or a combination of three methods: Adjusting the required reserve ratio, implementing open-market operations, and controlling borrowing from the central bank. Changes in reserves that result from changes in float, foreign transactions, Treasury operations, shifts among deposits against which different reserve ratios are required (if this practice is followed), and changes in the banks' and the public's desired holdings of excess reserves and currency can be offset with open-market operations.

For the effective control of the money supply via reserves, the central bank must have information on the banks' reserve balances and be reasonably assured that the relationship between the reserves and the money supply is stable or, at least, predictable—for example, there will not be unexpected shifts of deposits for money substitutes that it cannot effectively offset. For this purpose it is desirable (but not necessary) that the providers of demand deposits be subject to specified reserve requirements and that they be known to and possibly report to the Federal Reserve. (Reporting would not be necessary if the Fed could adequately estimate the needed data with sampling.)

Monetary policy would be more effective if velocity were more predictable. For this reason, and as an aid to identifying the assets that are used by the public as money, it would be desirable if the opportunity value to nonbanks of providing money substitutes were minimized. For these purposes (and for reasons of equity and the efficient allocation of resources), bank-provided money should not be taxed at a higher rate than other forms of money. This leads to the conclusion that the Federal Reserve should pay interest on the required reserves it holds against demand deposits. The rate of interest should offset the opportunity loss to the banks of the funds required to be held as reserves. With no other regulations imposed on banks (other than required deposit insurance) competition would

ensure that the demand depositors rather than the banks would benefit from the removal of this tax on their funds. While the government would lose this source of revenue, the public would gain from
the Federal Reserve's more effective control of the money supply
and from a more efficient allocation of resources. At the same time,
tax subsidies to banks should be removed, such as their right to earn
tax-free interest on state and municipal bonds while being allowed to
deduct against taxable income the cost of funds used to purchase the
bonds.

The Furtherance of Social Goals—The Provision of Banking Services

Three general types of social goals are distinguished: (1) provision
of the banking services of loans, fund transfers and savings; (2) support of housing and other attempts to allocate credit; and (3) prevention of individual discrimination and unfair dealing against individuals. Each is described and analyzed individually in the following
sections.

The Historical Record.   Until recently, commercial banks were expected to further social welfare primarily by providing businesses and
consumers with an efficient means of making transactions (bank
notes and checking) and borrowing and lending assets (loans and savings). The banks also served as a vehicle for collecting taxes (as is
discussed above). The additional goal of unrestricted access to these
facilities was characteristic of the United States. Hence a powerful,
national quasi-monopoly bank, such as the Bank of England, was not
permitted to develop, until the Federal Reserve was created in 1913,
and for most of the nation's history, bank charters were not difficult
to obtain.

It is important to note that the Federal Reserve was not conceived
of as a central bank but as a bank for and by bankers. Its function
was to facilitate check clearing and provide other banking services
for its members. After it was converted into a central bank by Senator Glass and President Wilson, a principal social purpose still was the
development of an efficient nationwide clearing system as well as a
vehicle for eliminating panics and providing the nation with an "elas-
tic" currency. The cost of the system was borne by the members

with the non-interest-bearing reserves they were required to keep at the Federal Reserve Banks. With the passage of the Depository Institutions Deregulation and Monetary Control Act of 1980, the Fed was directed to charge users of its services for the full cost of those services. By this action, the social desirability of publicly supporting a national payments system was recognized as being no longer a concern of the present.

The United States developed specialized financial institutions in large measure to serve perceived social goals. Mutual savings banks (MSBs) were established (the first in 1816) for the social purpose of providing a place where the working poor could save with safety (Benston 1972: ch. 2). These institutions were founded as mutuals because the costs of providing these services exceeded the revenues derived therefrom; hence space and personal services often were donated and the institutions were not taxed. The MSBs were established primarily in the northeast, where they dominated the market for savings. They did not develop much in other areas of the country, for two reasons; One is that the mutual form of organization made establishment of a new bank difficult, particularly when the charitable desire to help the poor in this way was not as strong as it was in the northeast. The second is that the newly established banks in the newer states were not averse to serving the less affluent individuals shunned by the well-established northeastern banks. Because their principal stated goal was service to the working poor, and as a consequence of some failures during the panic of 1873, the MSBs were legally prohibited from investing these peoples' savings in such risky and potentially fraudulent assets as business loans. Consequently, they tended to hold bonds. By 1910, though, about half of their portfolios were in mortgages. The percentage declined after the 1930s and did not get up to about 60 to 70 percent until the 1960s.

Savings and loan associations (S&Ls) were established principally to make mortgage loans. They developed from mutual building and loan societies. In the early years of the Great Depression federal chartering of mutual S&Ls was established with the goal of helping the housing industry recover. Thus, although the financial statements of the S&Ls and MSBs now look very similar, they were initially established to serve different social goals.

Consumer finance companies and credit unions also were established for a social purpose. Consumer finance companies were licensed by states (the first in 1916) to make small loans at gross rates that greatly exceeded the states' usury ceilings. The small loan laws were passed when it became clear that the urban population was prevented by the usury statutes from obtaining loans legally; those who were unable to borrow from friends and relatives had to turn to loan sharks. Credit unions similarly were established to provide a source of small loans to individuals. Churches, fraternal groups, and businesses supported their development with donations of space and labor, since they made loans to members of these groups. Their growth also was helped by exemption from taxation.

The Present Situation.   The laws and regulations that first forbade and now constrain thrift associations from serving their clients have had a negative social impact. As consumers' demands changed from wanting a safe haven for savings and for mortgage loans to also wanting a wide range of financial services (particularly checking accounts and consumer loans), the institutions should have been free to offer the products demanded. Furthermore, the institutions were prevented from offering business loans and other services that would have benefited their communities. Similarly, restraints on commercial banks (such as the Glass-Steagall Act) that prevent them from offering a full range of services and geographical constraints in the form of prohibitions against intra- and interstate branching have kept them from meeting the social goal of service to consumers. Laws that limit payments to savers—the prohibition of interest on demand deposits and Regulation Q—obviously are contrary to the social goal of not hurting consumers, particularly because these limitations affect mostly the depositors who are ignorant of such alternatives as money market funds or who hold balances that do not meet the funds' minimum requirements. Indeed, it is difficult to find any of the laws and regulations that prohibit or constrain banks or any enterprises from offering their services to the public as operating to further social goals as these usually are expressed. While these constraints may have been imposed to reduce the incidence of bank failure (although that motivation and the effectiveness of the laws and regulations for that purpose are very doubtful in many instances), the advent of deposit guarantees should have eliminated this concern.

    The continued provision of payments clearance and other banking services by the Federal Reserve also is no longer relevant for advancing the social concern of improved banking services. Alternative and supplementary services have been offered by nongovernment organizations for some time. Now that all depository institutions that offer third-party transfers are required to maintain reserves with the Federal Reserve Banks and all can obtain Federal Reserve services at a price, there seems no reason for these services to be provided by a government agency. Rather, this aspect of the Federal Reserves' operations should be split off into a separate corporation, with marketable stock distributed to member banks in exchange for their stock in the Federal Reserve. The Fed's related buildings, equipment, other assets and liabilities, and personnel would be ceded to their new private corporation.

Support of Housing and Other Attempts to Allocate Credit as Social Goals

The Historical Record.   Housing was adopted as a social goal in the 1930s, when federal chartering of S&Ls and federal guarantees of home mortgage loans were established. This goal was furthered by the creation of the Federal Home Loan Bank Board as a regulatory agency, and the Federal Home Loan Banks, the Government National Mortgage Association, and the Federal Savings and Loan Insurance Corporation as vehicles for diverting funds into home mortgages. The extension of Regulation Q ceilings to thrift associations in 1966 and their continuation at a level below market rates on the savings deposits of all insured depository institutions were justified as means of keeping funds flowing into mortgages. Other means of supporting home ownership were restrictions on the nonmortgage assets in which thrift institutions can invest and the granting of tax benefits if mortgages are above a given percentage of total assets. Most recently, the Home Mortgage Disclosure Act of 1975 and the Community Reinvestment Act of 1977 were enacted to encourage (or force) chartered financial institutions located in older urban areas to make mortgage and other loans in those areas. The former act is simply a disclosure statute that requires the institutions to identify publicly the volume and type of mortgages made by census tract. The Community Reinvestment Act requires institutions to demonstrate they have adequately served their local communities, particularly when they request permission to open or close branches.

Other attempts to allocate credit that can be mentioned include the Federal Reserve's down payment and maturity requirements for consumer cash loans that have been imposed at various times, margin requirements on loans secured by securities, and moral suasion (or threats) by the Federal Reserve Board designed to get banks to forbear from lending for what the authorities consider to be socially undeserving projects.[16]

The Present Situation.   Whether housing should be subsidized, while a valid question, need not be addressed here since the laws and regulations designed to support this industry have not achieved this goal. Indeed there is reason to believe that these constraints have had the opposite effect. These conclusions are based on considerations of the availability and cost of funds for house purchases.

Availability has two dimensions. One is the effect that the number and type of sources have on the quantity (or level) of funds that flow into mortgages. The second is the effect of the variation of the fund flows on house purchases. With respect to the quantity of funds, there is no reason to believe that the required specialization in mortgage lending by a particular set of institutions is either necessary or desirable for funds to flow freely into mortgages. Money is the most fungible of all assets. Mortgage lending requires skills, but there are no barriers or great costs that prevent people from acquiring them or lenders from hiring people who have these skills. As long as there are no constraints on the yields that can be earned by lenders, demands for mortgages will be met by a large number of sources. Even now, people obtain mortgages from mortgage companies and private parties as well as from chartered financial institutions.[17] In addition, people can use their own funds and obtain purchase money mortgages and land sales contracts from the seller (which often are not recorded as mortgages). Furthermore, all of these sources for mortgage funds are available to home buyers in most markets.

Not only are mortgage funds available from many sources, but the evidence does not support the essential assumption that there is a direct and necessary linkage between mortgages and home buying. Mortgages are but one of many means of borrowing money. A house can serve as collateral for funds that are used to purchase other assets. Thus, Dwight Jaffee (1975: 119), who reviewed the relationship between mortgage finance and housing, concludes: "The main effect of developed policies [subsidies and interventions in the mortgage market] has been to extend greatly the use of mortgage debt in the U.S., but without any appreciable payoff in terms of housing investment." From his review of several studies, Allan Meltzer (1975: 149) similarly finds "no evidence that the availability of the particular type of credit has any important or lasting effect on the type of assets individuals acquire. If the housing market is the market in which 'availability matters' or matters most, there appears to be very little if any empirical basis for the conjecture on the public policies based on it."

Variation in the amount of funds available for mortgages, though, is likely to be an important short-run deterrent to house purchases. If a mortgage cannot be obtained, at virtually any price, houses can be purchased by very few people. This situation can occur when thrift institutions dominate mortgage lending in an area because laws and regulations give them a comparative advantage over other lenders. (These advantages may be positive, in the form of tax breaks and other subsidies, or negative, in the form of penalties that other lenders can avoid.) Then, when an event such as an unexpected increase in interest rates results in a reduced flow of funds to the thrift institutions because they are unable to offer the market rate for deposits, a major source of mortgages is cut off. Unexpected increases in interest rates also can result in the failure of the specialized thrift institutions, because they are unable to match the maturity (or duration) of their assets and liabilities. Consequently, they are subjected to capital losses when the value of their assets (mortgages) decreases, but they must pay the market rate on their liabilities (time deposits) or face disintermediation. Such failures obviously reduce the flow of funds to mortgages, at least until other lenders obtain the required skills to meet the demand.

Expected variations in fund flows also tend to reduce the flow of funds to mortgages. In this situation, lenders usually find it desirable to maintain assets that can be sold and purchased at relatively low transaction costs. Nonspecialized lenders can hold a mix of assets and liabilities where the expected fund flows tend to offset each other. Since, until recently, thrift institutions generally were not permitted to invest in consumer and business loans and obtain checking account deposits, they tended to hold bonds as a buffer stock (secondary reserve). In those states (such as Connecticut) where the mutual savings banks could hold consumer loans, the institutions tended to hold relatively fewer bonds and more mortgages (Benston 1972: 174–76). Hence, enforced specialization tended to reduce the flow of funds to mortgages.

Turning now to the cost of mortgage funds, it is obvious that the greater the number of lenders vying to make mortgages, the lower the cost to mortgagors. And the greater the variation of funds to lenders and borrowers, the greater the costs to both. Therefore laws and regulations that restrict entry into the mortgage market and that require financial institutions to specialize in mortgages tend to increase the cost of mortgages.

A final question that should be considered is whether subsidies to thrift institutions in return for their specializing in mortgage lending are likely to be supportive of housing (whether or not these subsidies are otherwise justified). The subsidies take the form of lower taxes and legally imposed limits on the amounts that can be offered to depositors (Regulation Q). As is discussed above, the first form of subsidy is likely to increase the variation and reduce the flow of funds available for mortgages because of the enforced specialization of the institutions in mortgages and the reduced incentives of other lenders to make this type of loan (witness the virtual withdrawal of life insurance companies from one to four-family unit mortgages). The second is only temporarily useful, even if one assumes that the lower interest rates paid to depositors are passed on to home buyers. When market interest rates are above the Regulation Q ceilings, disintermediation occurs. The enormous growth of money market mutual funds are due entirely to the desire and ability of savers and entrepreneurs to get and offer the best return on funds. Unfortunately for those who want to obtain mortgages, the savers who take their money out of the thrift institutions that specialize in the mortgages and purchase money market mutual funds shares are actually redepositing their funds principally in commercial banks and are financing corporate and government borrowing. The money market mutual funds tend to hold commercial paper, U.S. Treasury issues, and the certificates of deposit (CDs) of large commercial banks. They held these CDs because only CDs over $100,000 could bear market rates of interest and CDs of these amounts are not guaranteed by the FDIC. Hence, the funds would have been foolish to risk investment in the CDs of thrift institutions, many of which are in danger of bankruptcy, or of smaller commercial banks, about which information is more expensive to obtain and which are more likely to be permitted by the FDIC to fail than are the very large banks.

The effectiveness of directing credit by regulation toward other specified assets and borrowers has also been found to be slight and often dysfunctional. A number of these studies are surveyed by Thomas Mayer (1975: 91), who concludes: "As the above has shown, credit allocation is not an efficient system. The shifts in the distribution of credit which it tries to bring about are of doubtful value, and, in any case, credit allocation would be ineffective in the long run." When the controls are effective (in the short run), they cause borrowers and lenders to incur the costs of complying with and attempting to avoid the controls. While some borrowers are advantaged and some set of social goals advanced, the effect, at best, is temporary. At worst, the benefits do not flow to those who are presumed to be aided, but to others who are more adept at using regulations to their advantage.

With such credit allocation laws as the Community Reinvestment Act of 1977, harm rather than good is likely to be done to those for whom the law presumably is directed. The law requires chartered financial institutions to direct loans to mortgages on local houses and businesses, particularly if these are in older, blighted areas. If lenders would make these loans without the law, compliance costs are needlessly imposed. If these loans would not be made because the risks exceed the interest rates that can be charged (given institutional or legal constraints), the law encourages institutions to leave the area and discourages others who are similarly regulated from opening branches in the area. In either event, while the volume of loans flowing into the area may be increased initially, the funds will tend to be directed toward the least risky borrowers. As lenders can adjust to the situation, consumers in the area will find fewer sources of funds and other banking services (Benston 1978). The law will benefit consumers only if bankers had been discriminating against borrowers for noneconomic reasons and, as a consequence of the law, they were led or forced to give up their taste for discrimination. With respect to mortgages particularly, almost all of the empirical studies find no evidence of discrimination against persons or areas (redlining) (Benston 1979: 144–45, 1981: 8–23).

Prevention of Invidious Discrimination
and Unfair Dealing against Persons

The Historical Record. Laws that explicitly prohibit invidious discrimination in the provision of banking services (especially loans) were first enacted in 1968 (Rohner 1980: 1–168). The Fair Housing Act of 1968 prohibited banks and other lenders from denying mortgages or home improvement loans on account of a person's race, color, religion, sex, or national origin. The Equal Credit Opportunity Act (Title VII of the Consumer Protection Act—CCPA—of 1968), enacted in 1974 and amended in 1976, added prohibitions against all credit discrimination on the grounds of age, race, religion, national origin, receipt of public welfare benefits, and exercise of rights under the CCPA. The Federal Reserve's Regulation B supplements the law. Regulations written under the dictates of the Community Reinvestment Act of 1977 forbid the alleged practice of denying mortgage and home improvement loans on properties solely because they are old or are located in older areas (redlining).

Several laws are directed at providing borrowers with complete information and forbidding certain practices in the belief that without these laws borrowers would be victimized. The Truth-in-Lending Act of 1968 (Title I of the CCPA) requires disclosure of credit costs and terms on consumer loans and long-term leases of consumer goods. It also regulates the content of credit advertising and regulates credit card distribution, terms, and liabilities. The provisions of the act are implemented by the Federal Reserve's detailed and lengthy Regulation Z. The Electronic Fund Transfer Act (Title IX of the CCPA), enacted in 1978, requires disclosure of account terms, documentation of transfers, and prompt error resolution; limits the consumer's liability for unauthorized transfers; and imposes liability for unauthorized transfers by financial institutions. The Real Estate Settlement Procedures Act, adopted in 1974 and amended in 1976, requires mortgage lenders to provide borrowers with a statement of actual charges, forbids kickbacks of settlement fees and tie-ins of sales of title insurance, and limits escrows for taxes and insurance. The Right to Financial Privacy Act of 1978 restricts the right of government agencies to gain access to a consumer's banking records.

Finally, some lending and collection practices of creditors are constrained or prohibited by various laws. The Fair Credit Reporting Act (Title VI of the CCPA), passed in 1970, regulates the content, accuracy, and disclosure of credit and investigative reports furnished to creditors, employers, and insurers in connection with consumer transactions. Title III of the CCPA establishes a minimum level of wages that are exempted from garnishment and prohibits an employer from firing an employee because of a single garnishment. The

Fair Debt Collections Act (Title VIII of the CCPA), enacted in 1977, prohibits abusive and coercive collection practices and requires bill collectors to provide debtors with certain information. It applies to banks only insofar as they collect the debts of other lenders. In addition, the Federal Trade Commission's holder-in-due-course rule, issued in 1975, effectively abolished this protection for banks that discounted consumers' notes made to retailers.

In addition, the states have enacted laws that similarly regulate credit practices. Some of these parallel the federal Truth-in-Lending and Equal Credit Opportunity Acts. In several states, notably California, the antiredlining regulations are more severe than the federal regulations. Most states have usury statutes that stipulate the maximum interest rate that can be charged on various types of loans. These laws are quite diverse and complex. The Uniform Consumer Credit Code, promulgated in 1969, has been adopted by only six states, and they changed various provisions. (In contrast, the Uniform Commercial Code has been adopted virtually intact by almost all states.) Finally, the laws of various states restrict creditors' collection remedies more severely than do the federal statutes. These restrictions on contractual provisions include prohibitions against confession of judgment clauses or cognovit notes, restrictions on collateral available as security, restrictions on deficiency judgments following repossession, and limitations on cosigner agreements.

The Present Situation.   Assuming (as I do as an ethical value) that invidious discrimination against individuals should not be permitted as a matter of social policy, two questions related to the laws and regulations should be considered. First, are these laws effective in eliminating or reducing invidious discrimination at a cost that is not excessive? Second, is the particular way in which these laws are enforced preferable relative to alternatives? While answers to these questions appear to require value-based assumptions about the meaning of the words *excessive* and *preferable* important aspects of the answers need not await agreement about their operational meaning.

A preliminary question, though, is whether invidious discrimination by financial institutions was a serious problem before the laws were enacted. If such were not the case, the laws simply impose costs on the institutions and their customers without yielding benefits to those whom the laws purport to help. Passage of the Equal Credit Opportunity Act was supported by testimony before the National Commission on Consumer Finance and before congressional committees that described incidents of invidious discrimination in lending to women (National Commission on Consumer Finance 1972: 153–56). However, any activity, including credit granting, is conducted with some error and insensitivity. When these occur to women, blacks, or other persons who have experienced invidious discrimination in other situations, the refusal of credit is likely to appear to have been deliberate and unfair. Since testimony by men and whites who were turned down for loans was not heard, it is not possible to know whether the lenders systematically practiced discrimination.

Several studies have been conducted since the hearings that find no evidence of invidious discrimination against women. Chandler and Ewert (1976) examined the records of slightly over 2,000 credit card applicants at a large metropolitan bank, drawn from applications made between 1971 through early 1974, prior to the passage of the Equal Credit Opportunity Act (ECOA). They constructed credit scoring models to determine the effect of using or not using an applicant's gender as a variable in rejecting or accepting applicants and, if the applicant was accepted, whether the person would be predicted to be a good or bad (loss) payer. They found that when the applicant's gender was included as a variable 22 percent more females would be accepted compared to excluding gender as is required by the ECOA. Among those accepted, use of gender would have identified 19 percent more good payers and the same number of bad payers (Chandler and Ewert 1976: table 6).[18] Thus, if these data are typical, the ECOA regulations tended to make credit cards more difficult to obtain for females and to have imposed greater losses on lenders.

The question of whether commercial banks discriminated against female small loan borrowers before enactment of the ECOA was studied with data obtained by the Federal Reserve from thirty banks in five regions, each consisting of a major metropolitan area plus surrounding environs (Peterson 1981: 547–61). Randomly selected data from the pre-ECOA period of 1966–71 included 3,000 charged-off, 12,000 good paid-off, and 13,500 new direct consumer loans. These were analyzed with a well-specified model to see if commercial banks systematically discriminated against one sex or another in granting consumer credit by oversecuring loans, thereby reducing loss ratios and probabilities, credit-rationing to reduce loss probabilities, or charging higher rates to certain borrowers based on sex. The study (1981: 560) found that "Overall, the tests provided extensive evidence that commercial banks did not discriminate against potential borrowers based on their sex before ECOA (Equal Credit Opportunities Act) was passed." The only other studies of which I am aware consider possible invidious discrimination in mortgage lending related to the area in which the home is located (redlining) or the race or other personal characteristics of the actual or potential mortgagor. With one exception, all of these find no evidence of invidious discrimination in the denials of loan applications, the types of loans made or the terms charged (Benston 1979).

Thus the empirical analyses do not find evidence of discrimination in lending by financial institutions in the years before or after the laws prohibiting such discrimination were enacted. This result is not surprising if one views lenders as people who prefer to maximize their wealth. If they are bigots and if they and their shareholders are willing to accept lower rewards (and it is likely that some are, considering that more than a few people speak and act in this way), it seems unlikely that they would indulge this taste on people with whom their principal contact is a loan agreement and the receipt of repayments (usually by mail).

While the benefits to those who are supposed to be protected by the antidiscrimination acts at best appear to be negligible (and possibly are negative), the costs to financial institutions (and therefore, to their customers) are substantial. James Smith (1977: 609–22) estimated these for compliance with the Federal Reserve's Regulation B that implemented the antidiscrimination provisions of the ECOA. He included the nonrecurring costs of legal fees, training, and obsolete form removal and the additional costs of printing and mailing notices, changing systems, and handling responses due to the requirement that women be informed that they can establish separate credit records. These costs are estimated to be $88.6 million for financial institutions (commercial banks, thrift associations, credit unions, and finance companies) and $78.8 million for merchants (retailers, oil companies, and other credit card issuers). Recurring costs include increased losses, collection expense, and record retention costs. These annual costs are estimated to be $68.8 million for financial institutions and $58.7 million for merchants.

Chartered depository institutions are subjected to additional costs in the form of compliance examinations. Rohner (1980: 107) reports that in the fiscal year ended June 1978, 9,117 compliance examinations were conducted and $7.1 million was spent by the federal banking agencies (FDIC, Federal Reserve, and Comptroller of the Currency.) Additional examinations and expenditures were made by state agencies. In addition, the banks incurred additional costs related to the examinations, including the cost of special computer runs, time spent with examiners, and the opportunity cost of constraints on banking operations that examiners might question. Indeed, bankers are reported to find these examinations particularly costly and of very limited benefit to consumers. In a study of the opinions of banks, regulators and consumer specialists toward federal and state regulation, Gloria Elhat (1980: 406–24, 492–502, 542–57) elicited opinions on the following aspects of consumer protection: Credit discrimination, disclosure, community reinvestment, creditor practices and remedies, and regulation of loan terms (interest rates, maturities, and amounts). She reports most (from 70 to 90 percent of the bankers saying that compliance with the consumer protection laws are "very or quite" costly and were not important in protecting consumers.[19] The regulators and examiners interviewed tended to agree with the bankers (though they were not as strongly negative, particularly with respect to the importance of the limitations on creditor practices). Not surprisingly, the professional consumer advocates were of the opposite opinion. Thus all except the consumer advocates believe that the consumer protection laws as administered are considerably more costly than beneficial. Assuming, though, that these laws are not repealed, it seems clear that they can be administered in a more efficient and more equitable manner than by compliance examinations.

CONTEMPORARY REASONS FOR AND METHODS OF REGULATING BANKING— A RECAPITULATION

No Longer Relevant Reasons

Taxation. Restriction of entry as a means of enhancing taxes, the initial reason for bank regulation, is no longer relevant. (The effect of differential taxation of depository institutions compared to other suppliers of banking services is discussed below.)

Prevention of Centralized Power. Restriction of entry for this purpose also is no longer relevant, if it ever was. In particular, there is no reason to believe that the removal of all restrictions on branching or holding companies would result in the demise of small, locally owned banks. Indeed, if further decentralization of banking services is desired, all legal restrictions on entry and the provision of services, by banks as well as other enterprises, should be removed.

Bank Solvency and the Effects of Failures on the Economy. The requirement of deposit insurance has eliminated concerns about bank runs and the consequent effects on the economy. While bank failures, as such, are not desirable, they now are likely to be somewhat less disruptive on employees, customers, and local economies than are the failures of most other types of enterprises. Therefore, special government supervision of financial institutions (with the possible exception of mutuals) is no longer justified for this reason.

The Social Goal of Available Banking Services. Regulations that prevent or impede organizations from providing services to the public violate this social goal. Consequently, such constraints as limitations on the banking services that thrift institutions can provide, securities services that commercial banks can offer, and interest that can be offered to depositors are undesirable. There also no longer is any reason to subsidize the payments mechanism by maintaining it as a Federal Reserve operation.

Support of Housing and Other Attempts to Allocate Credit. It is unlikely that enforced specialization of thrift institutions as providers of mortgages benefits the production and sale of houses. To the contrary, such specialization tends to increase the variance of funds flows into mortgages, which works a temporary hardship to those who want to buy and sell houses. Interest rate ceilings on deposits and mortgages also restrict the flow of funds to mortgages. Credit directing legislation, particularly the Community Reinvestment Act, raises the cost of lending and is unlikely actually to direct a greater flow of funds to the presumably favored borrowers, except perhaps in the very short run. Such legislation, though, tends to raise costs to bank customers and allocate resources inefficiently. Consequently, if support of the housing market is a social goal, the existing regulations on lenders and prices should be removed.

Possibly Relevant Reasons

Taxation. If the government wants to levy a tax on bank-supplied money, it can do so efficiently by requiring all enterprises that supply this product to maintain a given percentage of the relevant deposits as non-interest-bearing reserves with the Federal Reserve. With the exception of equality of reserve ratios among enterprises (larger banks are required to hold higher percentages than smaller banks), this procedure is presently being followed. Any regulation on entry, products supplied, interest paid or charged, and so forth, would either be unnecessary or counterproductive, since anything that impeded or made more costly the supply of bank money would favor nontaxed substitutes, such as credit cards.

Money Supply Control. The Federal Reserve can exercise control over the money supply by requiring all suppliers of third-party transfers (demand deposits and close substitutes) to maintain reserves and, possibly, to report statistics. Alternatively, the Federal Reserve could control the money supply simply by predicting the effect of open market operations, on the assumption that the relationship between voluntarily held reserves and money is predictable. In either event, unexpected changes in the money supply and velocity can be reduced by making substitutes for specified third-party transfers less desirable. This can be accomplished by removing the tax on required reserves represented by the opportunity loss on these presently non-interest-bearing funds. At the same time, tax subsidies to banks should be removed.

Avoidance of Competition. Regulations that restrict entry are particularly beneficial to those providing a product or service. Thus the present requirement that those who would open banks must obtain a charter, the granting of which is not automatic even if some basic qualifications are fulfilled (such as the obtaining of deposit insurance), provides an opportunity for existing bankers or other competitors to raise objections. Restrictions on inter- and intrastate branching also serve to reduce competition. Competition is reduced further by laws and regulations that restrict thrift associations from providing a wide range of banking services (most of which have now been removed or reduced), prevent commercial banks from providing securities services, impose interest rate ceilings on deposit accounts, and restrain nonchartered enterprises from providing depository banking services. Indeed, restraining competition is a relevant past and contemporary reason for regulation. However, as the advantages from avoiding restrictions grow and as technological change and innovations reduce the cost of avoiding the laws and regulations, the constraints serve predominantly to raise costs to consumers with fewer and fewer benefits to the increasingly less protected producers.

The Protection of Depositors and Bank Solvency.   Since the creation of the FDIC and the other federal deposit insurance agencies, this concern is relevant only insofar as the requirement of deposit insurance tends to restrict competition and innovation and increase the cost to consumers of credit and other banking services. Solvency, as such, is a currently relevant regulatory problem only for mutual associations, and then only because there are no stockholders and securities market to discipline wayward managers.

Prevention of Invidious Discrimination and Unfair Dealing against Persons.   The legislative history indicates that this concern is currently relevant, even though there is no scientifically acceptable evidence that supports the underlying belief that financial institutions invidiously discriminated, at least in recent times. The present procedure of compliance examinations, though, is neither cost effective nor fair.

NOTES TO CHAPTER 1

1. The principal regulators for banks would be the state banking commissions and the Securities Exchange Commission (SEC). For an analysis of the disclosure regulations of the SEC and proposals for reform, see Benston (1982).
2. Alternatives to the present system are not considered herein. See Smith (1936).
3. The Bank of England did not have a complete monopoly. A few smaller banks of issue were permitted to operate outside of London, and entry was essentially unlimited in Scotland.
4. See Carson and Cootner (1963: 56–59). They give three reasons for the limited lives of the two federally chartered banks: (1) concerns by agrarian

and small business borrowers with concentrated banking power; (2) sentiment for unit banking (the U.S. banks were establishing branches); and
(3) desire for inflation (the U.S. banks were conservative note issuers).

5. While there is reason to believe that this centralized power should be re-
strained, perhaps by repealing the legal tender laws and allowing alternative currencies and other means of payment to be used, the issue presently
is moot.

6. Even if banking were characterized by economies of scale, consumers still
would benefit by the removal of organizational constraints as long as entry
were unrestricted. In this event, should a bank drive out its competitors by
underpricing them, it could not subsequently raise its charges without
inviting in new competitors or reviving the old ones. Considering that there
are few physical, capital, or technological barriers to entry, predatory pricing would seem to be a foolish practice but one that is beneficial to consumers if it is practiced.

7. The most comprehensive work on the legislation lists the alleged abuses
but does not cite any evidence of their occurrence. See Peach (1941).

8. Between 1927 and 1930, the participation of banks in bond issues grew
from 36.8 to 61.2 percent (Peach 1941).

9. The Scottish experience is one of stable banking, much more so than the
experience of England with its central bank and restrictions on entry and
competition.

10. Clark Warburton carefully studies the relationship between bank failures
by county and the 1930s depression. He concludes (1966: 2) that

> There was a massive contraction of deposits nationally, during the early 1930s,
> relative to the rate of growth during the 1920s, of which less than one-fourth was
> accounted for by deposits in suspended banks. This indicated that the depression
> of the 1930s could not be explained by the impact of balances of payment result-
> ing from adverse conditions in particular industries or areas, but was due to, or at
> least associated with, some potent force operating on a national scale.

11. An exception is the small run on the Franklin Savings Bank when the
Franklin National Bank (an unrelated institution) failed. While depositors
attempted to withdraw funds from many non-federally insured Ohio savings and loans when Home State Savings failed, such withdrawals were not
experienced by FSLIC-insured institutions.

12. Note Warburton (1966), the concentration of suspensions among small
banks (particularly those in the agricultural areas described next), and the
very few failures of branch banks noted above.

13. The only important exception is the mutual savings banks. Apparently
because of a fraternity derived from shared mutualism, they provided each
other with the currency needed to pay off anxious depositors and then
stem incipient runs. They also benefited from not practicing reserve bank-

ing and from their concentration in long-maturity assets, the present values of which increased when interest rates declined unexpectedly.

14. If entry into banking is not constrained (as is suggested in this chapter), the gains to shareholders from risk taking will be greater, since they will no longer face the loss of rent from restricted entry.

15. However, it should be noted that the New York state system was phased out as bank charters were granted and renewed under the free (entry) banking law. As banks left the insurance system, the premiums went up considerably.

16. Subsidies to borrowers are a much more important means of allocating credit. These extensive (and expensive) programs include the FHA 221 (d)(2) and 235 programs that provide low-interest rate, low downpayment loans to lower-income persons and other house buyers in declining urban areas, education loans, farm loans, and small business loans. The cost of these programs in terms of the difference between market rates of interest and the rates charged to the borrowers has been very great and no doubt has resulted in the shifting of resources to those assets and activities that would qualify for the subsidies. An additional cost is the nonrepayment of the loans. Since these allocations of credit and their associated costs are not an aspect of banking regulation, they are not considered further here.

17. As an indication of this fact, note that the $1,503 billion of total mortgages and $992 billion of one- to four-family mortgates outstanding as of June 30, 1981, were held by the following:

	All	_One- to Four-Family_
Commercial banks	18.3%	16.8%
Mutual savings bank	6.6	6.6
Savings and loan associations	34.2	43.3
Life insurance companies	9.0	1.8
Federal and related agencies	7.9	6.3
Mortgage pools or trusts	10.1	13.0
Individuals and others	13.8	12.2
Total	99.9%	100.0%

18. The figures are for a 0.75 cutoff score (a number that determines how stringently credit is granted). At higher cutoff scores (to 0.80), relatively more applicants are accepted (including bad applicants who should have been rejected). At lower cutoff scores (to 0.55) the relative differences decline, but even then more rejected female applicants would be accepted, and more good and bad applicants identified.

19. Similar findings are provided by a "representative nationwide sample of 1585 chief executive officers of national, state member, and state non-

member banks" conducted in 1979 by the FDIC. An average of 91 percent said these examinations were "very or quite costly" (Miller 1980: 379–80).

REFERENCES

Benston, George J. 1972a. "Economies of Scale in Banking." *Journal of Money, Credit and Banking* 4 (May): 312–41.

_____. 1972b. "Savings Banking and the Public Interest," *Journal of Money, Credit and Banking* 4, pt. 2 (February): ch. 2.

_____. 1973. "Bank Examination." *Bulletin* of the Institute of Finance, Graduate School of Business Administration, New York University, 89–90 (May): 12, table 2.

_____. 1978a. *The Anti-Redlining Rules: An Analysis of the Federal Home Loan Bank Board's Proposed Nondiscriminatory Requirements.* Miami: Law and Economics Center, University of Miami School of Law.

_____. 1978b. *Federal Reserve Membership: Consequences, Costs, Benefits and Alternatives.* A study prepared for the trustees of the Banking Research Fund of the Association of Reserve City Bankers. Chicago: Association of Reserve City Bankers, ch. 3.

_____. 1979. "Mortgage Redlining Research: A Review and Critical Analysis." In *The Regulation of Financial Institutions*, Conference Series No. 21, Boston: Federal Reserve Bank of Boston (October): 144–95, and in *Journal of Bank Research* 12 (Spring): 8–23.

_____. 1982. "Security for Investors." In *Instead of Regulation: Alternatives to Federal Regulatory Agencies*, edited by Robert W. Poole, Jr., pp. 169–205. Lexington, Mass.: Lexington Books.

Benston, George J., Gerald Hanweck, and David H. Humphrey. 1982a. "Operating Costs in Commercial Banks." *Economic Review* of the Federal Reserve Bank of Atlanta 47 (November): 6–21.

_____. 1982b. "Scale Economies in Banking: A Restructuring and Reinterpretation." *Journal of Money, Credit and Banking* 14 (November): 435–56.

Carson, Deane, and Paul H. Cootner. 1963. "The Structure of Competition in Commercial Banking in the United States." Research Study Two in *Private Financial Institutions*, prepared for the Commission on Money and Credit, pp. 56–59. Englewood Cliffs, N.J.: Prentice-Hall.

Chandler, Gary G., and David C. Ewert. 1976. "Discrimination on the Basis of Sex under the Equal Credit Opportunity Act." Working Paper No. 8, Credit Research Center, West Lafayette, Ind.: Krannert Graduate School of Management, Purdue University.

Elhat, Gloria A. 1980. "The State and Federal Regulation of Banks: Interpretive Analysis and Principal Findings of a Survey of Bankers, Regulators and

Consumer Specialists." In *State and Federal Regulation of Commercial Banks*, edited by Leonard Lapidus et al., pp. 406–24, 492–502, 542–57. Washington, D.C.: Federal Deposit Insurance Corp.

Flannery, Mark J., and Jack M. Guttentag. 1980. "Problem Banks: Examination, Identification and Supervision." In *State and Federal Regulation of Commercial Banks*, edited by Leonard Lapidus et al., vol. 2, p. 218. Washington, D.C.: Federal Deposit Insurance Corp.

Golembe, Carter. 1975. "Memorandum re: Interest on Demand Deposits." Washington, D.C.: Carter H. Golembe Associates.

Jaffee, Dwight M. 1975. "Housing Finance and Mortgage Market Policy." In *Government Credit Allocation*, edited by Karl Brunner, p. 119. San Francisco: Institute for Contemporary Studies.

Mayer, Thomas. 1975. "Credit Allocation: A Critical View." In *Government Credit Allocation*, edited by Karl Brunner, p. 91. San Francisco: Institute for Contemporary Studies.

Meltzer, Allan H. 1975. "Credit Availability and Economic Decisions: Some Evidence from the Mortgage and Housing Markets." In *Government Credit Allocation*, edited by Karl Brunner, p. 149. San Francisco: Institute for Contemporary Studies.

Miller, Randall J. 1980a. "An Analysis of Chartering and Conversions, 1960–1977." In *State and Federal Regulation of Commercial Banking*, edited by Leonard Lapidus et al., vol. 2, pp. 495–96. Washington, D.C.: Federal Deposit Insurance Corp.

_____. 1980b. "On the Cost of Double Supervision for Insured State Chartered Banks." In *State and Federal Regulation of Commercial Banking*, edited by Leonard Lapidus et al., pp. 379–80. Washington, D.C.: Federal Deposit Insurance Corp.

National Commission on Consumer Finance. 1972. *Consumer Credit in the United States: Report of the National Commission on Consumer Finance.* Washington, D.C.: U.S. Government Printing Office.

Peach, W. Nelson. 1941. *The Security Affiliates of National Banks.* Baltimore: The Johns Hopkins Press.

Peterson, Richard L. 1981. "An Investigation of Sex Discrimination in Commercial Banks' Direct Consumer Lending." *Bell Journal of Economics* 12 (Autumn): 547–61.

Rockoff, Hugh. 1974. "The Free Banking Era: A Reexamination." *Journal of Money, Credit and Banking* 6 (May): 141–67.

Rohner, Ralph J. 1980. "Problems of Federalism in the Regulation of Consumer Financial Services Offered by Commercial Banks." In *State and Federal Regulation of Commercial Banks*, edited by Leonard Lapidus et al., vol. 2, pp. 1–168, esp. 16–75. Washington, D.C.: Federal Deposit Insurance Corp.

Smith, James F. 1977. "The Equal Credit Opportunity Act of 1974: A Cost/Benefit Analysis." *Journal of Finance* 32 (May): 609–22.

Smith, Vera C. 1936. *The Rationale of Central Banking.* London: P.S. King & Son.

Warburton, Clark. 1966. *Depression, Inflation and Monetary Policy, Selected Papers: 1945–53.* Baltimore: The Johns Hopkins Press.

Willis, H. Parker. 1902. "The Demand for Centralized Banking." *Sound Currency* 8 (March): 23–24.

2 RISKS AND FAILURES IN BANKING
Overview, History, and Evaluation

George J. Benston
George G. Kaufman

At least since the Great Depression of the 1930s, public policy toward banking and financial services in the United States has emphasized safety at the expense of competition and efficiency. The original rationale for this emphasis is understandable. The 1930s were an economic and financial holocaust. The U.S. economy experienced its worst crisis in history. The number of commercial banks declined by 40 percent from about 25,000 to near 14,000 between 1929 and 1933, and all banks were closed for at least three days during a national bank holiday in March 1933.

But times have changed dramatically since then. While not perfect, overall economic performance has been relatively satisfactory. Increases in the level and volatility of interest rates, in large measure the result of increases in the level and volatility of inflation, have provided depositors and suppliers of financial services with incentives to circumvent regulatory barriers—many of which were put in place in the 1930s to combat the actual or perceived problems of that day—that both imposed interest rate ceilings on deposit accounts and restricted transaction accounts to commercial banks. At the same time, advances in telecommunications and computer technology, which permitted the rapid and low-cost transfer of funds and information from both account to account and institution to institution, have provided the means to circumvent the barriers. The technology also has permitted banks to compete outside their traditional geographical and product market areas and allowed many other firms to offer financial services previously restricted to commercial banks. Thus, the number and type of firms comprising the financial services industry increased, and competition intensified.

While much in the public limelight, recent de jure deregulation has primarily validated the de facto deregulation already produced by market forces. It did, however, help to remove some remaining vestiges of regulation that, although mostly ineffective, produced inequities where still effective. At the same time, risk in banking increased because of higher levels and volatility in interest rates; rapid runups followed by equally rapid rundowns in the prices of real estate, energy, and agricultural products; financial difficulties in many less-developed countries; and advances in technology that permit almost immediate and costless transfer of funds and that greatly increase the importance, cost, and complexity of internal control and monitoring systems. As a result, the number of bank and other depository institution failures has increased sharply. What should be the response of public policy?

The answer depends greatly on how important individual bank (in the generic sense to include all depository and other financial institutions) failures are for other financial institutions, the banking system as a whole, and the national economy. If they are likely to ignite instability throughout the financial system and reduce economic activity severely, such as occurred in the 1930s, then adoption of new, more effective pro-safety and anticompetitive regulations could be in order. If failures of individual institutions are unlikely to spread to other institutions or to severely restrict national economic activity, then public policy need not be as concerned with bank safety and soundness and can be directed more at increasing competition and efficiency. This chapter first delineates the sources of individual bank risks and considers why and how they have become more important in recent years. It then analyzes the interrelationships between bank risk, bank runs, and bank failures and the conditions under which individual bank failures can spread to other banks and destabilize the banking system and economy as a whole. Next, it reviews the record of bank failures in U.S. history since the Civil War to determine the extent to which such failures and bank runs actually have been serious problems. Finally, the importance of bank failures in the current environment is analyzed and conclusions are drawn about the most effective ways to deal with them in the public interest.

SOURCES OF INDIVIDUAL BANK RISK

Individual banks face, assume, and even seek out risks that could lead to significant reductions in their net worth and, at the extreme, to insolvency and failure. The most important risk faced (as compared to sought out) by a bank is fraud. In this situation, only the defrauder benefits. But for other types of risk, bank owners and managers generally expect to benefit because the risk of loss usually is accompanied by an even greater expectation of gain. In contrast, banking authorities and the deposit insurance agencies, in particular, bear the cost of excessive risk taking of any type by banks. Besides fraud, risk taking can take the form of (1) credit risk, (2) interest-rate risk, (3) securities speculation, (4) foreign-exchange risk, (5) risk taking by related organizations, (6) operations risk, (7) regulatory risk, and (8) liquidity risk. Each of these sources of individual bank risk is discussed briefly.

Though each type of risk is discussed separately, the total risk of a bank's failing is not simply a function of the sum of the individual risks. As is well known in portfolio theory, one type of risk can offset another, and the acceptance of one risk can reduce the amount of another. For example, highly variable cash flows from individual activities taken alone might indicate high risk for each but when summed may yield lower overall variability and, hence, lower risk for the firm as a whole. Thus, real estate investment might be risky if done alone, but the cash flows derived therefrom may be imperfectly or negatively correlated with the cash flows from business loans and result in lower overall risk for the bank. It should also be noted that the cost of reducing risk may be greater than the benefits—risk reduction is not an end in itself.

Fraud Risk

Frauds—outright theft—are particularly troublesome because they result in the largest losses to depositors and other creditors, including the deposit insurance agency. In other failures, the banks' assets usually have substantial liquidation value, but in frauds the assets involved are frequently gone altogether. Fraud has always been a big problem for banks and their regulators. For example, the Comptroller of the Currency has cited fraud and violations of the law as the most frequent cause of national bank failures between 1865 and 1931, when the Great Depression took the honors. Over the years 1914 through 1920, citations for fraud comprised 63 percent of the total number of identified causes of bank failures. The percentage dropped to 16 over the decade 1921 through 1929, when local economic depression was identified as the principal cause (Benston 1973: Table VII). Between 1934 and 1958 the FDIC reported that in "approximately one-fourth of the banks, defalcation or losses attributable to financial irregularities by officers and employees appear to have been the primary cause of failure" (Federal Deposit Insurance Corporation 1958). One study found that 66 percent of the failures during 1959–71 were due to fraud and irregularities (Benston 1973: Table XI). Another study that covered much of the same period—1960–74—reported that 88 percent of the sixty-seven failures were due to improper loans, defalcations, embezzlements, and manipulations (Hill 1975).

The most recent studies show that fraud continues to be the principal contributor to bank failures. The causes of the failures of thirty-three banks in 1982 and forty-seven failures in 1983 and the first quarter of 1984 are identified as follows: malfeasance alone, 30 percent; malfeasance and low performance, 15 percent; malfeasance and rapid growth, 16 percent; and malfeasance and both poor performance and rapid growth, 5 percent. In sum, 66 percent of these failures are due in whole or in part to malfeasance (Peterson and Scott 1985). Similarly, a survey by a congressional committee found that in the seventy-five commercial bank failures between 1980 and mid-1983, 61 percent involved actual or probable criminal misconduct by insiders and 45 percent involved criminal conduct as a major contributing factor (Committee on Government Operations 1984).

Fraud can take many forms. Simple looting of vaults is rare, perhaps because more can be stolen at less risk in other ways. Perhaps the most popular way is making loans to confederates who use the proceeds in very risky ventures or just dissipate the funds. In such situations it is difficult for the authorities to prove that the bad loans were not the consequence of bad luck or bad judgment rather than fraud. Contemporary and rather spectacular examples of this practice appear to include the failures of the United States National Bank of San Diego, the Penn Square Bank of Oklahoma City, the United American Bank in Knoxville, Empire Savings and Loan of Mesquite, Texas, and possibly Home State Savings Bank in Cincinnati, Ohio. (See Committee on Government Operations 1984 for examples and an extensive analysis.)

Operations related to the normal lending and borrowing of securities can be another means by which banks are defrauded. Dishonest bank officers and customers can either gamble with or simply steal a bank's assets by using securities or other collateral that the bank did not keep under sufficiently close control. This appears to have occurred in the supposedly secured loans made by means of reverse repurchase agreements by Home State Savings of Cincinnati, Ohio, to ESM Securities. The collateral securities were not deposited with an independent third party but effectively remained under ESM control, which misused them. Partially as a result, Home State failed in 1985. Earlier fraudulent use of collateral securities by Drysdale Securities of New York had cost the Chase Manhattan Bank, which acted as a conduit in providing Drysdale with reverse repurchase agreement customers, nearly $300 million in losses (Welles 1982).

Moreover, few if any of the white-collar crime culprits are prosecuted, and those that are rarely serve significant time in prison. Thus, the penalties for fraud are relatively weak.

Credit Risk

A primary activity of banks, and one for which they have a comparative advantage over many other organizations, is the assessment, monitoring, and resolution of credit risks. Such risks are kept within acceptable bounds by means of regularized routines for documentation, approval, and follow-up of defaults. Diversification of loans by the borrower and restrictions on the amounts that can be lent to a single borrower or related group of borrowers are important in reducing catastrophic losses. Diversification among industries, countries, and other groupings of borrowers, who may be similarly affected by adverse economic events, also is useful for reducing risk.

Occasionally, such constraints on credit risks are not taken. A notorious example is the Penn Square Bank, where lending officers wrote over a billion dollars in loans, twice the size of the bank, to a single industry—petroleum—based on little more than the bankers' unsupported and undocumented belief that the borrowers were "good for it" and that the industry was booming and could be expected to continue to boom. Amazingly, the Penn Square Bank had little trouble in selling large amounts of such poorly or completely undocumented loans to such major banks as Continental Illinois, Seattle-First, Northern Trust, Michigan National, and Chase Manhattan (Singer 1985; Zweig 1985). A consequence of these risky and often fraudulent lending practices was the economic failure of both the Continental and Seattle-First banks as well as the Penn Square Bank.

Banks that concentrated their loans in a single industry have failed as a consequence, even though they may have used reasonable credit standards and controls when writing the loans. For example, the Public Bank of Detroit, which was one of the largest U.S. failures at the time it failed in 1966, concentrated in loans to mobile home dealers. When that industry became severely depressed economically, the bank's portfolio declined in value sufficiently to use up its equity. More recently, banks in Oregon that were heavily involved in the timber industry and banks in midwestern farm states have experienced relatively high rates of failure as the industries in which they specialized fell on hard times (see Bovenzi and Nejezchleb 1985). A similar situation explains the high rate of failure in the 1920s and early 1930s of banks in the western grain and southeastern and southwestern farm states (see Benston 1973: Table III).

"Country risk" is a related aspect of credit risk. It refers to the possibility that loans will not be repaid as promised because economic conditions in the borrowing country have deteriorated to the point where the foreign exchange needed to service loans made in foreign currency is unlikely to be available or because the government will not permit the loans to be repaid and/or will not repay the loans made to it. Some of the largest U.S. (and foreign) banks are currently experiencing considerable losses due to this type of risk from loans to Eastern European and Latin American countries.

Interest-Rate Risk

An unexpected change in market rates of interest changes the present values of fixed-interest-rate assets and liabilities because the interest payments are discounted at higher or lower rates. The greater the change and the longer the maturities (or, more properly, the durations) of the obligations, the greater the change in present values. When banks have assets and liabilities that are unbalanced with respect to durations, interest-rate risk can be very serious because, unlike many other risks, there is nothing to offset a negative event. Consequently, those who accept this form of risk may be characterized as "betting the bank."

As long as interest rates were stable, interest-rate risk was only a minor danger. But the interest-rate changes experienced since the late 1970s have shown that this risk quickly can become major with serious consequences. Thrift institutions, in particular, were adversely affected by the increase in the level and volatility of interest rates because they held predominantly long-term fixed-interest assets (mortgages) that were funded with short-term liabilities (savings deposits). They were able to hold this interest-rate sensitive portfolio because, to a large extent, deposit insurance removed the risk to depositors. As Kane (1985) explains, the fact that deposit insurance is not priced in relation to the risk assumed by the institutions gives them a strong incentive to gamble that interest rates will decrease rather than increase or remain unchanged. But many of them lost this gamble during the past seven years. Indeed, most of the official failures among thrifts were due to the unexpected increase in interest rates that occurred (Benston 1986). Few were the result of the misuse of new powers. Moreover, because a depository institution can continue operations even though it is economically insolvent if the authorities decline to declare it legally insolvent, interest-rate risk has resulted in many more insolvencies than failures. Kane estimates that as of December 31, 1983, the thrifts' aggregate net worth after deducting unrealized losses on mortgages was a negative $86 billion (Kane 1985; Tables 4–5 and 4–6). Other studies found similar results (Auerbach and McCall 1985; Barth, Brumbaugh, Sauerhaft, and Wang 1985; Barth, Bisenius, Brumbaugh, and Sauerhaft 1985).

Thrift institutions were not the only institutions to gamble on interest-rate declines, and mortgages were not the only means for gambling on interest-rate changes. Long-term bonds that are funded with short-term borrowings were used by the First Pennsylvania Bank, which failed economically, if not legally, in 1980. In 1979, when interest rates went up instead of down, the bank's bond portfolio is estimated to have declined in market value by $89 million, which contributed considerably to reducing its equity below zero if measured at market values (Maisel 1981: 123–34).

Forward or standby commitments to sell securities at a fixed price or yield on a future date at the option of the purchaser is another means of taking interest-rate risk. The banker selling the commitments gets a fee up-front and accepts the possibility of a large later loss. Such transactions appeal to risk-seeking bankers because they offer the prospect of immediate profits and increases in new work and do not require much expertise or expense.

Securities Speculation

The market value of equities changes more rapidly than that of many assets, and therefore they often are considered a vehicle for risk taking. Federal Reserve member commercial banks, however, are forbidden by the Glass-Steagall Act from underwriting and trading equities, and all banks are prohibited from investing in corporate equities. However, banks can hold corporate bonds and mortgages and other asset-backed bonds of varying degrees of risk. Depository institutions generally also can hold very high risk, high nominal yield "junk" bonds. However, while each of these assets individually can be risky, a portfolio of such and other assets need not be very risky if it is well diversified. The cash flows from the portfolios also might offset cash flows from other aspects of a bank's operations, which reduces overall risk.

Foreign Exchange Risk

Foreign exchange risk includes speculative dealings by means of options and forward contracts. Franklin National Bank of New York is the premier U.S. example of such risk taking. Before it failed in 1974, it was the twentieth-largest U.S. bank. When it failed, it achieved the distinction of being the largest U.S. bank failure up to that time. While factors other than foreign-exchange speculation caused Franklin's problems, as its financial situation worsened, it undertook increasingly risky foreign-exchange transactions. These transactions resulted in a $65 million loss for the first five months of 1974, the largest loss ever reported to that date by a U.S. bank

(Spero 1980: 126). Similar speculations were responsible in 1974 for the failure of Bankhaus I.D. Herstatt—one of Germany's largest private banks—and for sizable losses by other banks, including Citicorp.

Risk Taking by Related Organizations

Organizations related to a bank—such as subsidiaries and affiliates— can be used for excessive risk taking that is not controlled by the authorities, or as a means of separating risk-taking activities from ordinary banking. Affiliates are frequently said to have been used as a means of securities speculation and other risk-taking activities by banks prior to passage of the Glass-Steagall Act. However, evidence to this effect is not unequivocal (Peach 1941). A more current example is the Hamilton National Bank of Chattanooga, which was the third-largest U.S. bank failure when it failed in 1976. Hamilton invested heavily and disastrously in real estate loans that were recorded as assets of its holding company affiliate, Hamilton Mortgage Corporation of Atlanta. The bad loans were shifted ("sold") from the affiliate to the bank. Thus, the separate corporate form did not insulate the bank from the losses incurred because the practice violated banking regulations, however, the situation might better be described as a fraud (Sinkey 1979: 199–205).

The incentives for a banking organization to accept responsibility, even for entities to which they are not legally related, was demonstrated by many banks in their treatment of the real estate investment trusts (REITs) they sponsored. Though the REITs were not bank affiliates, the losses they took were absorbed by many of the sponsoring banks, which apparently feared a loss of their reputations, particularly when the REITs bore the bank's name (Sinkey 1979: 237–55). Thus, shifting activities to a related organization did not shield the banks from the losses incurred.

Operations Risk

Operations risk refers to the possibility that a bank's operating costs will exceed its operating revenues to the extent that its continued existence is threatened. This, of course, is not special to banking.

Because the risks discussed above are within the control of a bank's management, they are all forms of operations risk. For example, fraud, foreign-exchange risk, and credit risk are likely to increase when a bank does not have a well-maintained and monitored system of internal controls.

High operations cost because of mismanagement or overambition have led to the failure of a number of banks. Overambition apparently was the initial cause of Franklin National's failure. The bank incurred high operating expenses and credit losses in its attempt to expand quickly from a suburban Long Island bank to a major New York City bank after the New York state branching laws were liberalized to permit branching throughout the metropolitan area.

Fraud by customers is a form of operations risk, a risk that is made more serious by the increasing complexity of banking transactions and the advances in technology that permit large sums to be transferred almost immediately among accounts and institutions. Computer experts and skilled amateurs (hackers) attempt to and sometimes succeed in violating electronically a bank's security and funds-transfer systems. Recently, E. F. Hutton admitted to obtaining billions of dollars in interest-free funds by writing checks on uncollected balances, a form of check kiting made possible on a large scale by computers. As effective internal control systems become more difficult to construct, they also become more important to implement.

Daylight overdrafts are another form of operations risk. Banks can pay out amounts equal to many times their capital in funds that are uncollected from other banks at the time but that they expect to collect by the end of the accounting day. Should a paying bank fail during the day and these funds not be collected, the entire system could be severely disrupted and perhaps be forced to grind to a halt. This almost happened when Bankhaus Herstatt (Germany) failed in 1974.

Regulatory Risk

Changes in regulations can affect banks' ability to cope with risks and even to survive. Most notably, the prohibition of interstate branching and, in many states, of intrastate branching contributed to the large number of the failures of U.S. banks in the 1920s and

1930s. These laws hampered small banks in diversifying their portfolios efficiently. When local economic conditions declined severely, deposits at these banks were increasingly withdrawn at the same time, and an increasing proportion of their loans became uncollectible. Not having funds and gains from other areas to offset their losses, many of these banks had to close their doors. This situation is being repeated to some extent in the 1980s, as small agricultural banks have been failing when the economic condition of their homogeneous customers deteriorated.

Legislation, such as the Community Reinvestment Act, has encouraged banks to make loans to borrowers located in particular geographic areas (or punishes them for not doing so). The result can be inefficiently diversified portfolios. Should the value of the collateral or economic situation of these concentrated borrowers deteriorate, a bank could incur losses sufficient to wipe out its capital.

Legal and regulatory restrictions on bank investments can also impose inefficiencies on banking operations. The Glass-Steagall Act, which prohibits banks from offering corporate security underwriting, is one such example. Until recently, thrift institutions were constrained by laws and regulations that prohibited them from offering checking accounts, business loans, variable (adjustable) rate residential mortgages, and direct investments in real estate and other assets. Because of these laws (and tax subsidies), which rewarded thrift institutions for specializing in mortgages, the thrifts' portfolios were excessively vulnerable to unexpected increases in interest rates.

Interest-rate controls have also been another important example of the pernicious effect of regulations on bank risk. While the prohibition of interest on demand deposits and ceilings on savings and time deposit interest (Regulation Q) initially benefited banks, its long-term effect was to make it more difficult for banks to compete effectively for funds with "unregulated" suppliers of similar banking services. State-imposed usury ceilings on loans have led to similar inefficiencies.

Liquidity Risk

Many depositors have claims on banks that can be exercised at par value at any time without notice. Consequently, if they have reason to believe that these claims may not be honored because the bank has incurred significant losses, the depositors have incentives to remove their funds immediately—to run. The only constraints are the transactions costs of the transfer (which usually are very small) and the costs of disrupting banking relationships (which are likely to be more considerable).

Liquidity risk refers to the possibility that depositors will withdraw funds at a rate that exceeds a bank's ability to replenish their funds, except by borrowing at higher-than-normal interest cost (including emergency borrowing from the Federal Reserve window) or by selling assets at lower-than-normal (fire-sale) prices. Should these additional costs or losses exceed the bank's capital, it would fail.

COPING WITH RISK

Banks do not attempt to eliminate risks; indeed, to do so would be inimical to banking. Banks are organized to deal efficiently with risks—that is one of their principal comparative advantages over other types of firms. The bankers' skills consist of effectively equating at the margin the benefits and costs of risk taking.

For example, the risk of fraud can be reduced by expenditures on internal control systems. Credit risk can be reduced by administrative procedures for loan approvals and monitoring to assure that diversification, collateral, and repayment requirements are being met. But a bank would not want to eliminate credit losses because this could not be done without forgoing lending. Instead, banks charge customers for the risk of nonrepayment that is expected.

Interest-rate risk can be reduced by a bank's holding a more duration-balanced portfolio. Adjustable-rate mortgages can be made rather than fixed-rate mortgages, though at the expense of possibly greater credit risk because the mortgagor's income or the market value of the collateral may not increase, pari passu, with increases in market rates of interest. Unmatched cash positions may be offset by purchasing or selling interest-rate futures and options contracts.

Regulatory risk can be reduced by expenditures on lobbying and planning. Liquidity risk can be mitigated by a bank's holding greater amounts of readily marketable assets and establishing lines of credit.

Although risk may be reduced through diversification, sufficient risk reduction may not always be possible or pursued for at least three reasons. First, laws and regulations may not permit bankers to diversify optimally. As noted, until recently, such laws included restraints on branching and on the products that banks may offer and assets in which they can invest.

Second, diversification can be costly if a bank must give up advantages from specialization. For example, a bank in a small farming community benefits from specializing in farm loans even though this specialization subjects it to a higher risk of failure. Banks specializing in oil and timber loans benefited as long as the prices of these resources continued to rise.

Third, diversification is not undertaken by bankers who want to take risks. Banks continue to specialize in industries with which they have a special relation and expertise. Many, perhaps most, thrifts still hold duration-unbalanced portfolios of fixed-interest-rate, long-term residential mortgages. Managers of economically insolvent institutions have incentives to "bet the bank." As is discussed next, deposit insurance that is not priced to reflect the risks taken by bankers encourages bankers to take excessive risks or at least protects them from market constraints on such risk taking.

RECENT CHANGES IN BANK RISK EXPOSURE

Although incentives for risk taking have always existed in banking, they have been increased in a number of ways in recent years.

Risk Taking and Deposit Insurance

Depositors with account balances under $100,000 in banks and thrifts that are insured by the Federal Deposit Insurance Corporation or Federal Savings and Loan Insurance Corporation have no reason to be concerned about the risks taken by their banks. Uninsured depositors are at risk, unless they believe that their funds are de facto insured, as occurred when the Continental Illinois Bank failed, or that they can remove their funds before their bank is closed.

This is not to say that bankers are unconcerned about failure: It might cause bank owners to lose their investments and bankers their jobs. Indeed, if the amount of investment by owners and managers in a bank is sufficient, risk taking by bankers should be no more a problem than risk taking by anyone else. Alternatively, the deposit insurance agency could charge banks for the risks they undertake. Then bankers would be faced with the same problem faced by other decision makers: They must balance at the margin the benefits from additional risks undertaken with the costs of such risks.

However, deposit insurance is not now priced directly to reflect risks undertaken. Rather, banks are charged indirectly for risk taking in the form of more extensive and expensive monitoring by bank examiners and supervisors and by legal and regulatory constraints on their activities. Because federal deposit insurance premiums were not tied to a bank's risk exposure, the value of deposit insurance increased sharply as a result of the greater volatility of interest rates in the late 1970s and early 1980s (Kane 1985). Deposit insurance gave bankers, who held assets with greater duration than liabilities, a valuable option; they would benefit if interest rates decreased unexpectedly, while the deposit insurance agencies stood to lose if rates increased unexpectedly. Heads the bank wins, tails the insurance agency loses. The greater the volatility of interest rates, the greater the expected value of the gamble. Many, particularly thrift institutions, willingly took this gamble. More recently, many institutions have taken similar gambles on high credit-risk ventures.

Deposit insurance has also allowed banks and thrifts to hold lower amounts of equity capital. Were it not for deposit insurance, it is doubtful if depositors would keep funds in banks with capital ratios as low as those found in many banks and most thrift institutions. Bank capital ratios were substantially higher before the introduction of federal deposit insurance in 1934.

Finally, the increase in federal deposit insurance coverage in 1980 from $40,000 to $100,000 per account in each insured institution occurred just as computers sharply reduced the cost of transferring funds and keeping track of deposit accounts and as deposit-rate ceilings began to be removed. As a result, depositors were offered the opportunity of placing large sums in risk-free accounts without concern about the practices or even name and location of the institution. Bidding for insured deposits by institutions anywhere in the country, particularly by banks that engaged in particularly risky activities, became feasible. (Though brokers are useful for such fund acquisitions, they are not necessary because bankers can use their own personnel and newspaper advertising to contact depositors.) The removal of deposit-rate ceilings made it possible for banks to bid for funds in more efficient ways. Previously, banks could only offer depositors convenience in the form of branches and other services as a means of both making up the difference between the Regulation Q ceiling rates and higher market interest rates and competing for funds against other institutions. Thus, a bank's growth was pretty much limited by geography to its surrounding area. Now a bank's market can be the entire country, or even the world, if it so wishes.

Risk Taking and Bank Capital

The riskiness of banking activities was increased, in the sense that bank failures became more likely, by decreases in bank capital. Measured in economic rather than in accounting values, equity capital in banks and thrifts decreased as a consequence of two effects of the interest rate increases in the late 1970s. One was the entrance of non-chartered and "unregulated" suppliers of banking services into the banks' and thrifts' markets as market rates of interest greatly exceeded Regulation Q ceilings. The resulting growth of money market mutual funds and interest-bearing checking accounts offered by brokers decreased the intangible and unrecorded franchise value of bank and thrift charters. The other effect was the decrease in the present value of banks' and particularly thrifts' long-term, fixed-interest assets, which also is a decrease in their equity. The deregulation of deposit interest rates in the early 1980s served to increase the present value of the institutions' liabilities, which further decreased their equities.

Risk Taking and Deregulation

It is important to note that the increase in incentives toward risk taking is not due to the deregulation. Indeed, much of the deregulation that removed constraints on banks' ability to diversify and extend their activities and portfolios have tended to decrease risks. Almost all of the bank and thrift failures since have been the result of traditional frauds, previously permitted activities, and duration imbalances. In particular, commercial banks have not been permitted to offer many new products. The most widely publicized has been discount brokerage services, and these have not resulted in solvency-threatening losses. Few if any thrifts appear to have failed because they were given the power to offer checking accounts and consumer and business loans or to invest directly as majority owners in real estate and service corporations. They used more traditional ways to eliminate their net worth (Benston 1985). An analysis of bank failures in the post-deregulation period shows that no more than 17 percent involved sustained low performance without some form of malfeasance involved (Peterson and Scott 1985).

BANK FAILURES AND FINANCIAL INSTABILITY

We have argued above that, although bank risk taking has always existed, it has become more prevalent in recent years and has been accompanied by an increase in the number of bank failures to the highest levels since the 1930s. At least in part, the increase in bank risk, and thereby also in bank failures, is the expected outcome of not scaling federal deposit insurance premiums to the risk exposure of the insured bank. The balance of this paper examines whether the increase in individual bank failures threatens the stability of the national banking system and overall levels of economic activity.

Bank Failures

Banks fail in economic terms when the market value of their assets declines below the market value of their deposits and other borrowings. At that time, all depositors and creditors cannot expect to be paid in full and on time. The bank should be declared legally insolvent so that all depositors and other creditors can be treated equally. If not, those depositors who withdraw their funds from the bank first will be paid in full and those that wait, either because of ignorance or later maturity dates, will experience losses. Delay in declaring a bank legally insolvent does not affect its economic solvency or the size of past losses; they have already occurred. It affects only those who suffer the losses. But delays can increase future losses as the bank is encouraged to gamble to seek large gains. After all, with no capital left, the bank has little more to lose and much to gain.

As noted earlier, most depositors know that a large proportion of a bank's deposits have put options exercisable at par without notice at any time and that banks operate on fractional reserves and may have to take losses on hurried "fire-sales" of earning assets at below their fair equilibrium market values given normal search time. Thus, these depositors are motivated to withdraw their uninsured funds from a bank that is perceived to experience financial difficulties as soon as the difference between the value of the banking affiliation and the costs of fund transfer, which generally are low, fall below the expected loss. If the bank is economically solvent at the time a bank run starts, the only harm to the bank will be fire-sale losses on asset sales or losses from paying higher rates on hurried borrowings. If these losses exceed the bank's economic net worth, the bank would experience "fire-sale insolvency." Because all the bank requires to remain solvent is time, assistance from other banks or the Federal Reserve is appropriate and may reasonably be expected to be forthcoming. If the bank is economically insolvent when the run starts, additional losses attributable to the run per se would also be only fire-sale losses. They probably would be small relative to the bank's losses before the run, although larger than the fire-sale losses experienced by solvent banks, since the assets may, on average, be expected to be less marketable. In this case, assistance from other banks is unlikely to be forthcoming and from the Fed inappropriate. Such a bank particularly needs to be declared insolvent so that remaining depositors can be treated fairly, and owners/managers can be removed before they incur additional risk in a last-ditch effort to regain profitability and save their investment and/or jobs.

Bank Runs

The consequences of a bank run on other banks depend on what depositors do with the funds they withdraw. They have three alternatives: (1) redeposit at other banks, (2) purchase nonbank securities, or (3) hold currency outside the banking system. Which they do matters greatly.

If depositors perceive the financial difficulties to be limited to one or a few banks, they are likely to redeposit their funds directly at other, perceived safe, banks. After all, currency is an inferior form of money for almost everything but the purchase of small-ticket items. If redeposited, the deposits are only transferred within the banking system; they are not destroyed. Ceteris paribus, there is no decline in aggregate money and credit, and the problems of the affected banks are not transmitted to the system as a whole.

The larger the number or size of banks perceived to be in difficulty, the less likely are depositors to view as many other banks as safe and to redeposit directly. Many depositors are likely to purchase perceived safer securities, such as those of the U.S. Treasury—a flight to quality. The outcome now depends on what the sellers of the safer securities do with the proceeds. Because these transactions are likely to be relatively large, the funds probably will be deposited at a "safe" bank, possibly, particularly in the United States, quite a distance away. If so, aggregate deposits again would not change. But interest-rate spreads are likely to be changed somewhat as depositors bid up the yields (bid down the price) on riskier securities, including bank deposits, relative to safer securities. This is likely to dampen private investment and increase uncertainty. Although both effects may be expected to influence economic activity adversely, they are likely to be second-order effects. However, if the sellers of the safe securities hold the proceeds as currency, the implications would be different and more serious.

If the withdrawn funds are not redeposited at other banks either directly or indirectly but held as currency, they represent a reserve drain from the banking system as a whole. There is a run on the banking system rather than on only individual banks or group of banks. Unless offset by a Fed injection of an equal dollar amount of reserves, the banking system will undergo the much-feared multiple contraction in deposits and credit, and aggregate money will be reduced. The difficulties of one bank will spread to other banks as the instability is transmitted in domino fashion throughout the system. Banks are also likely to experience greater fire-sale losses as the number of sellers increases, and more banks are likely to be driven into fire-sale insolvency. In this scenario, private bank support is more difficult, and appropriate Fed action more important. Thus, a net currency drain from the system is a prerequisite for individual bank problems to contaminate a large number of other banks and the system as a whole.

But net currency drains are now unlikely and, as will be shown later, have not been frequent in U.S. history. As long as depositors are confident in the ability of the federal deposit insurance funds to pay fully and promptly and the minimum coverage per account is not too low, small depositors have no incentive to withdraw deposits from any bank and hold currency. Although Henry Ford threatened to do so in 1907, large depositors cannot conduct their operations efficiently with currency and are also unlikely to withdraw their funds from all banks. Thus, even in the absence of appropriate Fed policy to maintain reserves, contagious and severe bank problems are highly unlikely in today's federal deposit insurance environment. There is no reason, therefore, for the authorities to delay declaring a bank insolvent. Even if the declaration intensifies the run on the insolvent bank, it is unlikely to destabilize many other banks or the banking system. Furthermore, fear of runs by bank managers is a desirable constraint on their taking excessive risks. If they have reason to be concerned that depositors might withdraw their funds should they perceive that the bank might become insolvent, bankers would have greater incentives to operate their banks safely and to voluntarily inform depositors about their banks' condition and operations. The net result may be fewer, rather than more, bank failures.

Aside from contagiousness, how important is a bank failure on the community? As noted, banks fail economically when they experience losses on assets greater than their economic net worth. Other than fraud, losses are likely to reflect depressed economic conditions of the bank's loan customers, local lending community, or the nation, or sharp, unexpected increases in interest rates. Such losses represent feedback from the economy to the banks and must be distinguished from any further effects that bank failures have on the economy. Only the latter are of concern to us here. When a bank fails and is declared legally insolvent, employees, customers, and creditors as well as shareholders are harmed. However, with the exception of customized loans, bank services are more or less homogenous, and most employees and customers should not be inconvenienced greatly in transferring to other banks or providers of the particular service. Indeed, banking services are more homogeneous than the products of many other types of firms, and the cost of transfer among providers is less. Furthermore, under most circumstances, a failed bank is likely to be sold or merged so that the facility will remain, although possibly as a branch office. Under these circumstances customers with long-standing loan connections are likely to be disadvantaged most, but even they may not be harmed greatly because not all loan officers of the failed bank will lose their jobs. Thus, though bank failures are not costless, they also are not calamities for a community.

Evidence from History

Why then have we been so fearful of bank runs and failures and have we directed public policy at minimizing if not preventing them altogether? Our research suggests that many of the public's concerns are based on a brief and not very representative period in U.S. history— the Great Depression from 1929–33. As noted earlier, the number of banks declined by 40 percent from some 25,000 to near 14,000, while the economy declined to record depths. The financial system literally was in a shambles, banks in many states were closed for all business for days at a time during bank "holidays," and finally all banks were temporarily closed by President Roosevelt in March 1933. Depositors lost faith in almost all banks, and the currency to total bank deposit ratio jumped from 9 percent in 1929 to 19 percent in 1933 and to 23 percent, when government guaranteed postal savings are included as currency. Aggregate deposits and money declined by one-third, and banks appeared to fail in domino style. Many of the survivors of this financial holocaust were so traumatized by the event and recorded it with such emotion and flair that they affected public policy not only at the time but for decades to come. Most of the regulations stressing safety and anticompetitivenss—such as Regulation Q, separation of investment and commercial banking, and more restricted entry—were enacted at the time in response to the crisis.

A review of history, however, shows that the experience of the 1930s was the exception rather than the rule. Although there were some 10,000 commercial banks in operation in 1892, 20,000 by 1906 and 30,000 by 1920, there was only one year between 1865 and 1919 in which more than 200 banks failed (491 in 1893) and only nine years in which more than 100 banks failed. As can be seen from Table 2–1, the annual rate of bank failure averaged 0.8 percent in this period, well below the failure rate of 1.0 percent for other firms. And this was before federal deposit insurance and, except for the last six years of the period, the Federal Reserve! The annual losses suffered by depositors at failed banks during these years was estimated by the FDIC to have averaged only 0.2 percent of total deposits. (This estimate is somewhat on the low side, since the FDIC did not discount delayed payments by an interest rate; nevertheless, it does provide a ballpark figure.) Currency drains, as measured by

Table 2-1. Commercial Bank and Business Failures, 1865–1935.

	Mean	Standard Deviation	Coefficient of Variation
Number of bank failures:			
1865–1935	262	590	
1865–1919	64	71	
1920–1933	1,070	966	
1930–1933	2,274	1,062	
Bank failure rate:			
1875–1935[a]	1.82	3.88	8.27
1875–1929[a]	1.02	1.03	1.04
1875–1919[a]	0.82	0.96	1.12
1920–1933	4.61	6.65	9.60
1930–1933	13.05	8.89	6.06
Business failure rate:			
1875–1935	1.00	0.24	0.06
1875–1929	1.00	0.22	0.05
1875–1919	1.01	0.23	0.05
1920–1933	1.01	0.26	0.07
1930–1933	1.27	0.19	0.02

a. Available data substantially underestimates number of banks through 1896.
Source: George Benston et al. (1986: ch. 2).

an increase in the currency to total bank deposit ratio concurrent with a decline in aggregate deposits, occurred in only three years— 1874, 1893, and 1908. To the extent that currency drains are a prerequisite for contagious bank failures, before 1920, contagion could have occurred only in these three years and probably only in 1893.

This interpretation appears to be supported by studies made at the time. These tend to attribute the failures primarily to fraud, mismanagement, and depressed local economies. Hardly any mention was made of contagiousness or ripple effects. In the absence of federal deposit insurance and the Federal Reserve, private banks themselves undertook the task of offsetting the systematic effects of bank runs and failures during this period, thereby stabilizing the system. At times of serious runs, when depositors wanted to convert their deposits into currency (or earlier, notes into specie), the banks with the implicit approval of regulators called time out. They temporarily suspended convertibility but continued almost all other bank operations, including fund transfers by check and loan originations. The suspension provided banks with the necessary time to search out the highest bidders for their more specialized loans and minimize fire-sale losses. At the same time, bank clearing houses circulated their own transferable certificates, which the banks and the public used as a substitute for currency. Furthermore, financial panics, in which most bank failures occur, tended to lag national economic downturns (Cagan 1965). In short, the evidence is strong that at least in the period from 1865 to 1919, at least, the major direction of causation was from depressed economic conditions to bank failures rather than the other way around. (Similar evidence for the free banking era before the Civil War has recently been generated by Rolnick and Weber 1985.)

In the 1920s, the number of bank failures jumped sharply to an average of about 600 per year and the failure rate to more than twice that of other firms, yet there was no increase in nonbank failures. Nor did the national economy experience any downturns. Most of the banks that failed were small and in agricultural areas. The failures spread little fear. Indeed, the currency to deposit ratio declined steadily from 15 percent to 9 percent, indicating increased confidence in the banking system. The next section applies the lessons from history to the current environment.

CURRENT POLICY PROBLEMS AND SOLUTIONS

The introduction of federal deposit insurance in 1934, which may be attributed in large measure to the failure of the Federal Reserve to inject sufficient reserves to offset the currency drain of 1930–33 and prevent the money stock from declining, has further stabilized the banking system. Indeed, there has been little if any evidence of a currency run on the banking system in recent years despite the abrupt jump in the number of bank failures to the highest levels since 1933 and the well-publicized economic insolvency of many of the country's thrift institutions. This was true even in Chicago, which experienced the failure of the Continental Illinois National Bank (the largest bank in the city and seventh largest in the country) and its two largest savings and loan associations, as well as a series of negative reports about the financial condition of most of its other large commercial banks. A recent study by the FDIC also found no statewide contagiousness or adverse aftereffects of the twenty-six bank failures in Tennessee between 1982 and 1984. The failed banks held 7 percent of total deposits in the state and more than one-third of the deposits in the Knoxville standard metropolitan area. The study concluded that the failures did, however, increase depositor awareness of federal deposit insurance and induce more conservative bank lending policies (Nejezchleb and Voesar 1985).

Nevertheless, to allay any possible public concern about the sufficiency of the insurance fund, such as has recently happened for some state funds (such as Ohio and Maryland), deposit insurance should be transformed into a full faith and credit guarantee of the federal government. Another concern is the recent increase in both the means and incentives for individual banks to incur additional risk stemming from advances in technology that permit the almost immediate and costless transfer of funds both within and across institutions, high and volatile interest rates, and federal deposit insurance premiums that are independent of an institution's risk exposure. Although losses from such risk are unlikely to destabilize the banking system or the national economy, they are likely to result in losses to the deposit insurance agency (and thus the taxpayers) if the insolvent institutions are not caught soon enough and closed. Thus, there remains legitimate public concern about the financial health of individual banks.

The most efficient solution to excessive risk taking by individual banks is to increase the forces of market discipline to the levels in other industries. This can be achieved in a number of ways. Bank owners can be placed at greater risk by increasing capital requirements. As studies have shown, the major reason that bank capital is low has been the artificially low failure rate under regulation and the introduction of federal deposit insurance, including de facto 100 percent insurance of almost all depositors. Before the establishment of the FDIC, bank capital ratios were more than twice as high and exceeded 30 percent in the second half of the 1800s. In addition, national bank and some state bank shareholders faced double liability and were assessed for additional funds when banks failed. This, undoubtedly, was a major contributor to the relatively low bank failure rate noted earlier.

Bankers may object to a requirement that they raise more capital. But capital is a source of funds that is distinguished from deposits primarily in two ways: Dividends on equity are not a deductible expense for tax purposes, and capital funds are not insured. The tax disadvantage can be reduced by permitting part of the requirement to be satisfied by subordinated debt that is de facto as well as de jure uninsured. Some of this debt should be short term. By being forced to enter the market periodically, banks will be more sensitive to the interest rate required on such debt, and the rate will serve as a signal to depositors and the supervisory authorities of the bank's risk exposure that is perceived by the market.

Uninsured depositors should also be placed at risk de facto as well as de jure so that they behave more as do the creditors of other firms. This should encourage them to monitor the bank's activities more carefully. At the same time, senior management at insolvent banks should be penalized and removed, and directors should assume greater liability for major policies and control procedures at their banks.

No bank should be too large to fail, although some may be too large to liquidate, recapitalize, sell, or merge quickly. Failure implies that shareholders are wiped out and top management is removed. This is not an insurmountable problem. The FDIC can take temporary control of an insolvent large bank through a "trusteeship" program, introduce management changes, and mark down the value of uninsured deposits by the estimated prorated negative economic net worth (Kaufman 1985). Thus, the bank would be treated as smaller insolvent banks are treated, and competitive equity would be maintained. Because the bank is not "closed," there is no interruption in business, and customer relations would be basically undisturbed. The FDIC would be required to sell, merge, or liquidate the bank within a specified period of time. The Federal Home Loan Bank System has recently adopted a similar "management consignment" program for some failed savings and loan associations.

As discussed earlier, except for fraud (and unexpected interest-rate increases for thrift institutions), uninsured depositor losses are unlikely to be very large if an economically insolvent bank is caught quickly. The value of the bank's total assets is unlikely to drop suddenly anywhere close to zero. Contrary to statements by some regulators at the time of the Continental Illinois Bank rescue, nonfraudulent banks are rarely "totaled." A loss of a few cents on the dollar is most likely if the bank is declared insolvent soon enough. The largest losses to both uninsured depositors and the insurance agencies have come from fraud (which is difficult to detect before the assets are dissipated) rather than from ordinary lending and investing, which are easier to monitor. This suggests that bank examiners need to reduce their emphasis on loan quality and increase their concern for detecting and preventing fraud.

Finally, federal deposit insurance premiums need to be scaled, at least in part, to an institution's risk exposure. This is necessary more to reestablish market incentives than to collect actuarially fair premiums, which, as discussed above, are more a function of monitoring than of known risk exposure. Indeed, as the insurance agency would experience no losses whatsoever if it caught a bank before its economic net worth became negative, deposit insurance is really not traditional insurance but a guarantee. Risk scaling may also be achieved through variable capital requirements and per diem charges for examinations and supervision.

CONCLUSIONS

By its nature, banking is a risky business, and, as in any business, successful institutions must control their risk exposure. Though the risks faced by banks are similar to those faced by other businesses, the basic nature of banking exacerbates some risks. The risk of fraud is particularly serious because banks deal with an intangible resource that can be readily stolen or profitably diverted—money. Other forms of risk include credit risk, interest-rate risk, securities speculation, foreign-exchange risk, risk taking by related organizations, operations risk, regulatory risk, and liquidity risk. These risks can be managed through diversification (to the extent permitted by laws and regulations that constrain bank location and products) and internal controls.

Deregulation has in general not increased risk taking by banks or risks to the banking system. Indeed, the new product powers granted and liberalized inter- and intra-state branching authority have tended to reduce risk and strengthen institutions by permitting additional diversification. The gradual removal of ceilings on the rates of interest paid on savings and time deposits has resulted in a reduction of disintermediation and in more efficient means of paying for deposits, although higher operating expenses in the short run.

However, traditional sources of individual bank risk have increased in importance in recent years because of increases in the volatility of prices and interest rates and because of advances in technology that permit nearly instantaneous and costless transfers of funds. In addition, federal deposit insurance was increased from $40,000 to $100,000 per account. These events have provided both the incentive for individual banks to enlarge their risk exposure and the means by which they can do so quickly, cheaply, and greatly.

If depositors believe that their bank's risk exposure is too great and that they may not be able to redeem their deposits in full and on time, they are likely to withdraw their funds as quickly as possible, starting a run on the bank. But a review of U.S. history suggests that runs on individual banks or groups of banks only rarely spread to other banks that are not subject to the same conditions that started the initial run and that most bank runs were contained by appropriate action with only minimal and short-lived adverse effects on national financial stability and economic activity. That is, the instability of individual banks or groups of banks did not translate into instability in the banking system as a whole. The major exception was the run on banks during the Great Depression of the early 1930s, which caused the banking system to come almost to a complete halt and contributed significantly to depressing national economic activity. Although an exception, this event was so traumatic that it has colored our analysis of bank runs and failures ever since. In this way, this experience was not unlike that of the Vietnam War, which although not representative of previous U.S. wars and unlikely to be representative of future wars, so traumatized the country that it affected U.S. foreign policy for many years afterwards.

The introduction of federal deposit insurance with some sufficient minimum per account coverage and a more informed policy by the Federal Reserve as lender of last resort have all but eliminated the conditions necessary for nationwide bank failure contagiousness. Individual bank reserve losses should not result in reserve losses to the banking system as a whole through a drain of currency. By reducing uncertainty about the financial strength of the insurance funds, transforming deposit insurance into an explicit deposit guarantee up to the de jure insured amount by the federal government would altogether eliminate the possibility of such an event occurring again.

It is time to discard the fears of bank runs based on the experiences of the Great Depression and to adopt realistic attitudes and policies based on both the long sweep of U.S. history and the new institutions and arrangements now in place. Bank runs indicate actual or perceived depositor concerns. They can be prevented from destabilizing other, nontainted banks and economic activity either by validating justified fears by declaring the bank legally insolvent or by disproving perceived fears through assisting economically solvent banks experiencing liquidity problems to remain solvent and in operation. Both policies can be pursued successfully without either weakening market discipline or withholding punishing economically inefficient banks for fear of adverse externalities on other banks or the economy as a whole. The banking system is likely to operate most efficiently with some churning among individual institutions. Indeed, because runs are feared, they may intensify market discipline on other banks. Although some institutions will fail in the process, this should not be prevented in the interest of economic efficiency and more effective service to consumers. The incentive that deposit insurance gives individual institutions to increase their risk exposure can be constrained by (1) scaling the deposit insurance premiums to the degree of risk exposure, (2) increasing monitoring by depositors and other creditors by putting uninsured depositors at risk de facto as well as de jure, and (3) requiring bank stockholders to put more of their capital at risk. This, however, requires permitting uninsured depositors, other creditors, and shareholders greater access to the financial condition of their institutions. If permitted to work, the free market will be able to control individual bank risk exposure more effectively than government regulators and with far fewer undesirable side effects.

REFERENCES

Auerbach, Ronald P., and Alan S. McCall. 1985. "Permissive Accounting Practices Inflate Savings and Loan Industry Earnings and Net Worth." *Issues in Bank Regulation* 9 (Summer): 17–21.

Barth, James R., R. Dan Brumbaugh, Jr., Daniel Saucrhaft, and George H.K. Wang. 1985. "Thrift-Institution Failures: Causes and Policy Issues." *Proceedings of a Conference on Bank Structure and Competition.* Chicago: Federal Reserve Bank of Chicago.

Barth, James R., Donald J. Bisenius, R. Dan Brumbaugh, Jr., and Daniel Sauerhaft. 1985. "Regulation and the Thrift Industry Crises." Working Paper. Washington, D.C.: Federal Home Loan Bank Board.

Benston, George J. 1973. "Bank Examination." *Bulletin of the Institute of Finance*, Graduate School of Business Administration, New York University, 89–90 (May): entire issue.

_____. 1986. *An Analysis of the Cause of Savings and Loan Failures.* New York: Salomon Center, Graduate School of Business Administration, New York University.

Benston, George J., Robert A. Eisenbeis, Paul M. Horvitz, Edward J. Kane, and George G. Kaufman. 1986. *Perspectives on Safe and Sound Banking: Past, Present, and Future.* American Bankers Association. Cambridge, Mass.: MIT Press.

Bovenzi, John, and Lynn Nejezchleb. 1985. "Bank Failures: Why Are There So Many?" *Issues in Bank Regulation* 8 (Winter): 54–68.

Cagan, Phillip. 1965. *Determinants and Effects of Changes in Stock of Money, 1865–1960.* National Bureau of Economic Research. New York: Columbia University Press.

Committee on Government Operations. 1984. *Federal Response to Criminal Misconduct and Insider Abuse in the Nation's Financial Institutions,* Fifty-seventh Report, 98th Cong., 2d Sess. H. Rep. 98–1137 (October 4).

Continental Illinois Corporation. 1984. *Report of Special Litigation Committee of the Board of Directors of the Continental Illinois Corporation.* Chicago.

Federal Deposit Insurance Corporation. 1958. *Annual Report, 1958.* Washington, D.C.

Friedman, Milton, and Anna Jacobson Schwartz. 1963. *A Monetary History of the United States, 1867–1960.* Princeton: Princeton University Press.

Hill, G.W. 1975. *Why 67 Insured Banks Failed: 1960–1974.* Washington, D.C.: Federal Deposit Insurance Corporation.

Kane, Edward J. 1985. *The Gathering Crisis in Federal Deposit Insurance.* Cambridge, Mass.: MIT Press.

Kaufman, George G. 1985. "Implications of Large Bank Problems and Insolvencies for the Banking System and Economic Policy." *Staff Memoranda,* Federal Reserve Bank of Chicago.

Kaufman, George G. 1984. "Measuring and Managing Interest Rate Risk: A Primer." *Economic Perspectives.* Federal Reserve Bank of Chicago (January/February): 16–29.

Kennedy, Susan Estabrook. 1973. *The Banking Crises of 1933.* Lexington: University Press of Kentucky.

Maisel, Sherman J., ed. 1981. *Risk and Capital Adequacy in Commercial Banks.* National Bureau of Economic Research. Chicago: University of Chicago Press.

Mayer, Martin. 1984. *The Money Bazaars: Understanding the Banking Revolution Around Us.* New York: E.P. Dutton.

McCulloch, J. Huston. 1981. "Interest Rate Risk and Capital Adequacy for Traditional Banks and Financial Intermediaries." In Maisel (1981): 223–48.

Nejezchleb, Lynn, and Detta Voesar. 1985. "Tennessee's Bank Failures: The Aftereffects." *Economic Outlook.* Federal Deposit Insurance Corporation (October): 15–34.

Peach, Nelson W. 1941. *The Security Affiliates of National Banks.* Baltimore: John Hopkins Press (republished by Arno Press, 1975).

Peterson, Richard L., and William J. Scott. 1985. "Major Causes of Bank Failures." In "Recent Bank Failures: Determinants and Consequences." *Proceedings of a Conference on Bank Structure and Competition.* Federal Reserve Bank of Chicago.

Rolnick, Arthur J., and Warren F. Weber. 1985. "Banking Instability and Regulation in the U.S. Free Banking Era." *Quarterly Review* Federal Reserve Bank of Minneapolis (Summer): 2–9.

Singer, Mark. 1985. *Funny Money.* New York: Knopf.

Sinkey, Joseph F. Jr. 1979. *Problem and Failed Institutions in the Commercial Banking-Industry.* Greenwich, Conn.: JAI Press.

Spero, Joan Edelman. 1980. *The Failure of the Franklin National Bank: Challenge to the International Banking System.* Council on Foreign Relations. New York: Columbia University Press.

Welles, Chris. 1982. "Drysdale: What Really Happened." *Institutional Investor* (September): 73–83.

White, Lawrence H. 1984. *Free Banking in Britain: Theory, Experience, and Debate, 1800–1845.* New York: Cambridge University Press.

Zweig, Phillip L. 1985. *Belly Up: The Collapse of the Penn Square Bank.* New York: Crown.

3 FINANCIAL FAILURES AND FINANCIAL POLICIES

Allan H. Meltzer

The recent increase in the number of failures by financial firms has renewed interest in the fragility of firms in the U.S. financial sector. Finding the causes of fragility presumably leads to eliminating or reducing fragility wherever possible. For some people any financial failure is an evil to be avoided—a flaw, as it were, in the regulation or deregulation of the financial system.

The history of the U.S. financial system provides ample evidence of an association between financial panics, bank failures, and recessions. The association does not show that bank failures caused recessions. Typically, multiple bank failures occurred after a recession was already underway; the failures added to the depth and severity of some recessions but did not initiate them (Cagan 1965). Further, there are many examples of bank failures that did not culminate in panics or financial crises. During the mainly prosperous years 1923–29, bank closings, most of them in agricultural areas, occurred at the rate of 600 per per year.

U.S. and British monetary history provides a record of intermittent financial failures that has been studied many times. The best research suggests two important conclusions. First, there are many examples of bank failures that were not followed by financial panics. Second, the occurrence of financial panics always involved a failure by the central bank to discharge its duty as lender of last resort to the financial system (see Schwartz 1985; Bordo 1985). The problem

79

to be studied, then, is at the policymaking level. What is U.S. policy toward financial fragility? What procedures can depositors expect to see applied when financial failures occur? What policies should be applied, and what should the public expect policymakers to do?

The experience of the past two decades, during which the number of financial failures increased, reveals that the institutions responsible for the safety of the financial system do not have a stated policy or a set of procedures. The response by official institutions like the deposit insurance corporations and the Federal Reserve have been appropriate at times but inappropriate at other times. Even when the actions have been appropriate, they have not been based on principles known to the public and on which the public can rely. If the principles exist, there is not much evidence of their existence. They are unknown to the public. Failure to state these principles, or perhaps to define them, heightens uncertainty and encourages bank runs and financial panics.

BAGEHOT'S POLICY PRINCIPLES

A century ago, Walter Bagehot, the editor of the *Economist*, described the problem of crises in the British financial system and the need for a financial policy by the Bank of England (Bagehot 1873). Bagehot's work was stimulated by the problems of the British banking system in the nineteenth century. The end of inflation after the Napoleonic wars was followed by the disappearance of 240 banks in 1814–16. The return to the gold standard eliminated another seventy banks in 1825. Expansion of bank powers, and the growing use of new instruments, including checking deposits, was followed by additional failures (Genovese in Bagehot 1962). These latter changes roughly correspond to the deregulation of our day. Further, banks on the continent and elsewhere held reserves in London. As the century progressed, London became the center of a world financial market, just as the U.S. banks have a major role in the world financial system today. Banks in London lent all over the world, in the developing countries of that day (including Latin America), just as U.S. and other banks have done in recent decades. From time to time problems arose with loans to firms in the developing countries of South America, North America, or elsewhere.

Of course, the parallels to our own time are not exact. We no longer have the gold standard, an important element in Bagehot's analysis. Many of the foreign loans are now to governments of foreign countries or are "guaranteed" by such governments. Speed of communication takes minutes instead of weeks or months, so markets are more closely linked. These and other changes do not reduce the relevance of the principles that Bagehot presented.

Bagehot's main concern was the universal problem of confidence in banks and the financial system. The problem arises from the nature of the fractional reserve system; banks hold much less in reserves than in deposits, and all but a very minor part of their reserves are required by statutes. The required reserves provide no protection against a run on the bank by depositors wishing to withdraw their deposits. Only the central bank—the Bank of England in Britain or the Federal Reserve in the United States—can supply sufficient reserves or currency to prevent a bank, or banks, from becoming illiquid when faced with large withdrawals by depositors concerned about a possible loss of wealth if the bank should fail.

Bagehot saw this issue clearly and prescribed for it in a classic statement: "The holders of the cash reserve [the central bank] must be ready not only to keep it for their own liabilities, but to advance it most freely for the liabilities of others. . . . In wild periods of alarm, one failure makes many, and the best way to prevent the derivative failures is to arrest the primary failure which causes them" (Bagehot 1962: 25). The rule that Bagehot enunciated for a gold standard was a remedy for an external drain of gold and a domestic demand for gold or government currency issues: "Very large loans at very high rates are the best remedy for the worst malady of the money market when a foreign drain is added to a domestic drain" (Bagehot 1962: 28). The high rate of interest attracts deposits and gold from abroad; the large loans convince the public that currency is available and that the banks can pay off depositors.

Bagehot's *Lombard Street* is timely reading not only for its classic statement of the rule for central banks but for its history of the experience with banking panics up to that time and its critique of financial policy during crises. The main criticism is repeated several times: "And though the Bank of England certainly do make great advances in time of panic, yet they do not do so on any distinct principle. . . . To lend a great deal, and yet not give the public confidence that you will lend sufficiently and effectually, is the worst of all policies; but it is the policy now pursued" (Bagehot 1962: 31–32).

Bagehot understood that the central bank must state its principles *in advance* and must adhere to them. No distinction should be made—or can be made—about the quality of the troubled financial institution, its size, or its type of business. What matters is the collateral that is offered, the interest rate at which the central bank discounts, the speed with which the central bank acts, and the certainty about the policy that it conveys. The central bank must act to prevent a problem from becoming a crisis. To prevent a crisis, the central bank must follow two rules. Again, the statements are classic (Bagehot 1962: 97 (emphasis added)):

> First. That these loans should only be made at a very high rate of interest. This . . . will prevent the greatest number of applications by persons who do not require it [assistance.] The rate should be raised early in the panic, so that the fine may be paid early; that no one may borrow out of idle precaution without paying well for it. . . .
>
> Secondly. That at this rate these advances should be made on all good banking securities, and as largely as the public asks for them. The reason is plain. The object is to stay alarm, and nothing therefore should be done to cause alarm. But the way to cause alarm is *to refuse some one who has good security to offer*. . . . If it is known that the Bank of England is freely advancing on what in ordinary times is reckoned a good security—on what is then commonly pledged and easily convertible—the alarm of the solvent merchants and bankers will be stayed. But if securities, really good and usually convertible are refused by the Bank, the alarm will not abate, the other loans made will fail in obtaining their end and the panic will become worse and worse. . . . The only safe plan for the Bank is the brave plan, to lend in a panic on every kind of current security, or every sort on which money is ordinarily and usually lent.

The securities on which the central bank should lend include paper on which the central bank does not normally lend: "The *amount* of the advance is the main consideration for the Bank of England. . . . An idea prevails . . . at the Bank of England that they ought not to advance during a panic on any kind of security on which they do not commonly advance. But if bankers . . . do advance on such security in common times, and if that security is indisputably good, the ordinary practice is immaterial" (Bagehot 1962: 101).

Bagehot did not make the now common mistake of confusing the problems of an individual bank and the problems of the banking system. The aim of the central bank or monetary authority should not be to save an insolvent bank. Policy must prevent the effects of the failure from spreading to banks that are solvent and that will remain solvent and liquid if the financial crisis is prevented or properly managed by the central bank.

Insolvency occurs when the value of the bank's liabilities exceeds the value of its assets. Illiquidity occurs when a bank (or banks) cannot pay cash to redeem deposits. A liquidity crisis arises in a fractional reserve system if assets cannot be sold quickly at prices that permit the bank to repay liabilities on demand. Illiquidity is a temporary problem that arises only when there is a large increase in the demand for currency. If the central bank does not supply the currency, illiquid banks are forced to close. If the central bank supplies currency by buying assets at a discount, or lending at high rates of interest against collateral, illiquidity is removed and bank closings are avoided. The central bank is called the lender of last resort because it is capable of lending—and to prevent failures of solvent banks must lend—in periods when no other lender is either capable of lending or willing to lend in sufficient volume to prevent or end a financial panic.

I have quoted at length from Bagehot's rules for the lender of last resort, and his strictures about the lender's practices, because many of his criticisms and proposals are applicable in the circumstances in which we find ourselves. Let me summarize the main points:

1. The central bank is the only lender of last resort in a monetary system such as ours.
2. To prevent illiquid banks from closing, the central bank should lend on any collateral that is marketable in the ordinary course of business when there is no panic. It should not restrict lending to paper eligible for discount at the central bank in normal periods.
3. Central bank loans, or advances, should be made in large amounts, on demand, at a rate of interest above the market rate. This discourages borrowing by those who can obtain accommodation in the market.
4. The above three principles of central bank behavior should be stated in advance and followed in a crisis.

Nowhere does Bagehot suggest that all banks should be prevented from failing. On the contrary, he describes the failures of some leading financial institutions of his day, and he does not suggest that the failures should have been prevented. A main point of his book is that failures do not have large systemic effects if preannounced rules to prevent panic are followed. He cites several examples to show that when the Bank of England followed correct principles, without precommitment, financial panics ended within two days. He argued that precommitment would prevent the panic or reduce its length and severity.

The modern reason for permitting insolvent banks to fail is that an understanding by financial institutions that they will not be allowed to fail changes attitudes toward risk. Managements are encouraged to accept higher risks so as to earn higher returns. If managers are confident that the risk will be borne by the public and not the management and the stockholders, they face a one-way gamble: The owners and managers get the gains, and the taxpayers pay the cost of large errors.

Recent efforts by regulators to save insolvent banks suggests that a fifth principle is needed to clarify the conditions under which insolvent banks and financial institutions will be permitted to fail or be acquired by other financial institutions:

5. Insolvent financial institutions should be sold at the market price or liquidated if there are no bids for the firm as an integral unit. The losses should be borne by owners of equity, subordinated debentures, and debt, uninsured depositors, and the deposit insurance corporations, as in any bankruptcy proceeding.

Market discipline is essential for market efficiency, and failure is a form of discipline. An important point is to distinguish between (1) the risk of an individual firm or financial institution failing and (2) aggregate risk. Prevention of an individual firm or bank failure to avoid aggregate risk to the community accomplishes what it is intended to prevent. Society bears the cost and the increased risk. Individual firms are encouraged to take larger risks, since owners and lenders recognize that they can earn higher returns without paying the full price of the increased risk if it comes due. This encourages risk taking and leads to malallocation of resources and a maldistribution of the returns from risk bearing.

Allowing banks or financial firms to fail is *one part* of a policy toward financial firms. The other parts—represented by the four Bagehotian principles—work to separate the risk of individual financial failures from aggregate risk by establishing principles that prevent bank liquidity problems from generating an epidemic of insolvencies.

There have been many hundreds of financial firm failures in the United States and in Britain. Only a few have been followed by financial panics or crises, and many of these panics were short-lived. The worst cases—but the ones that are engraved deeply in the public memory—are those in which the central bank failed to act as lender of last resort. These cases, particularly the banking failures of 1931-33 in the United States, arose because the central bank did not follow Bagehotian principles. It is important, therefore, to ask whether banking policy today is based on sound principles—or on any discernible set of principles.

REGULATORS' RESPONSES

Regulators' responses to some of the banking problems of the last ten to fifteen years reveal a changing pattern that offers no reliable guide to the future. At times regulators acted promptly and effectively, but there is no evidence of a policy—a reliable set of procedures based on established principles—for dealing with financial failures.

From the many examples of banking policy in the last two decades, I have chosen six to illustrate some of the differences in approach. Two cases, Franklin National and First Pennsylvania, have some common features but some differences also. Both banks continue to operate, but Franklin National was sold and operates as a new institution. Penn Square was closed and liquidated. The Ohio thrift associations were closed temporarily by state action, but many of these institutions remained both liquid and solvent. They have reopened, but most should not have been closed. The privately insured Maryland thrift associations remained open, but the size of withdrawals was restricted. Continental Illinois was taken over by the government after large loans had been made by the Federal Reserve and bankers across the country had been urged to lend money to Continental Illinois.

The Federal Reserve's loans to Continental Illinois at below market rates of interest and the extended borrowing provision available to other troubled banks continue the practice used at Franklin National and First Pennsylvania. At both Franklin and First Pennsylvania the bank's problems either resulted from, or were magnified by, speculation on asset prices. The management of First Pennsylvania speculated on a decline in long-term bond prices that did not occur. The Federal Reserve's policy of lending at below market rates, for extended terms, subsidizes behavior of this kind. A bank faced with the prospect of low earnings can anticipate that successful speculation will raise earnings and that unsuccessful speculation will be subsidized by the Federal Reserve if the bank is in danger of becoming insolvent.

The Federal Reserve did not attempt to save Home State Savings in Ohio. At first, nothing was done; the thrift association was left to rely on its own resources, and to the best of my knowledge, no public statement was made about assistance. Several days after the problems at Home State became public, the policy changed. The Federal Reserve began to make loans against collateral. Since the portfolios at Home State and the other Ohio institutions faced with withdrawals consisted mainly of mortgages, the Federal Reserve accepted mortgages on one- to four-family homes, in good standing, as collateral. Loans were not made at a penalty rate, and no effort was made to publicize the policy. I believe similar policies were followed in Maryland.

Prompt action, promptly announced, is a means of reassuring the public, thereby reducing uncertainty and discouraging withdrawals at other institutions. A penalty rate prevents excessive demands for borrowing. The Federal Reserve deserves praise for lending to nonmember institutions in Ohio and Maryland against collateral that it does not normally accept. But it did not announce the principles on which the loans would be made—forestalling problems elsewhere, and perhaps in Maryland—and it delayed taking action, thereby increasing the alarm.

The Continental Illinois experience suggests a failure by the regulators to agree on a banking policy. Since the problems with foreign loans came to public attention about three years ago, active public discussion of the financial system has focused attention on fragility and the potential failure of a relatively large bank. Although foreign loans were not the major source of problems at Continental Illinois, the lack of policy to deal with the prospect of failure by a large bank became apparent.

None of these recent cases shows evidence that the financial regulators fully accept the policy proposed by Bagehot or have developed an alternative. These experiences suggest that the central bank's function as lender of last resort to the financial system is either not well understood or is not fully accepted. The request to private banks to lend to Continental Illinois raises questions, of a different kind, about the functioning of the central bank as lender of last resort.

The request to private banks to lend to Continental Illinois is puzzling and, I believe, was counterproductive. It raised questions about the quality of the collateral: Was the Federal Reserve unwilling to lend against the collateral at Continental Illinois? It raised doubts about the degree to which the Federal Reserve understood its function as lender of last resort: Why were commercial banks asked to accept the risk, however small, of participation in the losses? And it mixed issues of the soundness of the banking system with the growing concern about the soundness of an individual bank.

The public effort to sell the bank further eroded confidence and heightened uncertainty. The news media carried frequent stories about the discounts demanded by prospective buyers and hints about the negotiations between the insurance corporation and prospective buyers. Reports and rumors of this kind do little to convince depositors that they should retain their deposits at the bank or make new ones.

These actions suggest confusion between saving the bank and preventing a panic in the financial system. A policy of lending on demand, at a penalty rate, against ordinary financial assets eliminates many of the concerns that delay response, encourage inaction, and foster bureaucratic hesitation. Because the rate is a penalty rate, the central bank limits demand and makes loans only when others are unwilling to lend in sufficient quantity to prevent a bank run. The only judgmental issue is the quality of the collateral. If there is not sufficient collateral eligible for discount, or the discount from book value is too large to pay current claims, the financial institution is insolvent and should be closed promptly. A central bank should not prevent insolvency; its responsibility is to prevent financial panics.

Past experience, particularly the experience with bank failures in the early 1930s, clouds the issue and may mislead regulators. The failure of a single bank or financial institution is no greater calamity for society and imposes no greater loss than the failure of any other firm of comparable size. (See also Kaufman 1985.)

There is a need to distinguish between the individual's problem and the social problem. To the individual who is a depositor (creditor) or who owns shares, an isolated bank failure involves a loss of wealth. Those who work in the bank or uses its services suffer a temporary loss of income and services. These losses in wealth, income, and services are not different in principle from the losses individuals experience in a theft or a fire, the bankruptcy of a manufacturing or retailing firm, and many other events that occur commonly. If the failure of one bank was unrelated to the failure of other banks, losses to depositors could be insured privately just as losses from theft, fire, or accident are insured.

A collective interest in the problem of failures arises if the failure of one bank, or the anticipation of a failure, alarms the depositors of other banks. Uncertainty about the safety of a large class of banks leads to withdrawal of deposits by depositors at many banks. In a fractional reserve banking system, simultaneous deposit withdrawals can produce the wave of failures and closings anticipated by frightened depositors unless a lender of last result provides currency by discounting financial assets. A private insurance company cannot underwrite the losses from the series of bank failures that constitute a banking panic. Only a central bank, able to produce currency at close to zero marginal cost, can prevent the spread of failure and the social loss.

The U.S. regulatory system divides responsibility for banking policy among state regulators, the deposit insurance agencies, the Comptroller of the Currency, the Federal Home Loan Bank Board, the Federal Reserve; and a few others. This system makes it appear that the function of lender of last resort is not vested in a single agency: This is misleading.

The Federal Reserve is the only agency empowered to supply unlimited amounts of currency on demand, and so it is the only one of the financial regulatory agencies that can serve as lender of last resort. The government's insurance corporations can pay out claims arising from single bank or thrift institution failure, or a series of failures, but they cannot prevent runs on financial institutions. Because there are no rules stating the circumstances under which a problem in the thrift industry or among insured, nonmember banks becomes a responsibility of the Federal Reserve, there is unnecessary ambiguity about the conditions under which the Federal Reserve, as lender of last resort, accepts responsibility for lending against collateral offered by institutions that are not members of the Federal Reserve system. Recent experience in Ohio and Maryland suggests that delays can be avoided if policies are agreed on in advance and implemented promptly. Experience also suggests that policies will not be formulated as precommitted strategies unless the administration, Congress, or the public demands some agreement among the regulators in advance.

The deposit insurance system developed in the United States after 1930 because the central bank failed to function as lender of last resort. Deposit insurance reduces the risk to individual depositors of losses from bank mismanagement, error, excessive risk taking, and fraud. It does not and cannot insure the safety of the financial system. In a financial crisis, the insurance agencies, like the institutions they insure, can obtain currency only from the Federal Reserve— the lender of last resort.

Many have noted that there is a flaw in the deposit insurance system. The flaw results from the use of fixed insurance premiums. Since premiums are unrelated to the risks accepted by financial institutions, opportunities for shifting risk to the insurance agencies arise. The problem is more serious in the current less-regulated financial system, than in the past, and the problem is most serious when an institution is close to insolvency. The fixed insurance premium permits the management to accept large risks, to earn higher returns, without paying a risk premium. If the speculation is successful, the owners and managers gain, but if the speculation is unsuccessful, the insurance agencies pay the losses. Under current conditions, with many financial institutions holding portfolios of assets that have much lower market value than their book values, this problem is more important than it was a generation ago. Nearly twenty years ago, I proposed that deposit insurance premiums be related to portfolio risk (Meltzer 1967: 482–501). A reform of deposit insurance to relate premiums to risk is a more pressing need now.

RISKS IN BANKS AND FINANCIAL INSTITUTIONS

The problem of financial fragility will not disappear, at least not soon. Many of the thrift institutions own portfolios that the market values far below their book values. Banks in agricultural areas hold mortgage loans on farms with market value below mortgage value. At current prices for agricultural products, some of these loans will continue to go into default. Banks with foreign loans, particularly loans to governments, continue to carry the loans at book value if payment is current. In the market, Latin American loans sell for no more than 70 to 80 percent of their book value, an increase in recent months, but a substantial discount from book value. Energy loans and loans to land developers, in many cases used to speculate on rising prices of oil or land, are an additional source of losses that are not fully recognized on many banks' balance sheets.

To gauge the size of some of the differences between the market value and the book value of bank portfolios, I use a sample of banks drawn from the *Value Line* weekly financial service. The issue for March 22, 1985, reports on forty-one banks. One bank is in the process of reorganization, so it was omitted from my calculations.

To measure unrecorded losses on a bank's balance sheet, I used the ratio of reported book value (on December 31, 1984) to the "recent" market value of the common stock shown by *Value Line*. A ratio of book value to market value below unity indicates that market is willing to pay less than a dollar for a dollar of assets. I used the ratio to compute the implied reduction in the bank's loan portfolio by multiplying the ratio by the loan portfolio. The result is a market estimate of potential loss or shrinkage. I compared the implied shrinkage in value to the bank's net worth. *Value Line* also reports the percentage of foreign loans in the portfolio, which allows us to compare banks with a large percentage of foreign loans to other banks.

For the sample of forty banks, the mean ratio of market value to book value is approximately 1 on the date I used. If this sample, consisting of larger banks with publicly traded shares, is representative of the industry, there is no difference on average between book and market values. This number hides the considerable diversity within the sample. The ratio of market value to book value ranges from .55 to 1.77 for individual banks. The characteristics of the banks differ also.

The ten banks with the lowest ratios of market value to book value include several of the largest banks in the country. Their average size, measured by reported net worth, is $2.1 billion, and they range in size from $200 million to $5 billion. For these banks, market value is less than two-thirds of book value (0.64), and the range of the ratio is from 0.55 to 0.75. On average, one-third of the loan portfolio of these banks is in foreign loans, but the banks differ in this respect; the proportion of foreign loans ranges from slightly above zero to 62 percent. Using the ratio of market to book value to estimate shrinkage in the loan portfolio, there is an implied loss equal on average to 5.6 times the reported net worth of these banks. The market's estimate of hidden portfolio losses, or shrinkage, is somewhat lower for these banks than the market valuation of loss on Latin American loans that are sold.

The banks with the highest ratios of market to book value have very different portfolios. Foreign loans are 2 percent of total loans for the group. Not a single bank has more than 8 percent of its portfolio in foreign loans, and many banks have either a negligible percentage or none at all. The banks are much smaller; their net worth is $400 million, about one-fifth the net worth of the banks with lowest ratios of market to book value. The market values each of these banks above its book value, so there is no portfolio shrinkage. Market values range from 129 to 177 percent of book value.

Differences in foreign loans do not explain all of the differences in market valuation. Many of the smaller banks are regional banks in areas with relatively strong economic growth. Some are possible candidates for acquisition if interstate banking is allowed to spread. These circumstances or prospects attract buyers of the shares.

Two main lessons can be drawn. First, the problems of the banking industry are problems of individual banks. There is no evidence in these data that the banking system has a serious problem. The problem for the financial system will arise if regulators fail to function as lenders of last resort in the event of loan defaults or failures by insolvent banks or financial firms. Second, the market appears to discriminate between banks. Banks with high percentages of international loans sell at discounts (often substantial) from book value. The market appears to have appraised bank portfolios and recognized anticipated losses. Although I have not computed the market's estimates of portfolio values for publicly held savings and loan associations or for banks with relatively large portfolios of agricultural loans, the market probably values these shares at substantial discounts from book value also.

Managements' reluctance to recognize portfolio losses has not hidden the problem. Regulators' delays have raised the level of risk borne by society. And the absence of a clearly stated, widely known set of procedures for responding to financial failures adds to uncertainty and heightens the public's concern about financial fragility.

SOME PROPOSALS

The safety, or soundness, of the payments systems is, properly, a matter for public concern, because maintenance of an efficient payments system benefits the public as a group more than it benefits individuals acting alone. In the United States and a few other countries, banks are the principal agencies operating the payments system, so that lack of safety or insolvency of banks and other financial institutions is a threat to the payments system. An individual bank or financial failure imposes losses on depositors; an epidemic of failures weakens the payments system and imposes losses to society as well as to individual depositors.

Events of the past few years have shown that, while most financial institutions remain strong and profitable, some have failed and others seem likely to fail in the future. The reasons for failures vary, but many of the current problems have common causes. Inflation encouraged speculation in land and housing, much of it financed by banks and thrift associations. Many, including some bank and thrift institutions, favored deposit rate regulation that weakened the structure and its institutions. Presidents, Congresses, regulators, and many others, including some of the banks and thrift institutions themselves, resisted changes in policy that would have prevented the inflation of the 1970s and therefore the demand for disinflation in the early 1980s. Disinflation both contributed to and revealed the major problems in the U.S. financial system. Although some of the problems would have developed following declines in the relative price of oil and changes in the tax code that raised the expected after-tax return to investment in the United States and thus raised real interest rates, many of today's problems are the result of past inflation, disinflation, and uncertainty about future inflation.

The fact that not all banks and financial firms are experiencing difficulties suggests an element of choice or managerial discretion. Many banks have small portfolios of foreign loans. Many banks avoided the real estate loan problems, the agricultural loan problems, and the energy loan problems by following such time-honored principles as scrutinizing assets for quality, relating risk and return, or diversifying portfolios. I do not know of any major money market fund, for example, that was willing to forgo taking possession of securities to earn an additional 1/4 percent interest. We know, of course, that not all institutions were as prudent; the problems of the Ohio thrifts were the result of that lack of prudence.

Bank managements are not always prudent. Major banks with large foreign loans have been slow to recognize their losses. Dividend reductions to increase retained earnings are a relatively rare event. Since dividend payments are, currently, 5 to 6 percent of market value, a policy of eliminating dividends, if adopted in 1982 when problems with Mexican debt came to public attention, would have increased retained earnings by 15 percent of current market value and 10 percent of book value. By building capital in this way, managements would have recognized two problems that markets have recognized. First, many of the international loans are not likely to be repaid; second, interest earnings on international loans are paid in many instances only because the bank lends the debtor country the amount of the interest payment when the payment is due. If major banks reduced or eliminated their dividend payments, their reserves would be larger. The banks would be less risky because a major loan default would be less likely to be followed by insolvency. It is not clear that the market price of bank shares would fall. The market recognized the losses long ago.

There have been improvements in the financial position of some major debtor countries, but not all debtors have used the recent strong expansion in the United States to increase their ability to service debt. Even in those countries where exports and current account balances increased at a rapid pace in 1983 and 1984, the cost of servicing external debt is large relative to exports. And substantial risk remains because much of the improvement in Mexico and Brazil reflects the combination of strong expansion in the United States (which has now ended) and one-time reductions in imports that cannot be repeated. Bank management can reduce the risk to the payments system and their bank's risk of insolvency by reducing or passing dividends, by increasing capital, and by selling some of their foreign loans to financial and nonfinancial institutions willing to accept the risk at the rates of return implied by current market prices for these loans.

The most alarming feature of the international debt problem is the failure to recognize that errors were made and that losses have occurred. Instead of carrying loans at face value, banks should write down the value, increase reserves against default, and sell many more of their loans to others including nonfinancial corporations. Several years ago, I recommended that banks offer to exchange debt for equity in government corporations in Brazil, Mexico, or even Argentina. Many of the state-owned corporations are profitable. The shares would command a market. Of course, the banks would have to discount the debt, but in exchange they would have a better claim than they now have. By reducing the burden of Latin American debt, they also would improve their own and others' prospects of receiving interest and principal payments on the remaining debt.

Public policy has a role in lowering risk in the financial system. Regulators must improve their system of crisis management. Their concern must be with the risk of a financial panic leading to simultaneous withdrawals from many banks and financial institutions. I recommend that they develop and announce rules of procedure to replace the present ad hoc nonsystem.

The rules should clarify the conditions under which the deposit insurance agencies can discount at Federal Reserve Banks or call for assistance. The deposit insurance agencies have an important role with respect to individual institutions, but at many institutions they must have help in a crisis from the Federal Reserve. The Federal Reserve is the only institution that can lend unlimited amounts in a crisis, so it must function as the final lender—the lender of last resort.

The position of foreign banks in the United States and of U.S. banks or branches abroad should be clarified. The Federal Reserve can function as lender of last resort only for financial institutions with dollar liabilities, so it should not undertake responsibilities that may require large loans to foreign branches of U.S. banks with liabilities mainly in foreign currencies. The Federal Reserve is the only lender of last resort for foreign financial institutions in the United States that issue dollar liabilities. There is need for an agreement between the Federal Reserve and foreign central banks that delineates responsibility for foreign branches in advance of a problem. Current agreements on lending facilities are more ambiguous and subject to greater discretion than seems desirable.

The rules for domestic institutions should specify the types of collateral that will be accepted, the financial institutions that are eligible to use the facilities of the lender of last resort, and the price to be charged. A penalty rate is an effective means of reducing demands for emergency borrowing and is an effective warning system that alerts regulators to problems in the financial system.

A century ago, Walter Bagehot criticized the central bank for not stating its policy for lending in a crisis. His criticisms and the principles he recommended to the lender of last resort are as relevant now as when he wrote them. The lender of last resort should lend freely at a penalty rate against any collateral that is marketable in the ordinary course of business. The Federal Reserve should accept these Bagehotian principles and remove the ambiguity that now exists about the circumstances under which it lends. Further, the Federal Reserve should stop lending at below-market rates to troubled institutions. Loans made at below-market rates encourage risk taking.

The current system of deposit insurance also subsidizes risk taking by financially weak institutions. Premiums for deposit insurance should be related to the risk of a financial firm's assets. This reform would reduce the incentive for weak institutions to acquire risky assets at high rates of return as a means of increasing earnings or delaying insolvency.

The current fragility of the U.S. financial system is, properly, a cause for concern. The risk of loss to depositors, creditors, and owners imposes a burden that can be avoided by appropriate action by the managements of troubled institutions and by regulators. Recent experience shows that there are flaws in the system for handling bank runs and protecting the solvency of institutions that are temporarily illiquid. Experience during the last three years suggests that many bankers and the banking agencies have been slow to adjust their policies so as to reduce the risk of financial failures. These problems can be reduced without imposing costs on the much larger number of safe, well-managed financial institutions.

REFERENCES

Bagehot, Walter. 1873, 1962. *Lombard Street.* New York: Scribner, Armstrong, 1873. Reprinted with introduction by Frank Genovese. Homewood, Ill.: Irwin, 1962.

Bordo, Michael. 1985. "Some Historical Evidence 1870–1933 on the Impact and International Transmission of Financial Crises." National Bureau of Economic Research, Working Paper 1606.

Cagan, Phillip. 1965. *Determinants and Effects of Changes in the Stock of Money, 1975–1960.* New York: Columbia University Press for the National Bureau of Economic Research.

Kaufman, George G. 1985. "Implications of Large Bank Problems and Insolvencies for the Banking System and Economic Policy." Staff Memorandum. Chicago: Federal Reserve Bank of Chicago.

Meltzer, Allan H. 1967. "Major Issues in the Regulation of Financial Institutions." *Journal of Political Economy* 75 (August supp.): 482–501.

Schwartz, Anna J. 1985. "Real and Pseudo Financial Crises." In *Financial Crises and the World Banking System*, edited by F. Capie and G. Wood. London: Macmillan.

4 CONFRONTING INCENTIVE PROBLEMS IN U.S. DEPOSIT INSURANCE
The Range of Alternative Solutions

Edward J. Kane

Federal deposit insurance operates as a disequilibrium system. Explicit premiums (that is, fees paid in dollars) are calculated as a fixed percentage of domestic deposits. For forms of portfolio risk that complementary supervisory activity does not appropriately penalize, this leaves the deposit-insurance agencies (principally the FDIC and FSLIC) offering insurance on cheaper terms than the market is prepared to pay institutions for assuming these risks in the first place. To offset the subsidy to risk bearing that this structure of explicit premiums creates, deposit-insurance personnel have to monitor client risk taking and impose a series of administrative penalties on clients that they observe to be taking inappropriate risks. It is convenient to think of these penalties as implicit premiums.

This two-part pricing system has two serious weaknesses. First, political restraints inevitably protect particular forms of risk bearing such as housing and agricultural loans. Second, inescapable lags in recognizing the implications for agency risk exposure of emerging categories risk taking by clients reward deposit-institution managers for discovering innovative (and therefore unregulated) forms of bearing risk.

Unregulated risks are not only subsidized, they are largely unfunded. The burden of backing up FDIC and FSLIC guarantees falls

This chapter draws heavily on Chapter 6 of *The Gathering Crisis in Federal Deposit Insurance* (Cambridge, Mass.: MIT Press, 1985).

implicitly on the general taxpayer and on any conservatively managed institution that chooses to resist the siren call of subsidized opportunities for aggressive risk bearing.

This study argues that generally accepted accounting principles—which allow deposit institutions to carry underwater assets at historical cost and prevent the value of FDIC and FSLIC guarantees from being booked—routinely distort public perceptions of deposit-institution earnings and capital and understate the cost of the federal government's commitment to bail out troubled banks and S&Ls. In the face of an increasingly risky economic environment, the absence of effective taxpayer discipline of regulators and elected politicians who permit the market value of deposit-insurance guarantees to grow leaves the value of these guarantees out of administrative control. Because the distribution of implicit taxpayer responsibilities for redeeming unfunded deposit-insurance guarantees differs sharply from the apparent distribution of the benefits of deposit insurance (which figure to grow with accountholder wealth and to be greatest for the stockholders and creditors of very large institutions), this lack of control is not politically sustainable.

Whenever opportunities for institutional risk exposure expand, lags in regulatory response permit the deposit-insurance subsidy to risk taking to grow, increasing the fragility of our financial system. To cut back incentives for voluntary risk taking, it is necessary to reprice and to redesign the existing system of deposit-insurance coverage. The FDIC and FSLIC must develop incentive-compatible insurance contracts and monitoring arrangements and price their guarantees fairly. Under current arrangements, low-risk deposit institutions are asked to pay unreasonably high premiums for deposit insurance, while high-risk institutions are offered bargain rates. To limit insured institutions' opportunities for an adverse selection of risks, contractual incentives need to be established to allow a would-be low-risk institution to lower its effective premium by communicating the confidential information that its own managers possess about the institution's true exposure to both traditional and non-traditional forms of risk.

We may liken the current federal system of deposit insurance to an old and undermaintained automobile that after years of hard but reliable service is nearing a serious breakdown. In recent years the deposit-insurance car has become a smoke-belching jalopy that is being driven at high speeds up and down a series of steep interest-rate mountains and over unpaved backroads in agricultural regions of the United States, in less developed countries, and in energy-exploration regions all over the world. Because it has taken so much abuse, the deposit-insurance jalopy ought to be traded in before it lets its passengers down at an inopportune time.

This metaphor has two instructive features. First, it implies that the largely trouble-free operation that the deposit insurance system delivered during its first forty or fifty years is of no current relevance. In ignoring the momentum of the system, defenders of the status quo act like a pair of government building inspectors that accidentally tumbled off the roof of a sixty-story building. Devoted to duty until the very end, as they fell past the top fifty floors, they loudly reassured each other and the building's occupants, "So far, so good." Whatever good the system has accomplished in the past, politicians and taxpayers need to recognize that its momentum is carrying it in the direction of a bureaucratic disaster exemplified by the breakdown of the Ohio system for guaranteeing seventy-odd S&Ls in March 1985. When the Ohio Deposit Guaranty Fund was exhausted by a single failure, state authorities resisted for a few weeks political pressure either to supply credible deposit guarantees for the fund's other seventy member institutions or to idemnify the FSLIC against liabilities it might incur from accepting responsibility for insuring these institutions. This led to serious runs on the weakest of the survivors, which frightened state authorities sufficiently to call a banking holiday that temporarily shook confidence in state-insured S&Ls and even federally insured thrifts in the rest of the country. Unless market discipline is reimposed on deposit institution risk taking, the federal deposit insurance bureaucracy is eventually going to encounter similarly mismanageable obstacles. Eventually, one of these will be mishandled badly enough to call the credibility of federal guarantees into question.

Second, it is instructive to liken the problem of selecting a new framework for deposit insurance to the process of shopping for a new car. Given dealer prices, the main question is what features to have installed on the new-model insurance system—either immediately or in stages. Options available on both insurance contracts and cars expand secularly. Cruise control, pneumatic shock absorbers, power steering, power brakes, automatic transmission, remote releases for hood, trunk, and gas caps, power locks, and power antennas did not even exist in 1933. Systems of risk appraisal, risk sharing, and risk management have improved in parallel fashion. After years of driving an antiquated car, a potential buyer needs guidance as to which of many apparently luxury options a contemporary driver should regard as practical necessities. This paper's program for deposit insurance reform is conceived as a six-category catalog of optional technological improvements that knowledgeable federal taxpayers might ask politicians to include on the new deposit-insurance invoice.

In an economic environment in which deposit institutions are highly levered and entering new businesses every day and in which interest rates are highly volatile, systematically mispricing deposit-insurance guarantees encourages deposit-institution managers to position their firms on the edge of financial disaster. Metaphorically, deposit-insurance authorities are paying deposit-institution managers to overload the deposit-insurance jalopy and to drive it too fast as it careens through interest-rate mountains and over back-country roads. Reformers' ultimate goal must be to confront institutions whose risk taking imposes socially unacceptable risks on its federal guarantors with a combination of reduced coverages and increased fees sufficient to move them to adopt safer modes of operation. Their proximate aim should be to make the FDIC and FSLIC act more like private insurers, so that they better protect their and federal taxpayers' economic interests, treat large and small institutions more equally, and make uninsured creditors (including large depositors) and stockholders bear more of the risk inherent in deposit-institution operations. This probably involves making much more room for private and even interagency competition in the provision of deposit insurance.

Although politicians and regulators prefer to minimize failures during their term in office, if deposit-institution risk taking is to be controlled over the long run, it is necessary to expand opportunities for troubled individual institutions to experience runs and even to fail. Economic analysis indicates that as deposit-institution managers and customers more fully appreciate the extent of implicit or de facto federal guarantees, continuing to rescue insolvent firms becomes counterproductive. In the long run, regulatory efforts to prevent de facto deposit-institution insolvencies from becoming de jure insolvencies increase the size and extent of de facto insolvencies in the depository industry.

SIX-POINT CATALOG FOR DEPOSIT INSURANCE REFORM

The adjustments needed must include at least some of six basic changes in federal deposit-insurance contracts (Kane 1983). Viewing these proposals as six desirable features available to purchasers of new-model automobiles should clarify that this program is not conceived as an all-or-nothing package. Although the various elements in the package complement each other, adopting any subset of the reforms suggested should provide a better deposit-insurance system, one whose operation would be smoothed by the improved system of risk-taking incentives.

Market-Value Accounting

The heart of various deposit-insurance dilemmas is that a deposit institution's managers have more and better information about the riskiness of their firm's operations than its insurers and customers do. Since 1938 generally accepted accounting principles and regulator-imposed accounting rules have authorized deposit institutions to employ so-called intrinsic-value accounting, which permits assets whose scheduled cash flows are relatively current to be carried at book value equal to their acquisition cost. Reinstituting market-value accounting for deposit-institution loans and investments can be justified as an administratively cheap scheme for raising the implicit regulatory premium on deposit insurance in a risk-sensitive way. The most attractive aspect of this approach is that it makes traditional capital requirements and other elements of the implicit premium more effective, while letting market forces help bureaucrats to conduct regular assessments of an institution's risk exposure and to impose appropriate penalties on overly aggressive risk takers.

That muggers and burglars prefer to work in the dark is reason enough to propose brighter lighting. In a world where declines in market value are not obscured by book-value accounting, deposit-institution managers who contemplate aggressively pursuing unregulated risks would know that they would have to defend their risk-taking strategies against regulator and financial-analyst criticism and to offer correspondingly higher interest rates to uninsured depositors. Moreover, when and if these risks go awry, they would face quicker and more extensive damage to their careers and to the stock price and deposit flows of the institution they manage.

Contemporary accounting principles relieve managers that report book values (and absolve their outside accountants as well) from legal liability for communicating less than their best estimate of the value of an institution's portfolio. Legal authority to use book-value accounting to cover up adverse information gives financial-institution managers (especially unscrupulous ones) too much discretion over the extent to which current problems show up on an institution's income statement and balance sheet. This managerial discretion puts the burden of valuing deposit institutions on financial analysts such as David Cates and Harry Keefe and weakens the effect of market and political controls that would otherwise discipline institutions' and insurers' risk exposure. Having to worry about how insurers and depositors might respond to quick-breaking news about potentially injurious developments would establish incentives for deposit-institution managers to modify and bond their behavior in helpful ways. Even after the FDIC issued blanket guarantees of Continental Illinois liabilities in May 1984, institutional investors governed by prudent-man rules continued to withdraw maturing funds from the bank. The bank's market for letters of credit dried up as well.

If private parties are to bear more of the risk inherent in a de jure failure, accountants owe investors in deposit institutions and coinsuring depositors (those that are less than fully insured) a best-efforts estimate of the risk exposure and changing market value of the assets and liabilities that deposit institutions hold on their books. Investors and insurers need reliable information on the value of unrealized losses and gains at financial institutions, information of the sort that conscientious deposit-institution managers should be assembling and analyzing in the course of operating their firms. To produce estimates that would be accurate to within a few percentage points of market value, accountants need only to expand their concept of the bookable assets and to supplement their more-traditional bean-counting skills by developing and deploying reasonable competence in asset appraisal. As in real-estate appraisal, to value an asset that does not trade, an analyst must rely heavily on data covering current yields and prices in secondary markets for comparable investments.

As collateralized instruments develop for more and more kinds of cash flows, the range of available data becomes richer and richer. For an institution as a whole, as long as unbiased appraisal techniques are employed, errors in valuing the individual assets in its portfolio should tend to cancel out. A major role for government examiners would be to determine whether or not deposit-institution managers and accountants are in fact employing appraisal techniques that are unbiased.

To estimate the value of mortgages and directly placed loans (such as those to troubled farmers, energy firms, and less-developed countries), the major problem is to assess the reliability of lender projections of future cash flows and to obtain reliable estimates of appropriate market discount rates to use as inputs into present-value formulas. Practical implementation of these formulas has been greatly simplified by software that preprograms the necessary calculations onto floppy discs or hardwires them into the circuits of hand-held calculators.

If federal deposit insurers wanted to develop rather than to conceal such information, they could expand the set of transactions observed in secondary markets. Specifically, they could request their liquidation divisions to arrange for periodic auctions of assets chosen for their inherent comparability to the most important classes of hard-to-value instruments currently being held by troubled institutions. They could also set up a self-regulatory board to help identify emerging types of unbookable assets and to determine what valuation principles and procedures should apply.

Until very recently, neither government nor industry has *wanted* to publicize base-line values for troubled assets. Although we may cite some tentative administrative steps in the direction of greater disclosure, backsliding continues to occur with respect to politically protected risks. On the plus side, authorities have required banks to report their positions in troubled foreign loans and required S&Ls to report gaps between the interest sensitivity of their assets and liabilities. In 1984 the SEC and Comptroller of the Currency specifically forced several large institutions to restate their 1983–84 profits in a less self-serving manner. However, authorities have encouraged cosmetic accounting by permitting problem loans to less-developed countries to be carried at book value and by promising to take a flexible approach to valuing distressed farm loans at banks located in agricultural regions.

Opponents of greater disclosure offer two objections: first, that the costs of providing market appraisals might exceed the benefits, and second, that outside parties might dangerously misinterpret the accounting reports that result. Even though market-value accounting promises to increase the costs and complexity of outside audits, it should improve decision making at any firm whose internal information system does not already employ market value data. In addition, by simplifying the tasks of financial analysis and of deposit institution examination, it should release appreciable amounts of resources elsewhere in the financial industry. Opponents of market-value accounting worry that it will increase fluctuations in reported earnings; however, making changes in the portfolio values public creates incentives for managers to adopt policies that make the true value of these fluctuations smaller. Moreover, because capital markets must estimate current values in any case, better estimates of portfolio values may reduce (at least on average) the size of allowances that market participants make for the uncertain cosmetic nature of reports of institutional earnings and capital positions. Today, the need to allow for the degree of managerial artfulness permitted in assembling information for reports prepared under principles of historical cost accounting makes investors discount the reported earnings of even conservatively managed institutions.

On the regulatory side, if taxpayers were well informed, political pressure would have led Congress long ago to insist that deposit insurers collect market-value reports. Such information would help regulators to discover and resolve problem situations more quickly and generate popular pressure on authorities to make more timely and better focused interventions. As long as deposit-insurance agencies remain free to offer capital assistance to failing clients, market-value accounting would merely curtail rather than eliminate regulatory discretion as to whether and when to close an economically insolvent institution. However, by forcing more timely and more explicit forms of intervention, market-value accounting would reduce an insolvent institution's opportunities for pursuing go-for-broke strategies.

Accounting standards that make it ethical for individual deposit institutions to disguise insolvency and risk taking beyond all recognition undermine the effectiveness of existing capital requirements. Until these standards are changed, proposals to solve the deposit insurance problem by raising or restructuring deposit institution capital requirements may have effects that are more cosmetic than real.

EXPANDED OPPORTUNITIES FOR
DEPOSIT INSURANCE AGENCIES
TO MANAGE RISK EXPOSURE

To neutralize political pressure for forbearance, deposit-insurance agencies need enhanced rights and a greater determination to take timely action on three fronts: to force institutions to maintain the market value of their capital accounts, to cancel the insurance coverage of aggressively managed institutions, or to foreclose on the bank's charter before the market value of an institution's net worth is exhausted. The goal of this class of reforms is to make the current disequilibrium system less breakdown prone by making it easier to prevent institutions that are insolvent de facto from making spectacularly risky endgame plays with FDIC and FSLIC (that is, taxpayer) money. In recent years so many failing institutions have made last-ditch maneuvers with insured-brokered funds that aggressive deposit brokers appear to do a better job of identifying insolvent institutions than do FDIC and FSLIC examiners.

Of course, because insurers may track the same data on CD yields to which customers of CD brokers respond, this appearance is illusory. The jibe has force only because problem situations persist long after the desirability of preserving FDIC and FSLIC insurance reserves should have led the insurer to demand an institution's closure. This delay, which intensifies agency exposure to go-for-broke speculation by failing firms, traces in part to statutory constraints on FDIC and FSLIC problem-solving options. Unlike automobile insurers who routinely cancel their coverage of drivers they deem to be poor risks, deposit-insurance agencies do not have the right to terminate an institution's insurance on short notice. For example, unless a problem bank neglects to exercise some of its rights of appeal, it takes the FDIC a year to start to terminate its insurance of new deposits, while the process of fully phasing out its guarantees on a bank's existing deposits absorbs two more years. In 1983 the FDIC initiated a record-high twenty-six termination-of-insurance proceedings.

Nor do insurers have the right to close an institution they deem legally or economically insolvent. They may, of course, petition the institution's federal or state chartering authority to declare a legal insolvency. However, the interests of this second agency in resolving the problem typically differ importantly from that of the insurer. For federal S&Ls and some federal savings banks, this tension is contained within a single building, as the FHLBB balances the narrow economic interest of the FSLIC against broader concerns that make an impact on the board. However, whenever an insured S&L holds a state charter, its chartering authority must also be brought into the negotiations. For the FDIC, conflicts of interest also vary with the character of the regulatory climate chosen by the client. For national banks, the primary regulator and chartering authority is the Comptroller of the Currency. (However, in December 1983 the Comptroller agreed to give the FDIC blanket authority to examine all national banks whose condition falls in the lowest two categories of the agencies' five-point rating scale.) For FDIC-insured federal savings banks, the FHLBB holds regulatory and chartering authority. For state-chartered commercial banks that belong to the Federal Reserve System, the Fed is the primary federal regulator, but not the chartering authority. This means that, to close such a bank, the FDIC must rely on information developed by the Fed and deal both with its state banking commissioner and officials from the Fed.

For the banks that it examines itself (that is, insured state-chartered nonmember banks and mutual savings banks), the FDIC may issue cease-and-desist orders against specific practices it deems improper; remove bank officers who engage in substantial violations of laws, regulations, or sound banking practices; and even levy civil monetary penalties. For federal supervision of other insured banks, it must rely on the Fed and the Office of the Comptroller of the Currency to take parallel enforcement actions. During the early 1980s, the number of such actions has trended upward with the number of problem banks.

Because the effects of formally shutting down an institution are effectively irreversible, requiring that an independent agency concur in advance with an insurer's decision to declare a bank insolvent has the benefit of protecting deposit-institution customers, managers, creditors, and stockholders against abusive uses of FDIC or FSLIC regulatory authority. However, given that injured parties retain the right to sue for damages ex post, this benefit should be weighed against the costs that systematically delaying the failure of moribund firms visits on the taxpayer. The benefits of requiring the FDIC and FSLIC to win the assent of other federal regulators merely to alter the level and composition of capital requirements or to update procedures for monitoring client institutions are even more questionable.

Insurer rights could be strengthened in many ways. By far the simplest approach would be to consolidate federal deposit-institution regulatory functions wholly, or at least primarily, in the federal deposit-insurance agencies. However, this approach would reduce the bureaucratic dominions of the Federal Reserve System and the Comptroller of the Currency and threaten job opportunities for identifiable groups of these agencies' employees. Maintaining that their supervisory functions are essential to their greater missions, each agency's leadership is prepared to lobby vigorously to retain them. Because the weight of the Fed's macroeconomic responsibilities give it extraordinary clout in Congress, the chances of transferring its regulatory powers to the FDIC are miniscule.

Treating the structural partition of federal supervisory authority as a given, Congress has been willing to entertain proposals to increase the authority of the federal insurance agencies to examine insured institutions, to reduce procedural delays in terminating insurance, and to impose further regulatory and civil sanctions on institutions whose managers engage in abusive practices. However, in the absence of a perceived legislative crisis, deposit institutions may be expected to lobby effectively to prevent applicable sanctions and statutory redefinitions of abusive practices from gaining much sweep.

Even without new powers, the FDIC and FSLIC should adopt policies that commit them more determinedly to protecting their economic interests. It should be noted that not until economic pressure against their reserve funds became severe did FDIC and FSLIC officials begin systematically to take administrative actions designed to foster uncertainty about the extent of their de facto commitment to rescue uninsured creditors.

The most important of these administrative actions was to develop a new technique for resolving failures that is known as the deposit transfer or modified payoff. In one variant of these transactions, the insurer sells only a failing firm's *insured* deposits to an acquiring institution and leases rather than sells the dead institution's premises and equipment to the acquirer. In several 1983–84 failures, the FDIC's approach was to sell the acquiring institution only the sum of the failed firm's insured deposits and its estimate of the percentage of uninsured deposits that the FDIC would recover in liquidating the firm's portfolio. If not overruled by the courts, this technique promises to make uninsured creditors take their lumps in liquidation without overly disrupting the financial lives of a failed institution's insured customers.

However, when the use of this technique helped to increase uninsured depositors' anxiety about the viability of Continental Illinois, it was at least temporarily abandoned. In the long run, I believe that it will prove regrettable that the essentially political advantages of preserving the accounting value of FDIC reserves persuaded the agency against using some variant of the modified-payoff technique to resolve the multibillion-dollar insolvency of Continental Illinois. Whatever the short-run benefits of shoring up the agency's insurance reserves and sharply arresting the spread of depositor pressure to other large banks, destabilizing precedents have been set by permitting an insurer to issue de jure guarantees of both the claims of Continental's uninsured creditors and the debt of its parent holding company. Paying uninsured creditors of the bank 98 cents on the dollar could have controlled direct contagion without imposing such large implicit funding burdens on the taxpayer.

The precedent set by the Continental Illinois bailout undermines the potential effectiveness of the FDIC's current proposal to raise capital requirements sharply for client banks, while permitting banks to raise the incremental funds by means of subordinated debt or debt sold to a parent holding company (Silverberg 1985). To the extent that debtholders feel themselves to be in line for a bailout in the event the bank's ordinary equity is exhausted, they will not hold out for a risk premium high enough to bring risk taking under control. Because the conjectural probability of bailouts increases with the size of the bank being financed, this approach would reinforce the de facto discrimination in the perfection of deposit-insurance guarantees available to large and small institutions.

A second category of administrative action has focused on reducing the size of the endgame play that an insolvent institution can make between successive examination dates. The proximate goal of this line of action is to limit CD brokers' ability to pyramid the $100,000 insurance coverage granted individual depositors to create large blocks of fully insured funds. In early 1984 the FDIC and FSLIC proposed to limit insurance coverage on the aggregate of funds placed in any single institution through any one broker to $100,000. They were forced to backtrack from this initial proposal both by lobbying pressure that CD brokers channeled through Congress and by the federal courts. A June 1984 ruling in U.S. district court, affirmed by the U.S. Court of Appeals in January 1985, upheld a legal challenge the brokerage industry filed against their action. Related proposals under active FDIC consideration include dropping its coverage of any deposits owned by financial institutions and eliminating various forms of trusteed accounts' rights to what has amounted to virtually unlimited coverage. Both proposals are aimed at closing loopholes through which a CD broker could almost costlessly circumvent FDIC and FSLIC efforts to control the proliferation of brokered funds in failing institutions.

On the issue of brokered deposits, the FDIC's and FSLIC's only victory so far has been to increase reporting frequencies for institutions that rely heavily on brokered deposits. Since August 1984 FDIC-insured banks have been required to file monthly reports and to be prepared to submit to sudden examination whenever 5 or more percent of their deposits come from CD brokers. This asymmetric data-gathering requirement underscores the inadequacy of the FDIC's and FSLIC's overall information systems. Insurers' information systems have notably lagged behind those operated by large, well-managed commercial banks. As more deposit institutions adopt electronic record-keeping and as telecommunications systems improve, more frequent and more extensive readings of clients' electronic balance sheets become less burdensome. With a more adequate information base, agency asset-liability committees (ALCOs) could be set up to manage each agency's aggregate exposure to interest-volatility, industry, and country risk.

Recalibration of Insurance Coverages

The economic value of a dollar of deposit insurance varies in two ways: (1) At a given institution, it varies with the type of account covered, and (2) for a given type of account, it varies with the riskiness of the portfolio policies followed at the institution that issues the deposits. As a complementary way of improving insurers' information flow, Congress should permit deposit insurers to alter their coverages and fee structure to generate information on an individual institution's own perception of the benefits it reaps from insuring different types of accounts in different ways. As we noted earlier, deposit insurers and uninsured creditors have less information about an institution's risk exposure than a deposit institution's managers have. By developing a wider-ranging structure of insurance coverages and associated premiums, managerial assessments of the value of different kinds of coverage could be extracted from their willingness and unwillingness to pay a set of carefully varied asking prices for specific coverages. Even more information could be gathered if clients were permitted to switch insurers in pursuit of what they regard as cheaper or more reliable coverages.

Managers' selection of coverages signals how risky they and their customers perceive a given institution to be. Low-risk institutions should operate most profitably with minimal coverages. Money-market mutual funds provide an instance of conservatively managed near-depository institutions that operate effectively without any insurance at all. On the other hand, high-risk institutions should be able to compete best when they obtain maximal coverages from one or more extremely reliable insurers. If the representative institution were to demand maximal coverages on all account types, we could infer that the price of each type of insurance is too low across the board and that risk bearing is being subsidized industrywide.

What is needed is a strategy for assembling information on which a reliable process of risk rating could be based. While I prefer to leave detailed planning to insurance specialists, as a start I would recommend three changes in contract provisions:

1. Lowering (perhaps gradually) the basic coverage per account to a level sufficient to protect the transactions and precautionary balances of most household customers. An upper limit of $10,000 is particularly attractive, inasmuch as this is the minimum denomination on U.S. Treasury bills, which stand as a close substitute for large-denomination holdings of insured deposits. If such a limit is adopted, future values of the ceiling should simultaneously be indexed for inflation to make it more difficult for lobbying pressure to reintroduce the real value of maximum account coverage into the political arena. Congress needs to recognize that its decision to increase account coverage to $100,000 in 1980 was a serious mistake that it should strive to rectify as soon as possible. Fully insuring large-denomination deposits

effectively permits banks to issue high-denomination federally guaranteed debt that in divisibility and liquidity is actually superior to ordinary Treasury securities.

2. Differentially pricing successive layers of *optional* supplementary coverages (offered, say, in $10,000 slices) and adjusting these prices in accordance with market principles. These coverages could be purchased either by institutions acting on behalf of holders of specific classes of deposit accounts or by individual depositors acting on their own. Market-based pricing would seek to cover the implicit and explicit costs of producing FDIC and FSLIC insurance services at the level of client demand served. The aptness of the prices charged could be tested by laying off some or all of these contracts in the market for reinsurance.

3. Introducing provisions for deductible and coinsurance elements into this supplementary coverage. In introducing these elements, authorities could investigate the effects of relating progressive declines in coverage directly to account size and inversely to an account's maturity.

A complementary action would be to impose cumulative lifetime limits on the collectability of an individual or institutional depositor's aggregate claims on the federal deposit-insurance agencies. Adopting cumulative ceilings would parallel the coverage patterns employed in underwriting major medical insurance, making it important for even fully insured depositors to "care" whether CD brokers transfer their funds into insolvent institutions.

Opponents emphasize that these adjustments would penalize large depositors and increase deposit-institution funding costs. The other side of this criticism is that the existing pattern of subsidies is anti-egalitarian welfare for large depositors who are wealthy enough to buy nominally risk-free debt in large denominations directly from the Treasury. Taxpayers as a whole would benefit from reducing the true cost to government entities of underwriting deposit-institution risk taking.

Risk-Related Explicit Premiums

Risk rating is the process of analyzing and pricing the risk exposure inherent in a particular insurance contract. Explicit insurance premiums are fees that clients pay in the coin of the realm. The major benefit from realigning deposit-insurance coverages would be to produce information that an insurer could use to develop a premium structure that would curtail its moral hazard. Risk-sensitive explicit pricing is needed to relegate ex ante implicit premiums on previously recognized forms of risk taking to a lesser role.

Risk-related explicit premiums need not (and possibly *should* not) consist entirely of ex ante payments. Such payments may include procedures for an ex post settling up of gains and losses between an insured institution, its stockholders, and the insurer. To lessen the incentive for last-ditch gambles, ex post settlement schemes could usefully include provisions extending the limited liability of the stockholders of a failed institution or even of the stockholders of its parent holding company (as in the double liability that used to apply to holders of a national bank's stock) or to give the insurer the right to claim an appropriate share of any gains that a client reaps from forms of risk taking that FDIC or FSLIC policy statements declare to have been abusive.

If a firm records the market value of every other time on its expanded balance sheet, including sources of value that current accounting principles designate as off-balance-sheet or unbookable items, the value of federal guarantee services to an individual firm can be calculated as a residual from the value that the stock market places on the equity of the firm. In principle, a firm's stock value, S, equals the market value of bookable and unbookable assets, $A + A'$, minus the market value of bookable and unbookable nonequity liabilities, $L + L'$. If every other off-balance-sheet source of value is accounted for, the value of a firm's explicit and conjectural federal guarantees net of discounted future premiums, F_{CG}, may be calculated as

$$F_{CG} = S - (A + A') + (L + L').$$

The annual cost of providing this guarantee, $C(F_{CG})$, may be defined as the interest cost of supporting the average value the guarantee has during the year, $i_t \overline{F}_{CG}(t)$, plus the change in the market value that occurs from year end to year end:

$$C(F_{CG}) - i_t \overline{F}_{CG}(t) + F_{CG}(t) - F_{CG}(t-1).$$

If the liability of stockholders in every financial institution that enjoys a conjectural guarantee were extended to two (or more) times the par value of their stockholdings, as the liability of stockholders in national banks was until the 1930s, quarterly or annual charges designed to recover this cost could be levied on an ex post basis. Moreover, such a scheme could price away the advantages of the differentially stronger guarantee received by banks that the market currently perceives to be too large for regulators to liquidate.

The many opponents of risk rating emphasize that setting ex ante premiums or designing an equitable scheme for ex post settling up is a difficult task, requiring a considerably larger information base than is collected today (Horvitz 1983). However difficult it may be for isolated teams of regulators, it is not beyond the capability of the modern methods of contingent-contract writing and information processing. As Pyle (1984) points out, corporate bond markets undertake similar kinds of risk assessments every trading day. Nor are these risk assessments demonstrably more difficult than others that private insurance companies perform. Modern insurance companies price many exotic forms of risk, including damages visited on insured parties by computer crime, divorce, cancer, tax audits, and space debris. No matter how great the practical difficulties of rating a deposit institution's risk exposure, the current approach is defective in principle. To maintain permanently an unfunded system that insures risk borne by deposit institutions at a price that lies far below the return offered in capital markets for risk-bearing services is to establish a kind of Ponzi scheme. The longer such a system remains in place, the more severely it will be tested. As time passes, individual institutions become more fully aware of opportunities for exploiting the situation and develop less compunction about seeking to take advantage of them.

Although ex post settlement and extended stockholder liability would be administratively easier than ex ante pricing, these concepts frighten many deposit-institution managers. They point out that a return to double or triple liability on deposit-institution stock would raise the cost of raising private equity capital. They also express concern that FDIC and FSLIC policy statements could degenerate into devices for bringing political influence to bear on institutions' lending priorities. To make sure that these policy statements serve only the purpose of ruling out such demonstrably dangerous activities as betting an institution's very survival on the future course of interest rates or on the success of particular types of investment projects, it would be useful to assign the task of defining abuses to self-regulatory organization: a deposit-insurance standards board made up of leading practitioners and industry analysts.

What makes risk-sensitive pricing such a hard task is the essential fluidity of opportunities to take risk in financial markets. An institution's adaptive efficiency may be defined as its organizational resourcefulness, which reflects its managers' capacity to think deeply about simple problems and the flexibility they show in adjusting their administrative structure and procedures to cope with sudden or rapid change. To keep risk ratings and insurance premiums current requires considerable adaptive efficiency. For this reason, it seems dangerous to assign the function wholly to government officials. This leads to the fifth option in my program.

Meaningful Opportunities for Mixed Private and Governmental Competition in Deposit Insurance

To enhance incentives for deposit-insurance agencies to maximize their adaptive efficiency, it is necessary to provide opportunities for the FDIC and FSLIC to compete with each other (Benston 1983) and for private firms to issue or to reinsure at least some layers of supplementary deposit-insurance coverage. To neutralize political pressure for low prices and uneconomic coverages, authorities must invite into the contract-design and contract-pricing process decision-makers whose only stakes are economic—parties whose jobs and firms can and will be wiped out if they issue contracts that fail to make it a client's own best interest to keep its risk exposure within prudent bounds.

Private firms may be counted on to enter any business in which they can anticipate earning a fair return. As if to demonstrate this proposition, during the 1980s private insurance companies have begun to nibble eagerly around the edges of the deposit-insurance market. The biggest growth has been in guaranteeing cash flows to bondholders. In markets for deposit subsitutes, the insurance industry focuses principally on offering supplementary guarantees for individual account-holders that, beginning where federal guarantees stop, greatly extend the size of the balance covered. Such insurance is particularly attractive to nondepository institutions such as brokerage firms and insurance companies seeking to market nondepository accounts designed to function much like deposit balances. One notable example is Aetna's provision of supplementary guarantees that operate on top of the Securities Investor Protection Corporation's $500,000 basic guarantee to lift coverage for any holder of a Merrill Lynch's cash-management account to $10 million. Also, two money-market funds have secured coverage for their customers: one from St. Paul Money Fund Inc. in Minnesota and the other from the Travelers Corporation of Hartford. In a more exotic vein, Cigna Corporation temporarily issued Citicorp $900 million worth of insurance against the risk of currency inconvertibility in five countries. The policies covered the contingency that scheduled repayments by debtors in Argentina, Brazil, Mexico, Venezuela, and the Philippines would fail to be remitted because their governments might decide against permitting local currency to be converted into dollars. The contracts included a deductible equal to 25 percent of Citicorp's exposure in each country and a six-month delay before any unremitted debt proceeds may be collected. Affirming the interest of other segments of the industry, Cigna announced that it expected to reinsure over 95 percent of the coverage.

While private insurance of deposit-institution risks should continue to grow, as long as Congress requires the deposit-insurance agencies to maintain unrealistically low explicit premiums, the core of federal insurers' business will remain insulated from the discipline of private competition. It is this insulation that enables agency managers to emphasize political and bureaucratic objectives over their need to adapt economically to rapid change.

Statutory Constraints on FDIC and Federal Reserve Authority to Rescue Insolvent Large Institutions

Although deposit-institution regulators profess a sincere belief in the theoretical benefits of market discipline, practical circumstances inevitably make them reluctant to liquidate a large institution. Given the short terms of office that financial regulators enjoy, it makes little sense for them to take an appreciable chance that a spillover of financial pressure will damage other institutions or undermine public confidence in depository institutions as a whole. Why should an agency's leadership risk ruining their own careers when they can reliably truncate further damage with a readily obtained injection of federal funds and federal guarantees that serve to rescue a failing institution and its creditors from the need to sustain uncomfortable levels of losses. Confirming this analysis, Comptroller of the Currency Todd Conover went so far as to assert in September 1984 that the Federal government would not allow any of the nation's eleven largest banks to be liquidated.

To hear the sirens' song without being lured to his death, Ulysses had to arrange to have himself strapped to the mast of his ship. Similarly, the reliable way to lessen the probability that the Fed and federal deposit insurers will routinely bail out large insolvent deposit institutions and (potentially) private deposit-insurance companies is to place statutory limits on their ability to respond to the political and bureaucratic siren call of shortsighted opportunities for using federal resources to rescue firms that are insolvent de facto.

Although any proposal to limit the discretion of deposit-institution regulators is bound to be controversial, the potential for private loss must be strengthened if implicit federal guarantees are to be made imperfect enough for market discipline to operate properly. The first and most important step would be to require that federal deposit-insurance agencies (like private deposit insurers) leave the short-term responsibility for stabilizing the financial *system* wholly in the hands of the Federal Reserve, acting in its capacity as lender of last resort. Deposit insurance will not be properly priced as long as bailout responsibilities compromise the economic function of deposit-insurance reserves. Responsibility for stabilizing financial markets should not be crammed into the mission statement of federal deposit-insurance agencies. Second, even the Federal Reserve's capacity for bailing out insolvent institutions needs to be constrained. Except in the event of a bona fide crisis—as defined by the condition that a given percentage (say, at least 5 percent) of aggregate deposit-institution assets in a region has been involved in de jure failures within the last twelve or eighteen months—the Fed should not be allowed to lend funds to an institution whose capital net of the federal guarantee is negative in market value. This would increase the probability that one or two large institutions could fail de jure, but would leave the Fed free both to assist a troubled firm to arrange financing from private sources and to arrest a developing run on the system as a whole.

What this reform would not do is to let authorities repeatedly use the mere possibility of a systemic run as a justification for bailing out individual institutions as a matter of course. The policy of routinely bailing out financially devastated institutions imposes enormous unaccounted expense and unrecognized liabilities onto the deposit-insurance agencies and through them onto taxpayers and conservatively managed competitors who knowingly or unknowingly backstop the limited insurance reserves these agencies hold. As long as large deposit institutions and their creditors may count on drawing federal subsidies to extract themselves from what would otherwise be do-or-die situations, the potentially salutary effects of market discipline have little opportunity to make themselves felt.

THE POLITICAL DILEMMA OF REFORM

Conceived in 1933 as a device for protecting small depositors and bolstering public confidence in financial institutions, the subsequent interplay of political forces has assigned federal deposit insurance a far broader bureaucratic mission. It functions today as a system for implicitly guaranteeing the capacity of the deposit-institution *system* to make good on all but a small percentage of its outstanding debt. These implicit guarantees purchase the appearance of stability at the cost of undermining the fear of failure that ordinarily leads an institution's creditors to impose market discipline on its risk taking activity. They also shift the burden for financing unfavorable outcomes to taxpayers and conservatively managed financial institutions. The result has been a spate of de facto or market-value insolvencies among insured institutions that U.S. citizens would recognize as a national disaster if politicians had to present the bill for underwriting these insolvencies to the body politic.

To reduce the underwriting bill and to restore market discipline, it is necessary to make deposit-institution creditors fear failure again. To be meaningful, deposit-insurance reform must reduce the flow of subsidies to deposit institutions. It must endeavor to shift the burden of underwriting catastrophic financial risks from the general taxpayer back toward insured institutions and their creditors. We may count on political forces to see that Congress develops a set of rules that eases the burdens of transition. But before it can do that, it must agree on the nature of the system it wants to establish for the long run. A better deposit-insurance system must be one that increases the cost to insured institutions of following subsidy-exploiting strategies of funding, lending, and product-line expansion that have seemed so very profitable in the past.

Every one of this chapter's six varieties of reform promises to complicate the jobs of deposit-insurance bureaucrats and to hurt deposit-institution stockholders managers, and large accountholders to some degree. Because they see the need to restore financial stability, most of these parties support deposit-insurance reform in principle. But to keep their own oxen from being gored, individually they support and oppose different combinations of the six reforms. Industry trade associations must be expected to lobby vigorously against any subset of the six proposals that in the judgment of their membership threatens to hit the firms they represent with disproportionate force. This leaves every one of the six proposals with important enemies and with virtually no important friends.

Each trade association's greatest fears are that its sector of the deposit institution industry will suffer greatly during the transition to a fairer and sounder system and end up regulated more burdensomely than before. Each wants to minimize the extent to which deposit-insurance reform could reduce the value of its particular type of depository firm. Inasmuch as each association's membership acknowledges the nation's need for deposit-insurance reform, their active resistance to anything but token reform puts them in the position of a banker who decided to consult a psychiatrist about a problem his brother had been causing him and his family. The problem was that his brother had come to believe he was a chicken. His incessant cackling was upsetting everyone in the household and embarrassing them in front of their friends. The psychiatrist assured the banker that he was a leading expert on fixations of this sort and could cure his brother completely in no more than six sessions of therapy. But rather than being pleased by this news, the banker became more agitated than ever. "Hold on," he said. "We are only complaining about the cackling. No one in the family wants to do without the eggs he lays."

Deposit institutions are able to harvest eggs from the deposit-insurance system only because their deepest layers of risk bearing are being unintentionally subsidized. As long as this subsidy continues, incentives exist for managers to bet their firms on the future course of interest rates and on the prosperity of specific projects and geographic areas. Some of these bets must lose, and, for the losers, nationalization looms as an increasingly likely possibility.

Perhaps the greatest irony of financial regulatory reform in the United States is that a necessary condition for its occurrence—a spectacular scandal or financial crisis—is virtually a sufficient condition for a program of reform that pays too little attention to long-term problems. Although reform seldom occurs outside an environment of perceived crisis, a crisis atmosphere favors short-sighted solutions. In the midst of a crisis regulators and politicians pay far more attention to the system's immediate difficulties than to its long-run needs. A sympathetic analogy is to consider how hard it would be for a football coach to prepare his team to play its season on dry fields, when fate dictates that their training camp must be held on a quagmire.

Today two immediate difficulties frame the problems that regulators see. First, because authorities have proved reluctant to declare de jure failures in the past, the market value of the nonequity liabilities of most deposit institutions exceeds the market value of the assets that they may recognize under generally accepted accounting principles. Second, because of this, the staffs and explicit insurance reserves of the deposit-insurance agencies are overwhelmed. The inadequacy of explicit agency reserves leads agency managers to resort to selling regulatory exemptions and to emphasize noncash forms of assistance such as income-maintenance agreements and ownership positions. At the same time staff limitations permit them to discipline only a few of the many institutions that engage in excessive risk taking. These constraints make it hard for the average number of de jure failures to exceed two or three a week, while the pricing of deposit-insurance continues to lead insolvent deposit institution managers to pursue a go-for-broke strategy.

It is not necessary for Congress to incorporate all of this chapter's six options into the new model deposit-insurance system. Nor is it necessary that the options finally chosen be installed all at once. Although the complete package probably would produce the best results, adopting any subset of the six options would result in a system that operates with greater safety, reliability, and comfort. Of course, just how safe, reliable, and comfortable a ride the nation ultimately enjoys depends also on the macroeconomic policies that the government follows. If Congress could bring government spending under long-run restraint, monetary policy would not have to push interest rates over as wide a cycle as it has in the last decade. Reducing the volatility of interest rates would relieve the car's drivers of the need to take it over quite so dangerous a set of roads.

REFERENCES

Benston, George J. 1983. "Deposit Insurance and Bank Failures." *Economic Review* of the Federal Reserve Bank of Atlanta (March): 4–17.

Horvitz, Paul M. 1983. "The Case against Risk-Related Deposit Insurance Premiums." *Housing Finance Review* 2 (July): 253–63.

Kane, Edward J. 1983. "A Six-Point Program for Deposit Insurance Reform." *Housing Finance Review* 2 (July): 269–78.

Pyle, David H. 1984. "Deregulation and Deposit Insurance." *Economic Review* of the Federal Reserve Bank of San Francisco (Spring): 5–15.

Silverberg, Stanley C. 1985. "Resolving Large Bank Problems and Failures." *Issues in Bank Regulation* 8 (Winter): 12–15.

5 COMPETITION, EFFICIENCY, AND FAIRNESS IN THE FINANCIAL SERVICES INDUSTRY

Michael Mussa

The past decade has been a period of remarkably rapid change in the structure of the financial services industry. From the 1930s through the 1960s, old guidelines defined relatively distinct spheres of activity for different classes of institutions providing financial services: commercial banks, savings and loan associations, credit unions, securities dealers, mutual funds, insurance companies, and other types of commercial enterprises. Those guidelines have been breached or eroded by new laws and regulations, by new interpretations of old laws and regulations, and by creative innovation of business leaders devising new products and seeking new areas for expansion and profit. Large commercial banks once relied heavily on core deposits subject to controlled interest rates to fund short-term commercial loans to domestic enterprises. They now fund their commitments to domestic and multinational firms and foreign enterprises and governments with large doses of market-rate-sensitive borrowings in the federal funds market, the market for large negotiable CDs, and the market for Eurodollar deposits. Savings and loan associations formerly concentrated on long-term fixed rate mortgages funded by savings deposits with regulated interest rates. They have shifted increasingly toward variable rate mortgages, have diversified into commercial lending, and have become increasingly dependent on shorter-term deposits with market-sensitive interest rates. Securities dealers

121

have invaded the markets for transactions and time deposit accounts with money market mutual funds. Commercial banks and savings and loan associations have counterattacked with forays into retail securities brokerage and marketing of commercial paper and have aggressively sought authorization for expansion into other securities market activities and into insurance. Barriers to interstate branch banking have been eroded by loan production offices, by specifically authorized interstate acquisitions of banks and other financial institutions, by regional agreements for interstate banks, and by the creation of nonbank banks that accept (insured) deposits but do not engage in commercial lending. Large commercial enterprises led by Sears, American Express, and Prudential Insurance have become diversified providers of a broad range of financial services on a nationwide basis.

This rapid change in the structure of the financial services industry has generated and continues to generate great controversy concerning the laws and regulations that control or ought to control the activities of various suppliers of financial services. Quite understandably, every class of institution providing financial services seeks to protect its particular range of operations from encroachments by other institutions and seeks authorization to expand operations into previously foreclosed regions where additional profits might be earned. Almost universally, enhanced competition is cited as the principal benefit and justification for relaxing or removing barriers to expansion, and the desirability of ensuring "fairness" of competition is often cited as a key reason to retain or strengthen existing legal or regulatory barriers and restrictions. Virtually all potential players in the financial services arena announce their willingness to abide by the outcome of competition, provided that competition occurs on the proverbial level playing field.

In assessing the conflicting arguments and claims in the debate over regulation of the financial services industry, it is first important to clarify what benefits may be expected from enhanced competition and how the public interest is involved in ensuring the "fairness" of competition. Next, it is crucial to understand why the commitment to "safety and soundness" of depository institutions and to the policies necessary to maintain this commitment imply that totally unregulated competition among depository institutions and between such institutions and other suppliers of financial services does not serve the public interest. Finally, it is essential to examine the nature of the regulations of depository institutions and of other suppliers of financial services necessary to ensure that the outcome of the competitive process serves the public interest.

In discussing these issues, this chapter makes the following main points. Competition is already intense among existing providers of virtually all financial services. With a few possible exceptions, relaxation of restrictions on the scope of activities of particular classes of institutions is not needed to secure the usual benefit of increased competition—elimination of the ability of existing suppliers to use market power to raise prices above marginal costs. Rather, the potential public benefits from relaxing most existing restrictions come from efficiencies of production or consumption resulting from combinations of activities within individual enterprises that are not permitted by existing laws and regulations. Fairness of competition is important for the public interest not because it is desirable to protect vested interests that have developed as a consequence of restrictive laws and regulations, but rather because competition best serves the goal of economic efficiency when no player has an artificial, government-supported advantage over any other player. The policy of assuring the safety and soundness of depository institutions requires that the major creditors of these institutions—their depositors—be given explicit and implicit government guarantees concerning the value of their credits of a sort that are not extended to the major creditors of other types of enterprises. Because the government acts as the ultimate guarantor of the value of deposits, it is desirable that the government impose restrictions on the nature and extent of risk-taking activity by depository institutions and monitor their compliance with these restrictions. It may be appropriate for the government to regulate the nature and extent of competition among depository institutions in order to ensure that such competition does not itself stimulate excessive risk taking by these institutions. It is also appropriate that the government regulate the terms and conditions under which depository institutions are allowed to engage in a broader range of commercial activities, including the provision of some classes of financial services, in order to make sure that the special advantages that these enterprises enjoy as depository institutions are not used to support unfair and inefficient competition in other activities.

THE MEANING OF COMPETITION

From the perspective of the public interest, a principal benefit of a high level of competition in any business activity is that it severely restricts the ability of firms to raise price above marginal cost through the exercise of market power. Important obstacles to competition that may have facilitated use of market power in some areas of the financial services industry a decade ago have been virtually eliminated, and a very high level of competition now prevails in the provision of almost all financial services.[1] The anticompetitive agreement of members of the New York Stock Exchange that fixed commissions for stock market transactions was ended on May 1, 1975. The legal and regulatory restrictions on interest rates payable to depositors at most financial institutions were almost entirely removed between 1980 and 1983.[2] There are still, of course, restrictions on interstate branching of depository institutions and on entry of new banks and savings and loan associations. With the possible exception of a few local banking markets (especially in states with limited within state branching), however, there is no indication of a meaningful deficiency of competition in the ordinary sense. Virtually all customers of financial services are able to obtain these services from a number of different firms within a given class of institutions (commercial banks, savings and loan associations, credit unions, credit companies, securities dealers, or insurance companies), and the same or very similar services are frequently provided by different classes of institutions. Many financial services are advertised and effectively available from a multiplicity of suppliers on a nationwide basis through the mail or by means of electronic communication. On the basis of the standards normally applied in assessing competition (concentration ratios within relevant markets, barriers to entry, and so forth), financial services must surely be among our most competitive industries.

The legal and regulatory restrictions that are now usually cited as barriers to competition are restrictions on the range of activities that may be conducted by particular enterprises, especially by individual commercial banks. Commercial banks that would like to establish full-service branches outside of their home states are generally prohibited from doing so. Commercial banks are also prohibited from securities underwriting and dealing (but not retail brokerage), from selling most classes of insurance, and from providing other services not deemed to be "closely related to banking."[3] Symmetric restrictions generally preclude securities firms and insurance companies from engaging in commercial banking. Despite the fact that savings and loan associations are now permitted to engage in most of the activities of commercial banks, restrictions on activities that may be combined with those of a savings and loan associations are less severe than for commercial banks.

These restrictions on the range of activities of individual financial institutions are generally not restrictions of competition in the ordinary sense of restrictions that permit of support the exercise of market power. The market for commercial banking services in New York City, for example, is undoubtedly highly competitive, despite the preclusion of full-service branches of the Bank of America and other non-New York banks from this market, and despite the preclusion of securities underwriters from engaging in commercial banking. Maintenance of a high level of competition (in the ordinary sense) does not require that every firm be allowed to engage in every line of business in every area of the country. The restaurant business in New York City is not monopolized because commercial banks are precluded from engaging in general commerce and industry.

Given that most markets for financial services are already highly competitive in the ordinary sense, despite restrictions on the permissible range of activities for particular suppliers of financial services, the argument for removing or relaxing these restrictions usually must be based on something other than the ordinary benefits of competition. This argument must be that consumers of financial services lose the benefits of efficiencies of production or consumption that would result from relaxing restrictions on the permissible range of activities of particular suppliers of financial services. Production efficiencies could result from allowing more efficient producers into markets from which they are presently excluded or from efficiencies of joint production of combinations of financial services that are presently prohibited. Consumption efficiencies could result from allowing consumers to purchase combinations of financial services from single suppliers that are now available only from separate suppliers. For example, banking services might be more efficiently produced by branches of large nationwide banks than by smaller local or regional banks. The services of securities underwriting might be more efficiently produced in combination with the services of commercial lending. Consumers of banking services in several areas of the country might benefit from the services of a nationwide bank. Consumers might also find it efficient to deal with a financial supermarket that offers the whole range of financial services.

The potential benefits from increased efficiency in production and consumption might be subsumed into a broader definition of the benefits of competition. In this broader notion, competition not only limits the ability of suppliers to exercise market power, but it also ensures that the most efficient producers, who provide the most desired products and combinations of products, will ultimately prevail in the market. Adoption of this broader notion of the benefits of "competition," however, tends to confuse the debate over the appropriate regulations to impose on the financial services industry. It allows the suggestion to be made that existing restrictions on the range of activities of particular suppliers of financial services are anticompetitive in the ordinary sense that they allow greater latitude for the exercise of market power, when there is no sound reason to believe that existing restrictions have any significant effect of this kind. It also diverts attention from what should be the central issue in the debate over regulation of the financial services industry: to weigh the potential public benefits from possible gains in production and consumption efficiency against the possible losses and dangers from relaxing existing restrictions suppliers of financial services.

FAIRNESS AND EFFICIENCY

Almost inevitably, individuals who suffer economic injury as a consequence of changes in government policies are likely to feel that they have suffered unfairly. There is frequently some justification for this view, even when the policy change increases competition or economic efficiency. Individuals who have invested in physical or human capital specific to particular business activity that is protected by a longstanding government policy from other more efficient suppliers may be earning no more than the normal rate of return on their investment. If protection is removed by a change in government policy, individuals who have made such investments in reliance on the old policy will usually suffer economic losses that could legitimately be viewed as "unfair." A principle that requires that policy changes avoid "unfair" losses of this sort, however, is virtually a prescription against any relaxation of restrictions created by laws and government regulations. Adoption of this principle effectively legitimizes the vested interests created by restrictive laws and regulations and precludes reforms that clearly serve the public good.[4]

This principle aside, there is one important circumstance in which injury suffered because of unfair competition resulting from relaxation of restrictive laws and regulations is a valid argument against a proposed policy reform. This situation arises when proposed reform would allow participation in a business activity by enterprises that are beneficiaries of special government privileges or subsidies, in competition with enterprises that are not so similarly advantaged. In this situation, not only will economic injury be suffered by existing participants in the field, economic efficiency is likely to be reduced. The likely loss of efficiency arises when the new entrants into the field are able to expand on the basis of their special privileges, rather than because of a genuine efficiency advantage over existing participants.

The issue here is both the likely loss of efficiency and the private loss of those injured by unfair competition that is based on special government privileges of subsidies. Even if allowing participation by specially privileged or subsidized enterprises in a particular business activity improves consumer welfare by lowering prices or improving quality of product or service, this is not evidence of a gain in social welfare. Rather, to the extent that lower prices and higher quality of products or services are the result of exploitation of special privileges and subsidies, social welfare is being reduced because consumers are not paying the full social opportunity cost of the goods and services they are purchasing.[5] Apart from this loss of social welfare, other participants in the business activity that are not beneficiaries of the special privileges or subsidies have a legitimate grievance of private injury.

The clearest instances of "unfair competition" justifying remedial action arise when one class of enterprises receives a direct government subsidy not available to other enterprises participating in the same business activity. For example, a business receiving a 5 percent subsidy on each unit of output it sells can compete effectively against businesses that are 5 percent more efficient but do not receive a subsidy. Growth of the subsidized business at the expense of its nonsubsidized competitors reduces economic efficiency and unjustly harms these competitors.

In many cases, the special privileges that allow some enterprises to compete unfairly in certain business activities are more difficult to discern and quantify than they are in the case of a direct subsidy. This is so in the financial services industry where artificial differences in the competitive position of different classes of enterprises supplying financial services are due to complex and sometimes subtle differences in the regulations applied to these enterprises and especially to the explicit and implicit government guarantees provided to creditors of some of these enterprises. To understand why constraints on the activities of different classes of suppliers of financial services may be required to assure both economic efficiency in the supply of financial services and fairness of competition among the suppliers of particular services, it is necessary to understand the nature and extent of the differences in the regulations applied to different suppliers of financial services and the fundamental reason why all of these differences are unlikely to be completely eliminated.

SAFETY AND SOUNDNESS OF DEPOSITORY INSTITUTIONS

In the United States and in most other countries, maintenance of the safety and soundness of banks and other depository institutions is a firmly established and widely accepted objective of government policy. The exact nature of the commitment to safety and soundness of depository institutions and the policies used to carry this commitment into effect have varied widely from time to time and place to place. At a minimum, this commitment has meant that governments (usually acting through central banks) would forestall or limit any crisis threatening the overall stability of the financial system by providing liquidity in the event of a crisis. It has also frequently meant that governments or their surrogates would monitor and regulate the activities of private financial institutions in an effort to assure the soundness of their operations. More recently, in the United States, it has come to mean that the government would directly or indirectly insure the nominal value of most deposits in financial institutions and would seek, to the greatest extent possible, to assure the survival of individual depository institutions. The commitment to safety and soundness of depository institutions and to the policies required to carry this commitment into effect provide the fundamental reason why unrestricted competition in the provision of financial services is not generally the policy that best serves the public interest.

A purest believer in laissez-faire applied to financial services might argue that governmental assurance of the safety and soundness of depository institutions is unnecessary and that specific policies to provide such assurance are undesirable. In my view, such arguments have some intellectual interest but little practical relevance. Government policies are committed to assuring the safety and soundness of depository institutions because the public demands and expects such policies. Abandonment of a general commitment to safety and soundness of depository institutions is not politically feasible (nor in my view would it be desirable). Failure to pursue policies that effectively fulfill this commitment and thereby disappoint public expectations would be likely to transform a minor financial crisis (such as the recent collapse of Continental Illinois) into a financial disaster. Faced with the prospect of a potential financial disaster and with a public demanding and expecting government intervention to forestall such a disaster, the government would be forced to intervene to guarantee the overall safety and soundness of depository institutions.

It follows that analysis of the appropriate policies to regulate competition in the provision of financial services must take account of the general commitment to the safety and soundness of depository institutions and of an array of policies that carry out this commitment. Five main types of policies are used for assuring the safety and soundness of depository institutions in the United States: explicit insurance of most deposits up to $100,000; implicit guarantees to noninsured depositors and other creditors of depository institutions, especially depositors and creditors of large commercial banks; special government support either of depository institutions themselves or of those indebted to depository institutions; special accounting rules for depositor institutions; regulation of depository institutions especially with respect to their competitive behavior, to the quality of their assets, and to their capital adequacy. Each of these policies deserves brief description and discussion.

Explicit federal insurance is provided on deposits up to $100,000 at most commercial banks, savings and loan associations, mutual savings banks, and credit unions. An important characteristic of this deposit insurance is that the nominal value of the deposit (including accumulated interest) is fully insured up to $100,000. This is different from the federal insurance enjoyed by holders of federal agency obligations such as Ginnie Maes and Fannie Maes where interest payments and ultimate principal repayment are guaranteed by the federal government, but where the asset holder is still subject to risk of fluctuations in the market value of his asset (which can be quite substantial) until the date of its maturity. It is also different from the federal insurance afforded holders of brokerage accounts under SIPC, which insures against loss due to fraud or misadventure but not against declines in market value. Insured depositors are protected not only against losses from fraud or default by debtors of depository institutions, but also are protected against losses from fluctuations in the market value of the assets held by these institutions.

Implicit insurance is provided to holders of large noninsured deposits and to other creditors of depository institutions through a variety of mechanisms. One important mechanism is the "purchase and assumption" transaction under which the regulatory authorities (the FDIC or FSLIC) arrange for a failing institution to be acquired by a healthy institution, with the acquiring institution assuming responsibility for all of the deposits of the failing institutions and the deposit insurance agency contributing enough to make the deal attractive. An effort was recently made to instill greater market discipline on depository institutions by allowing noninsured depositors of failing institutions to suffer losses, most prominently in the failure of Penn Square National Bank in 1982. This effort was abandoned in the collapse of Continental Illinois when not only all depositors but also all creditors of the bank and the bank holding company (except holders of common stock) were guaranteed against loss by the regulatory authorities. In the Continental Illinois crisis as in the earlier crisis at the Franklin National Bank, the Federal Reserve provided substantial amounts of short-term credit to keep the bank afloat while a more permanent solution to its difficulties was found. The principle that now seems to be established is that the regulatory authorities (1) will not permit the failure of a large bank to injure substantially the noninsured depositors who provide the bulk of funds to such banks and (2) will also seek to protect other creditors of such banks, with the exception of stockholders. Any other policy is perceived to generate significant risk of a run by large uninsured depositors out of any large bank thought to be in difficulty, thereby raising the danger of disruption of the financial system. The notion that the regulatory authorities will do whatever is necessary to prevent a run by large depositors is almost a self-fulfilling prophesy. This notion is likely to be tested only in circumstances where the financial position of a number of large banks is somewhat question-able.[6] In this situation, failure of the regulatory authorities to pro-vide the expected support to a single large bank that is experiencing difficulties will remove a factor critical to confidence of uninsured depositors in all large banks. The authorities will very likely be forced to support uninsured depositors (and possibly other creditors) in the failing institution in order to avoid a general panic.

Special government assistance is sometimes provided to financial institutions or to those indebted to such institutions as a means of preserving the safety and soundness of depository institutions. One example of such assistance is the "all savers certificate." When de-pository institutions, especially savings and loan associations, were in deep difficulty in 1981, a law was passed that allowed deposits to be issued on which individuals could earn up to $1,000 of interest free of federal income tax. The ability to issue such deposits clearly re-duced the costs of funds for the issuing institutions and helped in attracting additional deposits, thereby assisting in the resolution of their financial difficulties. Another example is the shift in attitude of Chairman Burns of the Federal Reserve toward the desirability of financial assistance to New York City in 1975, which was due partly to the view that default on New York City notes and bonds would create important difficulties for the banking system. A third exam-ple is U.S. government support for financial aid to developing coun-tries experiencing difficulties in managing their foreign debt. Concern with the possible effects of default by one or more of the larger debtor countries on the U.S. banking system has probably been one of the important reasons why the U.S. government has extended direct financial assistance to these countries and has encouraged and cooperated in multinational assistance to these countries and in the efforts of the International Monetary Fund to ameliorate and resolve the financial difficulties faced by these countries.[7] At a more general level, there is little doubt that the conduct of monetary policy by the Federal Reserve is (and ought to be) influenced by the financial con-dition of depository institutions. When the actual or possible failure of some large depository institution or large nonfinancial enterprise, or any other event, threatens a general financial crisis, the Federal Reserve quite properly provides additional liquidity to the financial system.

The accounting rules that apply to depository institutions are dif-ferent from those that apply to other types of enterprises, and these special rules allow depository institutions to survive in circumstances where other types of enterprises would be insolvent. The most important aspect of the special accounting rules is that depository institutions are not required to mark to market the values of their portfolios of loans and investments but rather are allowed to carry their loans and investments at par or acquisition cost so long as they are not in default or excessively in arrears. Because of this special accounting rule, savings and loan associations did not have to recognize that between mid-1981 and mid-1982 the market value of their portfolio of long-term fixed-interest mortgages was probably $150 billion below book value.[8] Accordingly, the reported net equity value of savings and loan associations remained positive during this period, when on a market value accounting basis, net equity would surely have been quite negative, probably on the order of minus $100 billion. Because commercial banks generally have a much better match between the maturity structure of their assets and that of their liabilities, there is usually less of a divergence between their balance sheet position on a book value basis and on a mark to market basis than there is for savings and loan associations. Nevertheless, I suspect that many commercial banks, especially larger banks, would have been technically insolvent on a mark to market basis in 1974–75 and in 1981–82. This is partly because rapid run-ups in interest rates reduced the market value of longer-term assets held by these banks relative to their book values and partly because doubtful domestic and foreign loans continued to be carried at par when a market valuation would have been below par.

Special accounting rules for depository institutions are not limited to avoidance of mark to market principles for valuing assets and liabilities. Depository institutions are sometimes allowed special latitude in delaying recognition of losses and accelerating recognition of income. For example, savings and loan associations are generally able to count points charged on new mortgages as current income, rather than amortizing these receipts over the expected life of the mortgage. Under regulatory accounting principles applied to saving and loans associations, losses taken on assets (such as older mortgages) that are sold at below book value can be amortized over the remaining life of the asset, rather than recognized in the year of its sale. Commercial banks are generally not required to write down the value of doubtful loans until these loans have been nonperforming for six months. This rule has induced some fancy maneuvering to avoid write downs in the value of commercial bank loans to some foreign countries, such as was recently reported in the *New York Times* (June 7, 1985) for the case of Argentina:

> Argentine officials and American bankers are scrambling to avert a downgrading of Argentine debt next Monday, which could cut into bank profits and scuttle a long-delayed package to reschedule the country's foreign debt.
>
> The third-largest debtor in the developing world, Argentina is more than six months behind in its interest payment. . . . That could lead an interagency committee of American regulators to downgrade Argentine debt held by American banks. . . .
>
> To avoid a lower credit rating, Argentine negotiators in Washington are desperately trying to reach a new agreement with the International Monetary Fund . . . [to] replace the I.M.F. accord that was suspended in February when the Argentine economy failed to meet agreed-upon targets.
>
> . . . Meanwhile, the United States and several Latin American governments are contemplating a "bridge" loan to Argentina. . . . Such a loan would allow Argentina to pay commercial banks at least part of the roughly $1.2 billion in interest arrears accumulated since Nov. 14.
>
> . . . Unless an agreement with the I.M.F. is achieved in the next few days, bankers and others expect the regulators to drop Argentina's credit rating at least one notch, to "substandard." . . . If the regulators downgrade Argentina's debt two notches to "value impaired," banks would be required to set aside reserves against a portion of their loans to Argentina.
>
> . . . One reason why regulators would be unlikely to declare Argentine debt value-impaired, bankers said, is the fact that it would require institutions to set aside reserves equivalent to perhaps 10 percent of loans to Argentina's public sector.
>
> . . . "You have to think the way a regulator thinks," one banker suggested. "They have to maintain credibility. But they can't take steps that threaten the very system that they are trying to serve or even some big banks in it."

The point here is not that the accounting rules for depository institutions are manipulated for some evil purpose. The public interest would not be served if large numbers of banks and savings and loan associations were forced into insolvency by a run-up in interest rates, a recession, or credit difficulties of foreign countries. (On the other hand, the lending practices of banks and other depository institutions might be different if they were subject to different accounting rules.) Rather, the point is that to protect the safety and soundness of depository institutions, special accounting rules are employed that allow these institutions to survive when similar institutions following more standard accounting rules would be almost sure to fail. To use a maritime analogy: Ordinary commercial enterprises are like surface ships—when they sink, they sink. Depository institutions are like modern nuclear submarines—able to survive submerged at great depths for long periods.

Many other regulations applied to depository institutions were also adopted to protect their safety and soundness. This was the rationale for the prohibition of interest paid on demand deposits and the regulation of interest paid on time deposits. It was believed that excessive competition among banks in terms of interest paid on deposits was partly responsible for the failure of many banks in the early 1930s. Restrictions on creation of new banks and new bank branches were also justified on grounds of protecting the safety and soundness of existing banks. It is noteworthy that both the restrictions on interest paid depositors and on entry of new banks and bank branches are clearly anticompetitive. The virtues of competition, however, were deemed to be secondary to the objective safety and soundness of banks and other depository institutions.

Depository institutions are also regulated with respect to the nature and distribution of their assets. Commercial banks are generally prohibited from holding common stocks and other "speculative" investments such as low-grade corporate bonds. Until recently, savings and loan associations were required to hold most of their assets in the form of mortgages or mortgage-based securities. All federally insured depository institutions are subject to periodic examinations in which the quality of their assets comes under regulatory scrutiny. Remedial action can be ordered to correct deficiencies uncovered during such examinations.

During the past decade, regulatory authorities have become increasingly concerned with the capital adequacy of depository institutions, as measured by the ratio of capital (equity, accumulated surplus, and subordinated debt) to total assets. For commercial banks, this ratio has been declining almost continually from the start of the national banking system during the civil war. Regulators have sought, without much success, to increase capital ratios for three reasons related to the objective of safety and soundness of depository institutions. Higher capital ratios contribute directly to safety and soundness by providing a larger cushion to absorb losses and avoid insolvency. Higher capital ratios supposedly give stockholders (and holders of subordinated debt) greater interest in monitoring and controlling risk taking by bank managements. Higher capital ratios provide greater protection for deposit insurance funds and longer lead times for regulators to enforce remedial actions to protect bank solvency.

In summary, there is a strong governmental commitment to maintaining the safety and soundness of depository institutions. A whole host of special government policies applying to depository institutions have been adopted for the purpose of serving this critical objective.

APPROPRIATE REGULATION OF DEPOSITORY INSTITUTIONS

The commitment to safety and soundness of depository institutions and to the government policies necessary to effectuate this commitment imply that some restrictions should be imposed on the behavior of depository institutions and on the range of activities in which they are permitted to engage. These restrictions are required both to protect the safety and soundness of depository institutions (at reasonable cost to the taxpayer) and to ensure that the special privileges afforded such institutions to protect their safety and soundness are not used as the basis of unfair and inefficient competition in other business activities.

There is fairly broad agreement that some limitation of risk taking by depository institutions is necessary to protect their safety and soundness and to limit the potential cost to the taxpayer of explicit and implicit government insurance of deposits at such institutions. Limitations of risk taking by depository institutions imply some restrictions on the nature and extent of competition of these institutions in their lending activities. Competition in lending activities among depository institutions that benefit from explicit and implicit government insurance of their deposit liabilities may contribute to excessive risk taking by these institutions. Individual depository institutions may get into difficulty because of stupid or irresponsible management. The general difficulties recently experienced by commercial banks and by savings and loan associations, however, cannot exclusively be ascribed to this cause.[9] Competitive pressure to make loans on terms and conditions comparable with those offered by other depository institutions has also probably contributed excessive risk taking by depository institutions in their lending activities. Competitive pressures surely prevent individual savings and loan associations from charging potential borrowers a premium that compensates for the risk of funding long-term fixed-rate mortgages with short-term interest-sensitive deposits. Competitive pressures also help explain why commercial banks extended large loans to developing countries at very low spreads over their costs of funds.

Risk-related charges for deposit insurance have been suggested as a method for controlling risk taking by depository institutions while avoiding explicit regulation of the lending activities of these institutions. I believe that a movement to risk-related charges for deposit insurance is feasible and desirable, but I doubt that this alone can resolve the problem of excessive risk taking by depository institutions. So long as accounting measures of the values of assets of depository institutions are based on acquisition costs rather than current market values, accounting measures of risks associated with lending activities of these institutions will not reflect true economic risks, and deposit insurance rates based on accounting measures of risks will not induce appropriate risk management by depository institutions. Deposit insurance based on economic risks with accounting done on acquisition costs could produce anomalies such as economically viable institutions that are insolvent on an accounting basis because of high deposit insurance charges. Deposit insurance rates based on economic risks together with market valuation accounting would probably be the best combination. But there are considerable difficulties in measuring economic risks and market values for many assets held by depository institutions, especially loans of commercial banks.

Moreover, constraints and restrictions typically used in private insurance policies and credit agreements suggest that solution of the problem of excessive risk taking by insured depository institutions ought to involve constraints and restrictions on the activities of these institutions. A private insurer or creditor is exposed to "moral risk" when the insuree or the debtor has some control over the extent of risk and has an incentive to exploit this control for his own benefit at the expense of the insuror or creditor. To deal with moral risk, private insurors and creditors not only charge a higher price to compensate for a higher risk, they also attempt to limit the ability of the insuree or debtor to manipulate the degree of risk. Stipulations, conditions, and exclusions in insurance policies and covenants and restrictions in loan agreements are mechanisms used to achieve this result. In extending insurance to depositors in depository institutions, the government exposes itself to moral risk. The managers and stockholders of these institutions have an incentive to increase the risk of their lending activities because part of this increased risk is effectively borne by the government. To deal with this problem of moral risk, it is appropriate not only for the government to charge a higher premium for insurance at riskier institutions, but also for it to impose regulations that restrict the extent of risk taking by depository institutions.

One problem of risk taking in lending activities of depository institutions that requires special attention is the issuance of long-term fixed-rate mortgages funded by short-term interest-sensitive deposits. A shift of accounting practices to mark to market valuation of assets would do a great deal to eliminate this highly risky lending activity, for it would force the gains and losses of this activity to show up on the balance sheet and income statement of the institutions engaging in it. Risk-related deposit insurance rates would also discourage this risky lending activity. Absent a change in accounting practices or adoption of risk-related deposit insurance rates, some quantitative restriction should probably be imposed on the fraction of assets that depository institutions could hold in the form of long-term fixed-interest instruments. This fraction should depend on the amount of longer-term fixed interest deposits at the institutions. This restriction would still allow depository institutions to originate large amounts of long-term fixed-rate mortgages to be resold to individual investors, pension funds, insurance companies, and other holders of such investments. Mortgages held by depository institutions, however, would have to be more heavily concentrated in variable rate forms.

Another area where it may be appropriate to place some limits on competition among depository institutions is in interest rates and bonuses paid to attract deposits. The old regulations that kept a constant effective maximum on interest rates paid depositors for long periods is no longer viable in the present era of rapidly changing market interest rates. A regulation that limited interest rates on deposits to a premium over the Treasury rate for the same maturity, however, probably would be viable. The argument for such a regulation in the case of federally insured deposits is quite clear. These deposits are ultimately a liability of the federal government if the issuing institution should fail. It makes no sense for the government to allow a private institution to attract federally insured deposits by offering a rate substantially above the Treasury rate, to use these deposits fo finance speculative loans and investments that pay high yields when they do pay off, and to leave the government holding the bag when these loans and investments do not pay off. A small-interest premium for depositors over the Treasury rate (adjusted for the maturity of the deposit) might be justified to take account of differences in liquidity and in state tax treatment of interest income, but differentials as large as 3 or 4 percent that have recently been offered by some institutions have little justification.[10]

A similar argument applies to uninsured deposits in insured institutions, especially large commercial banks. As previously discussed, most uninsured deposits benefit from some de facto insurance because the government is not prepared to tolerate the financial crisis that would likely result from inflicting substantial losses on uninsured depositors of a large bank that gets into financial difficulty. If the government extends de facto insurance to most uninsured depositors in large commercial banks, then it makes sense to place some limit on the interest rates paid on these deposits, relative to interest rates paid on Treasury securities of comparable maturity.

Competition between depository institutions issuing insured deposits and other suppliers of financial services or more general types of business also requires scrutiny. There are two important reasons why depository institutions may be able to compete on an unfair and inefficient basis in activities outside of the main scope of their functions as depository institutions. Both are related to the artificially low, risk-adjusted cost of capital for business activities of depository institutions that are outside the scope of their functions as depository institutions. First, the creditors of depository institutions benefit from the explicit and implicit government insurance of deposits at these institutions and from all of the other special actions that the government takes to prevent the failure of depository institutions. As a consequence, the risk to which creditors of depository institutions are exposed is smaller than the true economic risk arising from the activities of these institutions. This is true not only for depositors but also for other creditors. As the recent experience with the collapse of Continental Illinois makes clear, it is not only depositors (insured or uninsured) who are likely beneficiaries of government support: All of the creditors of the bank and the bank holding company, except the stockholders, were bailed out. Because of anticipated government support in the event of difficulties, creditors of depository institutions will demand lower rates of return on funds lent to finance the activities of depository institutions than would normally be consistent with the economic risk associated with these activities.

Second, restrictions on risk taking by depository institutions in their main line of business (imposed for the valid purpose of protecting the insurer of deposits in these institutions) create an incentive for excessive risk taking in other business activities of these institutions (see Black, Miller, and Posner 1978: 379–412). Because the government acts as the insurer of depositors and other creditors of depository institutions, the managers and shareholders of these institutions have an incentive to expand the risks of these institutions in their primary functions to beyond socially optimal levels. The government seeks to prevent such an expansion of risk taking by imposing capital adequacy requirements and regulating the lending activities of depository institutions. Frustrated in their desire to expand risk to privately optimal levels in the primary business activities of depository institutions, their managers and stockholders will seek to expand risks in other unregulated business activities. This means that these institutions will be willing to accept lower expected rates of return in these activities than would normally be justified by their economic risks.

Based on the general notion that diversification reduces risk, it is widely believed that extension of depository institutions into businesses where profits are not strongly correlated with profits from the normal activities of depository institutions reduces the risk of failure of such institutions. With regard to this proposition, it is important to remember that risk-reducing diversification occurs when equity capital is spread more evenly or more widely across a range of investments with less than perfect correlation of returns. For an enterprise with a given amount of equity capital, risk-reducing diversification requires that involvement in some activities be curtailed while involvement in others be expanded. Risk-reducing diversification does not occur when an enterprise expands into new businesses on a given base of equity capital, without an offsetting reduction of involvement in previously conducted business activities. This point is especially relevant for banks and bank holding companies because much of the expansion of these institutions into other lines of business has not been accompanied by a corresponding increase in their equity capital or a corresponding reduction in their involvement in traditional banking activities. Moreover, the effects on the overall risk of a depository institution from expansion into new businesses depends on how these businesses are conducted. For example, it appears that businesses run as components or subsidiaries of depository institutions are frequently more highly leveraged than similar businesses run as independent entities or as components or subsidiaries of other types of businesses. Awareness of such opportunities to increase risk through increased leverage or other business practices is especially important if, as has just been argued, owners and managers of depository institutions have an incentive to increase the risk of their enterprises (with the expectation of higher returns) beyond the level that is desirable from the perspective of the governmental insurer of their deposit liabilities.

The willingness and ability of depository institutions to accept artificially low risk-adjusted rates of return in business activities outside the scope of their main functions implies that these institutions have an unfair competitive advantage over other participants in these business activities, and that exploitation of this artificial and unfair advantage can reduce economic efficiency. To guard against such an outcome, it is appropriate to limit the nature and extent of participation of depository institutions in business activities outside of the scope of their main functions. The desirability of such limitations has long been recognized in U.S. law and regulatory policy. Banks have long been prohibited from engaging in most forms of commerce. Bank holding companies are legally restricted to performing only those nonbank functions that are "closely related to banking" and for which it can be demonstrated that the likely public benefit outweighs the possible public harm. Banks are legally prohibited from engaging in securities underwriting and from selling and underwriting a wide range of insurance.

Recently, however, the barriers that used to separate banks and other depository institutions from suppliers of other types of financial services, especially securities dealers, have been eroded, and there is the prospect of further erosion through legislative and regulatory changes, changes in the interpretation of laws and regulations, and innovation of business practices. The point to be made here is that all this change should not be presumed to be for the better simply because it is consistent with a general policy of "deregulation" and with a vague notion of the likely benefits of increased competition. There are good reasons why the activities of depository institutions should be regulated and why they should not be allowed to compete on an unrestricted basis among themselves or with other types of businesses.

One proposal for allowing broader participation of depository institutions in a wider range of business activities is that activities outside the main functions of depository institutions be carried out by separately capitalized, separately managed, and separately regulated subsidiaries of holding companies of depository institutions. This proposal has substantial merit and has enjoyed broad support. In many ways it extends the principle presently embodied in the approach to regulation of bank holding companies with respect to their nonbank activities. An important potential advantage of this proposal is that it allows for exploitation of some of the economic efficiencies of joint production or joint consumption of products and services supplied by a single business organization. It also allows for more symmetric treatment of depository institutions seeking to expand into other businesses and of other businesses seeking to offer the services of depository institutions.

The principal challenge facing this proposal is the need to structure and regulate holding companies for depository institutions so as to maximize the efficiencies of joint production and consumption while protecting against excessive risk taking and unfair competition. The bailout of all creditors of Continental Illinois illustrates the difficulty of maintaining financial separation between different subsidiaries of a holding company of a depository institution in an environment of potential financial crisis. The converse problem is that too rigid separation among subsidiaries may impair efficiencies of joint production and consumption. Ultimately, the viability and desirability of the holding company approach to extending the range of activities of depository institutions depends on successful resolution of the fundamental tension between too rigid and too lax separation of the activities of different subsidiaries.

CONCLUSION

This chapter has emphasized the desirability of maintaining some restrictions on the nature and extent of competition by suppliers of financial services in order to serve the objectives of efficiency and fairness in the supply of such services. In this conclusion, it is appropriate to emphasize the benefits from encouraging a high level of competition among suppliers of any particular financial service and the threat to these benefits posed by excessive or inappropriate regulation.

When alternative suppliers of a good or service operate on the same footing, without benefit of government-supported privileges and advantages relative to each other, competition promotes survival and prosperity of the most efficient suppliers. Thus, competition among equally advantaged firms promotes economic efficiency. It is also consistent with objective of "fairness" of competition, defined as the opportunity to participate on the same basis as other firms in a particular line of business. The only important difficulty that may arise when a particular financial service is supplied by equally advantaged and equally regulated competitors is that the overall supply of this service may diverge from the social optimum. For example, explicit and implicit insurance granted to holders of deposits may induce a suboptimal excess supply of intermediation services, at the expense of greater use of direct credit market instruments.

The principal threat to the beneficial outcome of a high level of competition in the provision of financial services comes from excessive or inappropriate regulation. Absent legal restrictions on entry and on competition in price and service quality, suppliers of financial services have little latitude for the exercise of market power. When legal or regulatory restrictions are imposed on the nature and extent of competition, however, even the presence of a large number of suppliers of a financial service does not guarantee an efficient competitive outcome. This was surely the case when regulated maximum interest rates payable on deposits at banks and savings and loan associations were kept well below market equilibrium rates at various times in the 1960s and 1970s. These regulatory restrictions prevented depositors from earning the higher interest rates that would have resulted from greater competition among depository institutions, and they encouraged depository institutions to compete for regulated deposits by providing services (such as a large number of branches) that probably had a greater resource cost than their value to depositors.

This unfortunate situation was finally ended by the removal of most controls on interest rates paid by depository institutions in the early 1980s. The major impetus behind this reform was the development and growth of money market mutual funds that offered many of the deposit services of depository institutions (without federal insurance on the nominal value of deposits) and paid market-related interest rates. This episode testifies to the virtue of having a lightly regulated sector of the financial services industry that competes with depository institutions the provision of some services but without the benefit of the same form of federal deposit insurance. The existence of such a sector, beyond the control of the regulatory authorities for depository institutions, provides a useful check on the adoption and maintenance of excessive or inappropriate regulations and restrictions on the activities of depository institutions, and thereby contributes to a more efficient financial services industry.

NOTES TO CHAPTER 5

1. I am not sufficiently knowledgeable about the insurance industry to know whether there are significant problems of deficient competition in this industry.

2. By law, commercial banks still may not pay interest on demand deposits held by firms (as distinct from individual transactions accounts). In many cases, however, competition forces banks to provide services to firms holding deposits that reflect the interest income forgone by these firms on their demand deposits.

3. Bank holding companies are restricted by the Bank Holding Company Act to activities "closely related to banking." In addition, there is the general prohibition on banks engaging in industry and commerce.

4. Theoretically, if a proposed reform enhances general welfare, it should be possible to compensate those who lose as a consequence of the reform and still end up with a net gain for everyone else. In some circumstances, payment of total or partial compensation may be practical and desirable. In many situations, however, there will be no effective method for identifying and appropriately compensating the losers from a policy reform.

5. There may be a gain in social welfare if consumers of the product or service are initially taxed and the subsidy partially offsets the effects of this initial tax. Complex issues of welfare analysis arise in second-best situations where there are a multiplicity of interacting distortions created by different government policies.

6. At the time of the collapse of Continental Illinois, other banks were experiencing difficulties with respect to domestic and foreign loans. In 1974, at the time of the failure of Franklin National Bank, many other banks were experiencing difficulties. More generally, we should expect individual banks and other depository institutions to fail when conditions in financial markets and in the economy are such that other banks and depository institutions are also experiencing difficulties.

7. The financial assistance that the U.S. government has provided to debtor countries may well serve important objectives of government policy other than preserving the stability of the U.S. financial system and protecting individual financial institutions. Similarly, financial assistance provided to New York City in 1975 and 1976 served a variety of important purposes. In each of these cases, maintenance of the safety and soundness of depository institutions was among the reasons for granting special assistance.

8. The market value of an 8 percent Ginnie Mae that sold at par in 1979 was reduced to 60 cents on the dollar when interest rates peaked in 1981. Assuming a comparable reduction in the market value of long-term mortgages held by savings and loans implies approximately a loss of $150 billion of market value relative to book value. Calculation of the overall position of savings and loan associations on a mark to market basis is more complicated and controversial because it requires assumptions about the market values of longer-term deposits most of which could be cashed with only small penalties.

9. Because the government usually acts successfully to prevent widespread failure of large numbers of depository institutions, the particular institutions that do fail are special cases that frequently suffer from poor management. This tends to create the incorrect impression that poor management is the basic reason for the difficulties suffered by depository institutions.

10. Regulators have been concerned with institutions that pay high interest rates to attract insured deposits. This concern has been expressed in efforts to suppress "brokered deposits" in which securities dealers market a diversified portfolio of high-interest insured deposits to individual investors. The problem, however, is not with securities dealers that market high-interest deposits; it is with the institutions that issue these deposits in the first place.

REFERENCES

Black, Fischer, Merton H. Miller, and Richard A. Posner. 1978. "An Approach to the Regulation of Bank Holding Companies." *Journal of Business* 51: 3 (July): 379–412.

6 CONCENTRATION IN BANKING
Problem or Solution?

Franklin R. Edwards

The fear of power in the hands of bankers is as old as banking itself. Credit and money are viewed as imbued with mystical powers that bestow on bankers a pivotal role in economic systems. The fear that bankers, by amassing resources, could gain control of these mystical powers is responsible for many of the banking laws and regulations that we have today. Prohibitions against branching, restrictions on nonbanking activities, and a constricting antitrust policy have all worked to keep banks smaller than they might otherwise be. As these laws and regulatory barriers crumble under the pressures of competition and advances in technology, it is understandable that there should be renewed concern about prospective increases in bank size and about the concentration of bank resources.

A substantial increase in (average) bank size is worrisome for several reasons. First, large bank size may, by increasing market concentration, diminish competition. Less competition is of concern not only because of its potential impact on the economic performance of banks, but also because it may intersect with other concerns about "bigness," such as the potential political influence of large banks. Second, the "conflicts of interest" problem, a perennial banking issue, may be accentuated by larger bank size. Third, larger average bank size may require significant changes in that part of our regulatory structure designed to assure the soundness of the financial system. Present FDIC deposit insurance, bank capital requirements, and so forth may be inappropriate for a world of predominantly large banks. Fourth, there is some concern that large banks will allocate credit in ways that are injurious to small businesses and small communities. Finally, the political ramifications of going from a system of many small banks to one of a few large banks are unclear. Will bankers have more political influence than they already have?

The focus of this chapter is on concentration, and not bigness per se. It examines the concern that the financial evolution now underway will lead to greater banking concentration, or to higher levels of market concentration among financial service firms. However, "bigness" and concentration are often interrelated, so along the way I have a few things to say about "bigness" as well.

IS CONCENTRATION A NECESSARY RESULT OF THE CURRENT FINANCIAL EVOLUTION?

A curious element of the current financial upheaval is the widespread acceptance of the notion that large bank size and increased concentration will be a natural by-product. It is as if everyone already knows that the present crazy-quilt financial structure of thousands of small banks and other nonbank financial institutions is a relic of the past—somehow disconnected to present realities. There seems to be little doubt that, left to find its natural state, the U.S. financial structure will quickly evolve toward a more concentrated financial system, populated by large, multiproduct, financial service firms.

Like many intuitions, this inference is founded on some solid inductions. To begin with, there are clearly economies of scale in banking—just how much is a never-ending debate. There is no doubt that the vast majority of today's financial institutions are operating at a scale less than the minimum efficient size. They exist only because they are protected from having to compete with larger, more efficient banks. Once the protective regulations are removed, as is already happening, these small institutions will no longer be able to compete. They either will have to leave the business or be absorbed by larger institutions. Either way, the larger institutions will take over their market shares, becoming even larger.

Whether there is a limit to bigness depends partially on the extent of economies of scale and scope, about which we are uncertain.

There have been many academic studies of cost economies in banking, but there are few clear answers. Several studies show that diseconomies of scale occur at a surprisingly small size (under $25 to $50 million); others show that the average cost curve, after a rather small scale is reached, becomes permanently flat. Few adequately account for the possibilities of economies of *scope* (through multiproduct firms) and for the cost savings to a customer of his being able to buy many financial services from a single entity.[1] Capital market scale economies also are poorly understood. My own view is that these studies are not so persuasive that we should base public policy on them. Further, current and prospective changes in technology, regulation, and the market itself make past studies obsolete.

Advances in communications and information technologies have undoubtedly increased the possibility of greater economies of scope and in all likelihood have already significantly increased the minimum efficient size of "bank." This technological evolution is also in its early stages, and it is not yet clear just where it will lead.

In a freely competitive environment these questions will be resolved by the market test. Indeed, in a free-market setting the most efficient institutional structure will emerge no matter whether there is competition or monopoly (at least in a static sense). Monopolists, too, wish to make as much profit as possible and so will operate in the most efficient way possible. (There are, however, good arguments to be made that, in the long run, industry efficiency is best assured by the existence of vigorous competition. Competition is also necessary if we are to have allocational—as opposed to operational—efficiency.) Thus, given a freer competitive environment, I believe we will see a financial structure emerge with larger banks and, at least in some areas, greater concentration.

More particularly, I would expect the percentage of U.S. assets or deposits accounted for by the largest three, five, ten, or fifty banks in the country to rise. Concentration at the state level may also rise: The share of state deposits or assets held by the largest banks operating in the state will probably increase. These dimensions (or measures) of concentration, however, may not be relevant to the central question of competition—the central issue. To assess that issue we must explore the question of what the market structure will be in "relevant" markets.

DOES GREATER SYSTEM CONCENTRATION
IMPLY LESS COMPETITION?

The view that high market concentration in banking is associated with less competition rests on a large number of empirical studies (Heggestad 1979). These studies have shown that concentration does adversely affect several aspects of bank performance: loan rates, deposit rates, managerial efficiency, and so forth. As one who pioneered these studies (Edwards 1964), however, I know only too well that they were conducted in a financial environment quite unlike what the future financial environment will be (and unlike the present one as well), New developments in regulation and technology make past studies of the effect of market concentration obsolete and misleading as policymaking directives.

The key issue, as all of these studies point out, is the level of concentration in a *relevant* (or meaningful) banking market. With this perspective in mind, it is very possible that the current financial revolution will not result in higher levels of concentration. First, traditional banking markets have been viewed as being quite small: a town, city, SMSA, or county. In many of these there are presently only a handful of banks—often less than two or three. The reason is simple: The markets are too small to support many competitors. Concentration is already high in most of these banking markets, and competitive vigor already low. By permitting fuller branching, the number of competitors in these markets will be increased not reduced. It is well known that the minimum efficient size of a branch office is considerably smaller than of an independent bank. Thus, with branching, the same size banking market can support a greater number of independent, efficient competitors. In addition, technology has made it possible for a competitor to have a presence in a market without even incurring the costs of the traditional branch office facility (electronic teller machines, for example). In many customary banking markets, therefore, concentration is likely to decrease not increase; and the result should be more, not less, competition.

But there is more to the story. Technological advances are expanding the boundaries of relevant banking markets. Banking by mail, telephone, electronic card, and computer gives customers more competitive alternatives, located both inside and outside the boundaries of traditional banking markets. Information flows between customers and firms are much better than they were in the past, which lowers the cost of dealing with distant institutions. In addition, deregulation makes it possible, and very likely, that there will be new local nonbank competitors with a low minimum efficient size (for example, Sears, Roebuck). All of these factors reinforce the view that higher systemwide concentration does not imply either higher concentration in *relevant* banking markets or less competition.

EVEN IF CONCENTRATION IN RELEVANT MARKETS WERE TO INCREASE, DOES THAT IMPLY POORER COMPETITIVE PERFORMANCE?

The emphasis on concentration as a key determinate of competitive performance and behavior is basically an emphasis on *internal* market conditions. *External* conditions, such as new entry and the threat of such entry, do not play an integral role in this analysis. Under some market environments this analytical dichotomy is perfectly acceptable; under others it is obviously deficient.

Banking regulations made the traditional analytical focus on market concentration in banking both understandable and acceptable. Legal obstacles largely made new entry and the threat of such entry irrelevant. Thus, the statistical nexus between concentration in banking and competitive performance uncovered by researchers was not unexpected.

The new regulatory world changes all that. Many regulatory barriers to new entry have been discarded or soon will be. Technology has also lowered the costs associated with entry and exit. Whether barriers to entry will soon be so low in banking as to make external conditions dominant remains to be seen. However, it should be noted that a large inventory of research findings, from many diverse industries and accumulated over a long period of time, suggests that market concentration may still be important even where entry is considerably easier than it has historically been in banking (Scherer 1980). Nevertheless, it is clear that in the coming regulatory environment concentration will not be as significant a competitive factor as it was once. It would be useful to redo with contemporary data some of the past concentration/performance studies. If entry and potential competition have increased in importance (or become the dominant factor), we would expect to observe little or no statistical relationship between concentration and various measures of competitive performance.

Whether or not entry and potential competition turn out to be the dominant factors, it is crystal clear that the enhanced threat of entry in the present (and future) financial environment reduces the importance of concentration in competitive analysis. Merger analysis and antitrust policy must realistically focus on entry barriers and the threat of entry as major competitive forces.

MERGER ANALYSIS AND ANTITRUST POLICY

Given the structural changes that are occurring, it is hardly surprising that the regulatory standards being applied to proposed bank mergers are rapidly becoming outdated. The traditional policy emphasis on local markets (towns, SMSAs, and counties) needs to be reevaluated. Defining relevant markets is always difficult. It is even more complex in markets undergoing significant technological and regulatory changes.

Similarly, the historical focus on banking as a line of commerce needs rethinking. There are few significant bank products for which there are not reasonable consumer alternatives. In addition, the synergy among financial services that was once unique to banks is no longer unique but can be found in many other nonbank financial institutions as well.

Finally, the acceptable levels of market concentration (or of the Herfindahl Index) that have been proposed by the Department of Justice are unrealistic, at least if applied to the usual narrowly defined geographical markets. They virtually prohibit mergers among even moderately large banks. While the Department of Justice recognizes the significance of entry and of potential competition, there is no clear guideline as to the tradeoff between internal market concentration and external competitive factors. This is a critical aspect of present (and future) financial markets and needs to be explicitly related to acceptable levels of concentration.[2]

CONFLICTS OF INTEREST AND BANK SIZE

Conflicts of interest occur when there are two or more competing interests present and the person (or firm) making the decision, which will affect those interests, has a larger stake in one of the interests than in the other's but is nevertheless expected, indeed required, to serve each interest equitably, regardless of his own stake.

Conflicts, so defined, are pervasive and are not intrinsic either to business firms or to large size. Nevertheless, since banks and bankers are seen as having a higher order of fiduciary responsibility than others, the question of such conflicts has always been important in banking.[3]

The present evolution in banking, I submit, is likely to lessen rather than increase the likelihood of bankers' taking advantage of conflict situations. Such conflicts have always existed in banking and continue to exist even in the smallest of financial institutions. While larger bank size, with its multiproduct dimensions, may possibly increase the scope for potential conflict situations, it is doubtful that large size itself is a significant contributor to this problem (if it is a problem).

To begin with, the predominant form of organizational structure among large financial institutions today is the holding company, in which the parent owns all (or the vast majority) of the equity of the subsidiaries. This should be contrasted with the historical situation in banking, where the bank owner (or manager) often had *personal* equity interests in the business activities of the bank's customers. The incentive to favor one set of customers to the detriment of others is considerably muted if the bank has total ownership of all of its subsidiaries. The bank has a common interest in serving all of its customers equally well (Edwards 1978: 273–94). Thus, large size accomplished through the organizational umbrella of the contemporary bank holding company may pose less of a potential problem than already exists among smaller financial institutions. It is therefore a considerable leap of the imagination to associate an accentuation of the conflict of interest problem with either larger bank size or with greater market concentration.

The changes occurring in financial markets may also mitigate the potential adverse effects of managerial conflicts. First, discriminatory treatment of certain interests (or customers) by managers implicitly assumes that these interests are not in a position to know what banks are doing to them—that they cannot monitor the bank effectively. Large banks, to the extent they discriminate at all, are likely to do so between different kinds of interests (or types of customers) and not between *individual* customers. It would be too bureaucratically cumbersome to discriminate any other way. Thus, if there is any single customer within that group who can monitor the bank effectively, all customers within that group will be adequately protected. This, together with the current regulatory trend toward greater disclosure by banks, may provide a significant check on abusive managerial behavior.

Second, competition is an important check on managerial behavior. If customers have alternatives, they will go elsewhere if they feel they are not being fairly treated. The current evolution, although it will result in larger bank size, will increase competition significantly and therefore may eliminate many possibilities for managerial abuse.

Thus, there is no reason to think that larger firm size (or greater market concentration) in banking will increase the kinds of problems commonly associated with conflicts of interest. Indeed, the reverse may be more likely.

SAFETY AND SOUNDNESS

Another consideration often incorrectly associated with higher concentration but really relevant only to large bank size is the safety and soundness issue. Will a system of predominantly large banks be more or less susceptible to instability than the present one? Or, alternatively, must our present regulatory structure for maintaining financial soundness be altered to accommodate a system of large banks?

This question has several dimensions. First, will large banks, taken independently, be more or less prone to insolvency? I think they will be less vulnerable to insolvency. Large banks are more diversified, have better access to capital markets, and, in general, are probably better managed. Thus, I believe that the probability of the failure of a large bank is less than that of a small bank.

The second dimension, however, is that the consequences of a large bank failure may be more widespread and severe. The interdependence among large banks may be such that one failure may precipitate others. In addition, even without this interdependence the failure of large banks may subject us to greater risk (or expose the Federal Deposit Insurance System to greater risk).

The Law of Large Numbers, a basic law of mathematics (and insurance), states that as the number of exposure units increases, the more certain it is that actual loss experience will equal probable (expected) loss experience. Hence, risk (or uncertainty) diminishes as the number of exposure units increases. More specifically, given certain assumptions, such risk varies inversely with the square root of the number of exposures.

With respect to banking, certain key assumptions must be met for this implication to be relevant. First, the probability of bankruptcy must be the same for all banks. Second, bank insolvencies must be completely independent of one another; and finally, all units must be of identical size. None of these assumptions is likely to be valid for banking: Large banks should have a lower probability of insolvency, interdependence is likely, and large banks are obviously bigger than small banks.

Without specifying an explicit conceptual and empirical framework for making the implied risk tradeoffs, it is not clear whether a system of large banks will pose a greater or lesser threat to financial soundness. It is clear that we need to give some thought to our present solvency regulatory structure. Large bank size, I believe, makes it more urgent that we rethink the current deposit insurance system, with its flat premium structure, and that we review our policy of de jure less-than-full deposit insurance but de facto full deposit insurance. Further, a world of large banks may require a more active central bank lender-of-last-resort policy, and we need to determine the parameters of such a policy.[4]

CONCENTRATION AND POLITICAL INFLUENCE

There are some who fear that firms in concentrated markets may be able to exercise more political power than they might otherwise be able to if they operated in unconcentrated markets. This concern, I believe, is often confused with the allegation that *large* firms have disproportionate political power (relative to smaller competitors). While high concentration may be associated with large firms, it is not a necessary relationship. Large firms can exist in markets without necessitating high concentration, and high concentration can occur without necessitating large firms. Moreover, the theory that might be used to analyze the political influence of large firms is not the same as would be used to explore the impact of concentration on political power. It is important, therefore, that we be clear about which issue concerns us.

The issue of firm size does not seem particularly germane to the changes currently taking place in financial markets. First, there already are very large firms outside of banking and finance (such as IBM and Exxon). Thus, the "bigness" issue is not unique to banking. There would seem to be little difference between a large bank and a large manufacturing firm with respect to political influence. Second, while we can expect existing banks to become even larger, as well as the average size of banks to increase, it is likely that the size distribution of banks will become less skewed. The size differences between banks will very likely be less in the future than at present. This may work to neutralize (or offset) any disproportionate political power that large banks may now have.

What is the reasoning behind the notion that firms in concentrated markets can exercise greater political power? It would seem to rest on two premises. First, firms in concentrated markets may have greater (monopoly) profits. If the managers of these firms have discretionary authority—perhaps because stockholders either have difficulty monitoring management or must bear significant costs to do so—they may elect to use some of the firm's profits to "buy" political influence. Indeed, stockholders might even approve of such activity if it increased profits. Thus, in its most simplistic form, firms in concentrated markets may simply have disproportionately more resources to employ to win political concessions.

The second argument is a "transaction cost" one: In concentrated markets there are relatively fewer firms with relatively more homogeneous interests, so it costs less to organize a given political campaign. The costs of having to bring together many firms with diverse interests is avoided. If both the average and marginal costs of a given political action are less, it stands to reason that the marginal (net) benefit to such action for a given total resource expenditure will increase. Thus, firms may choose to spend more on political action and less on something else. The result may be that they have greater political influence.

This view has found credence in the political economy literature as well. For example, David Vogel in a recent paper (1984: 374) argues that

> companies in concentrated industries do appear to enjoy an important advantage: firms in these industries are more readily able to perceive their political interests and can more easily communicate with each other. To the extent that firms in more concentrated industries are often relatively large, this

advantage is reinforced: larger firms are more able to monitor political developments, analyze and document the impacts of various public policies, and support a Washington office than are smaller firms. While this does not automatically translate into political power, it certainly constitutes a necessary condition for its exercise.

In addition, fragmented or unconcentrated markets may be subject to free-rider problems. An individual company may be unwilling to put substantial time, effort, and money into a political campaign for fear that others will not do the same.

With respect to banking, both of the foregoing theories require some questionable assumptions. To begin with, I have already argued that the current financial evolution may not result in higher concentration in *relevant* markets. Thus, the monopoly profits earned by large banks *will not* be greater in the future than at present. They may even be less, given the increased entry that will occur and the threat of such entry. Second, to the extent that concentration contributes to "efficiency" of political action, that may not necessarily be bad. In a democratic (indeed, any) society, political action and influence are a fact of life. It is not clear that if large banks are a more effective vehicle for political action the result will be a worse "social contract" outcome. There are large firms in other industries, large unions, and many other influential organizations that represent other economic interests. Small banks may be more sacrosanct than sacred.

There also is little empirical evidence to suggest that large banks (or, more generally, large firms) actually wield disproportionate political power (see Epstein 1980). The few studies of which I am aware fail to find a relationship between bank size and concentration and political influence. For example, Rose (1976) tests the hypothesis that domination of a state by a few banks may enable large banks to get laws passed that are favorable to themselves. However, he can find no relationship between state banking concentration and the votes of state senators on a bill to delay the introduction of nationwide NOW accounts.

Thus, there is no reason to allow concern about the political influence of large banks to dictate policy. If issues arise where large size may have an undesirable influence on policy—for example, through PAC contributions—these are probably better handled by a policy that deals directly with the source of the problem and that applies to all large firms and not only to banks.

IN A WORLD WITH FEWER REGULATORY CONSTRAINTS, WHAT SHOULD OUR POLICY BE TOWARD CONCENTRATION?

Assuming that nationwide banking were to become a reality, either through branching or holding company affiliation, should there be explicit legislation or policy aimed at controlling the level of concentration? For example, legislation could prohibit any single financial firm from having more than 20 percent of total deposits or "bank" assets in a state. Alternatively, if no such policy is adopted, and the free market is permitted to be the sole determinant, what level of concentration can we expect to occur? And would we be content to see this happen?

In the absence of constricting regulation, the two major determinants of financial structure would seem to be economic efficiency (broadly defined) and merger policy (primarily the antitrust laws). Economic efficiency encompasses both internal efficiency (economies of scale and scope) and external efficiency—the benefits to the customer of his being able to deal with a single financial firm for all of his or her financial services and in all geographical locations. The latter economy brings to mind credit cards. It is clear that credit card holders and participating merchants do not need more than a few universally accepted credit cards. Indeed, credit cards may be a kind of "natural monopoly," where one universally accepted card is the most efficient card for all customers (not considering the benefits of competition, of course). Is banking similar to credit cards? Some banking services are (such as payment services); others, such as "business loans," are not. It is reasonably clear, however, that external economies dictate a financial system with far fewer banks, and probably more concentration at the national and state level, than we have now.

Internal efficiencies also obviously exist, despite the absence of supporting econometric studies (Lawrence and Shay 1985; Gilligan, Smerlock, and Marshall 1984; Benston et al. 1983). How large they are, nobody knows. My guess is that they are becoming substantial and that they will drive our financial system to many fewer banks than at present.

But how many fewer? There is, unfortunately, no way to answer this question other than allowing the market to resolve it. Given a competitive environment, a market-determined size distribution of banks should be the most efficient financial structure.

Whether a competitive environment can be maintained brings us to the question of merger policies and the antitrust laws, the second determinant of the future financial structure. The crucial element of future merger policy will be how "entry" (or barriers to entry) is treated. The present merger guidelines issued by the antitrust division of the U.S. Department of Justice (1984) state that if entry is easy and rapid, a merger will not be challenged, regardless of market concentration. However, the guidelines do not devote a great deal of attention to discussing the measurement of entry barriers and do not discuss the weight to be placed on "moderate" as opposed to "substantial" entry barriers. In general, the merger guidelines identify firms as potential entrants if they do not presently sell in the market but could do so easily within two years.

With respect to banking, and assuming the elimination of regulatory entry barriers, I believe the critical economic questions that will have to be evaluated to determine the level of entry barriers are:

1. How significant are economies of scale? In particular, what is the minimum efficient scale (MES) for a branch or affiliate office? Are there cost savings from multioffice operation? What is the minimum viable scale (MVS) for an entering firm? What are the MES and MVS as a percentage of total market sales?

2. Do established firms have any advantages on the demand side that entrants will find difficult to overcome? Must the entrant spend considerable time and money to establish a reputation before attracting a significant market share? Is it difficult to establish a geographical service network?

Without going into detail, our present level of knowledge about banks suggests that many banks and other financial service firms would be able to enter most banking markets quite easily. These firms are not burdened either by cost or demand-side disadvantages. Thus, according to the criteria of the present merger guidelines, the level of concentration in a banking market should not receive much weight in determining the legality of a proposed merger. Accordingly, under the present law, restrictions on mergers among banks and other financial firms should not be a major obstacle to the widespread increase in concentration in the financial services industry.

Where will the unconstrained forces of market economies and competition take us? To fewer banks, clearly—but how few? My guess is that we will eventually have only twenty or thirty nation-wide banks or financial services firms but will continue to have several hundred smaller, more specialized banks. Many thousands of existing banks and financial services firms will cease to exist as independent entities. Concentration will be higher at national, regional, and state levels but will be lower in smaller geographical market areas. Finally, competition will be greater because concentration in most "relevant" markets will probably be lower and, most important, entry barriers will be lower. Entry and the threat of entry will provide the dominant competitive check.

In summary, in a world without significant regulatory restraints on competition, there would seem to be little reason to allow concern about market concentration to dictate social policy towards financial industries. We are, of course, still a long way from attaining a world without regulation-imposed competitive constraints. Thus, until we know what the future regulatory environment is going to be, it is difficult to adopt a clear policy toward concentration.

CONCENTRATION AS A SOLUTION

If in the absence of regulatory protections many thousands of banks and financial firms become economically unviable, the question arises as to how to eliminate that many institutions without disrupting our financial system. Widespread bankruptcy is not a reassuring scenario. Indeed, it is a frightening one, and one that we cannot tolerate. The orderly liquidation of that many financial institutions through insolvency would take years, during which time our financial system would be vulnerable to recurring financial panics of the kind that recently beset the states of Ohio and Maryland. It is unreasonable to subject our system and economy to that kind of risk.

The solution is to permit widespread mergers among existing financial institutions. That is the clear intention of Chairman Volcker's recent interstate banking proposal. Under his proposal full interstate banking would be phased in over a predetermined period of time. For the limited period of three years regional interstate banking compacts would be permitted, as would be prohibiting entry by banks outside the region ("Volcker Banking Compromise" 1985: 31, col. 3). Regardless of the merits of this proposal, it does accept the idea that consolidation is a necessary solution to the current regulatory and technological evolution.

Thus, more mergers and increased concentration at least at some market levels is a necessity if we are to make the journey safely from our present patchwork financial system to one that is more in tune with current and future economic realities. In this sense increased market concentration can be seen more as a solution than as a problem.

APPENDIX 6A. MERGER TRENDS IN THE FINANCIAL SERVICES INDUSTRY

Mergers and acquisitions involving banks, finance companies, and insurance companies doubled between 1978 and 1982. Between 1982 and 1984 they increased fivefold. In 1982 mergers in the financial services industry already accounted for one-quarter of all mergers in the United States and exceeded those of any other sector by a factor of three. In 1984 their relative importance was even greater (see Figure 6A-1).

The same picture emerges if we examine the total dollar volume of merger transactions. The dollar volume of financial services mergers and acquisitions increased more than fourfold from 1978 to 1983, but from 1983 to 1984 it increased more than sevenfold (see Figure 6A-2).

In addition, the average size of mergers and acquisitions increased from about $22 million in 1982 to about $48 million in 1984. While the largest banks are partially responsible for this trend, the activity of regional banks may be an even more important factor.

Figure 6A-1. Number of Merger/Acquisition Transactions, Banking, Finance, and Insurance Firms, 1978-84.

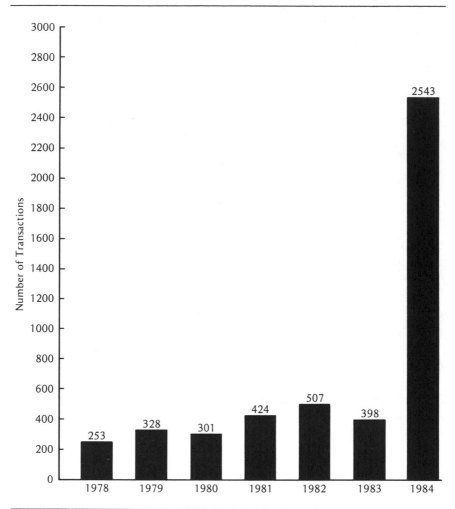

Source: W.T. Grimm & Company, Chicago.

Figure 6A-2.   Total Dollar Volume of Merger/Acquisition Transactions, Banking, Finance, and Insurance Firms, 1978-84.

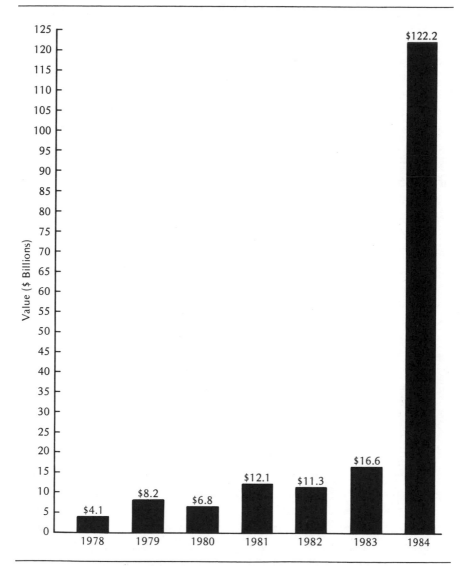

Source: W.T. Grimm & Company, Chicago.

APPENDIX 6B. CHANGES IN BANKING CONCENTRATION, 1966–81[5]

Trends in Local Market Concentration

The general tendency has been for concentration (defined by CR_3: the three-bank deposit ratio) to decline in most local banking markets. Tables 6B–1, 6B–2, and 6B–3 describe the changes in concentration over the period 1966–76 in 152 SMSAs and in 129 counties. The concentration data are presented separately for SMSAs and counties according to whether they are in states classified as expansion or nonexpansion states. Expansion states are those considered more liberal with respect to either bank holding company affiliates or branch offices.

Tables 6B–1 and 6B–2 show that in a large majority of local banking markets there have been decreases in concentration. Further, this tendency, surprisingly, is more pronounced in markets in nonexpansion states.

Table 6B–3 shows the magnitude of changes in local market concentration that have occurred between 1966 and 1976. While the changes in expansion and nonexpansion states are quite similar, nonexpansion states show a somewhat larger decrease.

Finally, Table 6B–4 shows the average percentage changes in local market concentration separately for all states for the period 1966–81. The mean decrease in CR_3 is –10.28 percent. Thus, concentration is clearly declining in local banking markets.

Trends in Statewide Concentration

The data summarized in Table 6B–5 indicate that there has been a general tendency for statewide concentration to increase in expansion states. For the period 1960–77, more than two-thirds (or fourteen of the expansion states experienced an increase in statewide concentration as measured by the CR_3 ratio. Only twelve of twenty-eight nonexpansion states had increases in concentration during the same period.

Table 6B-1. Number of SMSAs with Changes in Concentration in
Expansion and Nonexpansion States.

Period	Number of SMSAs in Expansion States with Changes in CR_3			Number of SMSAs in Nonexpansion States with Changes in CR_3		
	Increases	Decreases	None	Increases	Decreases	None
1966-70	15	86	1	7	41	2
1970-76	22	79	1	5	45	0
1966-76	16	86	0	2	48	0

Table 6B-2. Number of Counties with Changes in Concentration in
Expansion and Nonexpansion States.

Period	Number of non-SMSA Counties in Expansion States with Changes in CR_3			Number of non-SMSA Counties in Nonexpansion States with Changes in CR_3		
	Increases	Decreases	None	Increases	Decreases	None
1966-70	15	32	6	18	45	13
1970-76	13	32	8	11	57	8
1966-76	15	34	4	11	58	7

Table 6B-3. Average Change in Concentration in SMSAs and Counties
in Expansion and Nonexpansion States.

Period	Average Change in SMSA CR_3		Average Change in Non-SMSA County CR_3	
	Expansion States	Nonexpansion States	Expansion States	Nonexpansion States
1966-70	-2.37	-2.71	-1.12	-1.05
1970-76	-4.02	-4.88	-1.89	-2.63
1966-76	-6.39	-7.60	-3.01	-3.69

Table 6B-4. Average and Average Percentage Change in Concentration Ratio in SMSAs and Selected Counties by State and Year, 1966-81 (*commercial banks only*).

State	Average Concentration, by Year			Average Percentage Change[a]		
	1966	1973	1981	1966-73	1973-81	1966-81
Alabama	83.5	77.3	72.5	-7.5	-6.2	-13.2
Alaska	96.6	89.8	71.7	-7.1	-20.1	-25.8
Arizona	91.9	89.9	86.4	-2.2	-3.9	-6.0
Arkansas	81.9	79.7	79.0	-2.6	-0.9	-3.5
California	79.2	73.4	68.3	-7.3	-6.9	-13.7
Colorado	76.9	71.7	67.1	-6.8	-6.4	-12.8
Connecticut	85.3	79.5	73.7	-6.8	-7.3	-13.6
Washington, D.C.	41.6	38.3	38.5	-8.0	0.4	-7.6
Florida	65.9	62.0	54.6	-5.9	-11.9	-17.1
Georgia	91.8	86.0	83.6	-6.4	-2.7	-9.0
Hawaii	78.0	74.5	77.2	-4.5	3.6	-1.1
Idaho	93.7	88.6	82.1	-5.4	-7.3	-12.3
Illinois	63.7	59.4	55.8	-6.7	-6.2	-12.4
Indiana	80.3	78.0	76.2	-2.8	-2.4	-5.1
Iowa	77.5	74.7	73.5	-3.7	-1.6	-5.2
Kansas	76.8	68.8	66.9	-10.4	-2.7	-12.9
Kentucky	84.4	82.9	81.2	-1.8	-2.1	-3.8
Louisiana	85.8	81.9	76.8	-4.5	-6.3	-10.5
Maine	95.9	92.9	95.5	-3.2	2.9	-0.4
Maryland	55.1	51.0	51.0	-7.4	0.1	-7.3
Massachusetts	82.6	80.5	77.2	-2.5	-4.2	-6.6
Michigan	82.2	78.6	76.3	-4.4	-2.8	-7.1
Minnesota	69.8	67.2	63.7	-3.7	-5.3	-8.8
Mississippi	96.0	93.2	87.9	-2.9	-5.7	-8.4
Missouri	67.9	64.3	63.8	-5.4	-0.8	-6.1
Montana	96.7	90.7	87.8	-6.2	-3.1	-9.1
Nebraska	89.8	84.0	76.2	-6.4	-9.3	-15.1
Nevada	93.7	90.0	84.9	-4.0	-5.7	-9.4
New Hampshire	92.3	89.9	75.9	-2.6	-15.5	-17.7
New Jersey	66.9	61.2	59.1	-8.5	-3.4	-11.6
New Mexico	99.0	96.6	87.8	-2.4	-9.0	-11.3
New York	80.8	77.8	71.1	-3.7	-8.6	-12.0

Table 6B-4. continued

State	Average Concentration, by Year			Average Percentage Change[a]		
	1966	1973	1981	1966–73	1973–81	1966–81
North Carolina	84.9	76.6	72.9	-9.7	-4.8	-14.0
North Dakota	79.8	77.2	73.3	-3.3	-5.1	-8.2
Ohio	74.4	72.1	72.5	-3.1	0.5	-2.6
Oklahoma	77.7	73.3	66.7	-5.7	-9.0	-14.2
Oregon	91.1	87.5	77.0	-4.0	-11.9	-15.4
Pennsylvania	64.2	65.3	64.8	1.7	-0.8	0.9
Rhode Island	97.0	93.2	79.5	-3.9	-14.7	-18.1
South Carolina	75.5	59.4	57.5	-21.3	-3.1	-23.8
South Dakota	85.7	84.4	74.5	-1.6	-11.6	-13.0
Tennessee	76.7	71.6	64.5	-6.7	-9.9	-15.9
Texas	78.6	75.8	70.2	-3.5	-7.4	-10.6
Utah	58.8	62.2	54.6	5.9	-12.2	-7.0
Virginia	66.4	62.5	60.8	-5.9	-2.8	-8.5
Washington	83.8	81.2	77.6	-3.0	-4.5	-7.4
West Virginia	76.8	74.5	67.4	-2.9	-9.6	-12.2
Wisconsin	64.6	59.6	58.1	-7.8	-2.6	-10.2
Wyoming	96.5	95.9	90.0	-0.6	-6.2	-6.8

a. These percentage changes cannot be calculated from the data on the left side of the table. The changes shown are based on the average of the changes in individual markets.

Table 6B-5. Number of Expansion and Nonexpansion States with Changes in Concentration.

Period	Number of Expansion States with Changes in CR_3		Number of Nonexpansion States with Changes in CR_3	
	Increases	Decreases	Increases	Decreases
1960–70	11	9	10	18
1970–77	12	8	11	17
1960–77	14	6	12	16

Table 6B-6. Percentage of Commercial Bank Deposits Accounted for by the 100 Largest Banks, 1925-78.

Year	Percentage of Deposits Held by 100 Largest[a]	Year	Percentage of Deposits Held by 100 Largest[a]
1925	33.7	1953	45.1
1928	39.3	1958	46.3 (49.0)
1933	52.4	1963	47.4 (50.1)
1938	53.3	1968	48.2 (50.8)
1943	51.4	1973	49.6 (54.0)
1948	44.5	1978	51.4 (55.4)

a. Concentration ratios for 1925-78 are based on foreign and domestic deposits for the 100 largest banks, *not* banking organizations. For the period 1958-78 it was possible to construct deposit data for banking organizations, and the concentration ratios based on these data are shown in parentheses beginning with 1958.

Table 6B-7. Percentage of the Largest 100 Banks' Deposits Accounted for by Different Groups, 1925-78. Percentage of Deposits of 100 Largest Accounted for by:

	Top 5	Top 6-10	Top 11-25	Top 26-50	Top 51-75	Top 76-100
1925	19	12	24	22	13	10
1928	23	14	23	20	12	8
1933	28	16	22	17	10	7
1938	30	15	23	15	10	7
1943	30	14	22	17	10	7
1948	30	13	22	16	11	8
1953	29	14	20	18	11	8
1958	31	13	20	17	11	8
1963	33	14	20	15	10	9
1968	33	14	20	16	10	7
1973	35	16	21	14	8	6
1978	36	15	18	13	7	6

Trends in Nationwide Concentration

Analysis of trends in nationwide concentration indicate the following: (1) Concentration of deposits in the largest 100 banks increased from 33.7 percent in 1925 to 51.4 percent in 1978 (see Table 6B-6);

(2) deposits have become increasingly concentrated *within* the top 100 banks (see Table 6B-7); and (3) the pattern of changes and the absolute levels of concentration for the 100 largest banks is very similar to what has occurred for the 100 largest industrial firms over the same time period.

NOTES TO CHAPTER 6

1. Three recent studies find some evidence of economies of scope: Lawrence and Shay (1985); Gilligan, Smirlock, and Marshall (1984); and Benston, Berger, Hanweck, and Humphrey (1983).
2. For a review of the state of the law in the bank merger area, see *United States v. Virginia National Bankshares*, 1982-2 CCH Trade Cas. 64,871 (June 21, 1982).
3. It is, for example, a critical aspect of the debate over the Glass-Steagall Act. See Edwards (1978: 273-94).
4. For a more complete discussion of the safety issue, see Kaufman (1985).
5. The information in Appendix 6B is taken from two papers by Stephen A. Rhoades (1978, 1982).

REFERENCES

Benston, G., A. Berger, G. Hanweck, and D. Humphrey. 1983. "Economies of Scale and Scope in Banking." Research Paper in Banking and Financial Economies. Washington, D.C.: Board of Governors of the Federal Reserve System.

Edwards, F. 1964. "Concentration in Banking and Its Effects on Business Loan Rates." *Review of Economics and Statistics* 46: 3 (August): 294-300.

_____. 1978. "Banks and Securities Activities: Legal and Economic Perspectives on the Glass-Steagall Act." In *The Deregulation of the Banking and Securities Industries*, edited by L. Goldberg and L. White, pp. 273-94. Lexington, Mass.: Lexington Books.

Epstein, E. 1980. "Firm Size and Structure, Market Power and Business Political Influence: A Review of the Literature." In *The Economics of Firm Size Market Structure and Social Performance*, edited by John H. Siegfried, pp. 240-81. Washington, D.C.: Federal Trade Commission.

Gilligan, T., M. Smirlock, and W. Marshall. 1984. "Scale and Scope Economies in the Multiproduct Banking Firm." *Journal of Monetary Economics* 13 (May): 393-406.

Heggestad, A. 1979. "Market Structure, Competition, and Performance in Financial Industries: A Survey of Banking Studies." In *Issues in Financial Regulation*, edited by F. Edwards, ch. 9. New York: McGraw-Hill.

Kaufman, G. 1985. "Implications of Large Bank Problems and Insolvencies for the Banking System and Economic Policy." Staff Memorandum, SM-95-3. Chicago: Federal Reserve Bank of Chicago.

Lawrence, C., and R. Shay. 1985. "Technology and Financial Intermediation in a Multiproduct Banking Firm: An Econometric Study of U.S. Banks 1979–1982." Paper presented at the Columbia University Business School's Conference on Technological Innovation, Regulation and the Monetary Economy, New York, March 14.

Rhoades, Stephen A. 1979. "Georgraphic Expansion of Banks and Changes in Banking Structure." Staff Memorandum. Washington, D.C.: Board of Governors of the Federal Reserve System.

_____ . 1982. "Size and Rank Stability of the 100 Largest Commercial Banks, 1925–1978." *Journal of Economics and Business* 34, no. 2: 123–28.

Rose, John T. 1976. "Industry Concentration and Political Leverage: An Empirical Test." Washington, D.C.: Board of Governors of the Federal Reserve System, unpublished.

Scherer, F.M. 1980. *Industrial Market Structure and Economic Performance*, 2d ed. Boston: Houghton Mifflin.

U.S. Department of Justice. 1984. *1984 DOJ Merger Guidelines.* In *Antitrust & Trade Regulation Report* (BNA) special supp. 1169 (June 14): sec. 3.3.

Vogel, David. 1984. "A Case Study of Clean Air Legislation 1967–1981." In *The Impact of the Modern Corporation*, edited by Betty Bock, p. 374. New York: Columbia University Press.

"Volcker Banking Compromise." 1985. *New York Times*, April 27, p. 31, col. 3.

7 RISK AS A CRITERION FOR EXPANDING BANKING ACTIVITIES

Robert A. Eisenbeis

Significant competitive forces are working to change the service mix permitted to banking organizations. Thrift institutions have found ways to offer transaction accounts and other deposit liabilities in an attempt to avoid binding Regulation Q ceilings and resulting disintermediation.[1] Nontraditional suppliers have also begun to diversify into financial service markets, offering service packages not always available from commercial banking organizations.

These new suppliers are taking advantage of regulatory constraints and innovative ways to provide services on terms that commercial banks cannot legally meet (see Eisenbeis 1985). As a consequence banking organizations feel increasing competitive pressures to broaden their services and the geographic areas over which they are delivered.[2] These competitive pressures and the possibilities of capturing scale and scope economies are inducing banking organizations to seek loopholes in laws and regulations (such as the nonbank form and innovative interpretations of Glass-Steagall) to expand into new geographic markets and widen their service offerings (Table 7–1, from Koch 1984, compares powers of different categories of financial and nonfinancial institutions presently competing actively in the provision of financial services.) In addition, banking organizations are exploiting computer and related technological advancements in communications in an attempt to deliver services at lower cost,

Table 7-1. Financial Services, 1960 and 1984.

	Banks		Savings & Loans		Insurance Companies		Retailers		Securities Dealers	
	1960	1984	1960	1984	1960	1984	1960	1984	1960	1984
Checking	*	*		*		*		*		*
Saving	*	*	*	*		*		*		*
Time deposits	*	*	*	*		*		*		*
Installment loans	*	*	*	*		*		*		*
Business loans	*	*		*		*		*		*
Mortgage loans	*	*	*	*		*		*		*
Credit cards		*		*			*	*		*
Insurance					*	*		*		*
Stocks, bonds, brokerage, underwriting		*		*		*		*	*	*
Mutual funds						*		*	*	*
Real estate				*		*		*		*
Interstate facilities		*		*		*		*		*

Source: *Banking Expansion Reporter* 3: 23 (December 3, 1984).

presumably to benefit consumers.[3] The new technologies promise the capabilities to deliver not only traditional banking services but also both financial and nonfinancial services not presently permitted to be offered by banking organizations. To the extent these new packages of services enable banks to realize possible scale and scope economies and to provide services at lower cost and greater convenience to consumers, then the public may benefit from allowing banking organizations to offer services not presently permitted under current law or regulation.

Against this changing situation, individual states and the federal regulatory agencies are being pushed to respond to these market forces and expand the range of services permitted to banking organizations to assure their competitive viability. Some states have already passed or have proposed changes permitting a number of new service offerings, especially in the insurance and real estate areas. Similarly, the federal banking agencies have also become much more sympathetic to banking organizations' requests for new powers. The FDIC, for example, has recently proposed regulations to permit state-chartered insured nonmember banks to engage in a number of activities through their subsidiaries (state law permitting), including real estate development, real estate syndication, real estate equity participation, and real estate underwriting. In addition, under a literal reading of the Glass-Steagall Act, the FDIC has issued an interpretive ruling that the mandated separation between investment and commercial banking does not apply to state-chartered banks not members of the Federal Reserve System, which threatens the traditional separation between banking and investment banking. The Federal Reserve Board has requested comment on whether to permit BHCs to engage in real estate investment activities under section 4(c) 8 of the Bank Holding Company Act as amended. The Comptroller of the Currency is being urged by national banks to expand their powers. The Comptroller has played a major role in the expansion of nonbanking firms into commercial banking with the liberal policies toward the chartering of special purpose banks (the so-called nonbank banks). Lastly, numerous legislative proposals have been made in the Congress to modify and liberalize the criteria contained in the Bank Holding Company Act, expanding the permissible nonbanking activities of bank holding companies, including securities brokerage and underwriting (so long as the activity is conducted within nonbanking subsidiaries).

The failure of Continental Illinois bank, however, has been raised as a justification for restricting the powers of banking organizations. The argument is that banking organizations have become too risky. Bankers cannot control their existing products, and thus further product expansion will only exacerbate the risk exposure of the banking system. As a result, the issue now is how much liberalization of powers is warranted for banking organizations, if at all, consistent with maintaining safety and soundness and protecting the deposit insurance funds.

To address these issues it is first useful to review the rationale for restricting banking organization activities. Subsequent sections present criteria for evaluating new activities for banking organizations and available evidence with respect to these issues for those activities presently under consideration.

RATIONALE FOR RESTRICTING BANKING ACTIVITIES[4]

A number of historical events help explain why banking in the United States has long been heavily regulated. First, the general distrust of banking and the fears of the potential abuse of political and economic power have their roots deep in our economic history and gave rise to the separation between banking and commerce. These concerns played an important role in shaping the financial structure beginning with the First and Second Banks of the United States. This distrust was manifested in the "Free Silver" movement in the late eighteenth century and in 1864 when the National Banking Act was passed, which strictly limited the powers of National banks.[5] Later in the century, the Sherman and Clayton antitrust laws were passed in response to the concentration of industrial and financial power that arose during the early late 1800s. Second, the combination of Senator Glass's populist concerns about big banks, together with the supposed abuses and conflicts of interest during the late 1920s and early 1930s involving affiliations between banks and investment banking affiliates, resulted in their separation by the Glass-Steagall Act.[6] Finally, historical experience demonstrated the importance of a sound banking system and stable currency to a smooth functioning economy. As a result banks were subject to regulations to ensure they were operated in a safe and sound manner. In addition, we had the establishment of the Federal Reserve with its lender-of-last-resort function and the FDIC to protect the money supply and financial wealth of small, unsophisticated depositors.[7] Thus, concerns for safety and soundness, concentration of power, and the potential for abuses have played major roles in explaining why U.S. banking has been regulated.[8]

These same issues arose in 1956, when Congress passed the Bank Holding Company Act. Largely due to concerns about "bigness" and concentration of power, unfair competition through possible preferential treatment of subsidiaries, and safety and soundness considerations, the 1956 act provided for the separation between banking and commerce (Natter 1978).[9] This separation was reaffirmed in the 1970 Amendments to the Bank Holding Company Act of 1956. These Amendments provided that permissible activities should be "so closely related to banking or managing or controlling banks as to be a proper incident thereto." Furthermore, the performance of these activities by an affiliate of a bank holding company had to "reasonably be expected to produce benefits to the public, such as greater convenience, increased competition, or gains in efficiency, that outweigh possible adverse effects, such as undue concentration of resources, decreased or unfair competition, conflicts of interests or unsound banking practices." Thus, the rationale today for restricting banking activities and maintaining the separation between banking and commerce still rests primarily on safety and soundness grounds and concerns for concentration of power and conflicts of interest.

More recently, Corrigan (1982) has claimed that banks are "special" and should remain separate from commerce. This "specialness" arises not because of the traditional concerns but because of (1) the unique role that bank liabilities play as money, (2) the importance of banks to the conduct of monetary policy, and (3) the role that banks serve as a source of liquidity to the economy. Careful review of the issues, however, suggests that these arguments are not valid.

Demand deposits, for example, are but one of several types of liabilities issued by both banks and other suppliers making up the payments medium. NOW accounts and automatic transfer accounts issued by both banks and thrifts serve the same function as demand deposits for many customers. Transactions are also routinely made using credit cards, drafts on money market funds, cash management accounts, credit union share drafts, and other liquid asset accounts.

Similarly, although commercial banks' share of intermediation activity has remained relatively constant since 1950 (see Ford 1982), it is also true that more and more commercial entities have direct access to the open market and nondomestic sources of credit, which are reducing the banks' role as a backup source of liquidity and credit. Again, the expansion of electronics—and more important, the ease of obtaining reliable information on prospective borrowers at lower and lower cost—will reduce even more the traditional information advantage that banks have enjoyed.[10] The consumer, perhaps more than any class of customer, has benefited from the explosion of alternative sources of financial services.

Finally, reserve requirements facilitate the conduct of monetary policy only when they are binding; otherwise, it is institutions' desired holdings of liquid reserves that serve as the constraint on behavior when the Federal Reserve engages in open market purchases and sales of securities. However, the elimination of required reserves on other than transaction accounts and short-term CDs and the general reduction of the level of reserve requirements as the result of the Monetary Control Act of 1980 are making reserve requirements less binding and, hence, less relevant to monetary control. Recent statistics from the Federal Reserve indicate that for banks under $100 million, cash holdings to meet day-to-day currency and transfers exceed required reserves. Should this trend continue, the transmission belt argument will be all but moot.

Careful reflection reveals that what makes banks "special" today is not that they offer a wide range of services and perform varied functions but rather that they have access to government deposit insurance. Government guarantees make insured institutions "special" because of the potential subsidies they carry with them, especially if the guarantees are underpriced. Thus, there is always the danger, either because of moral hazard or through mispricing, that incentives may be created for the insured institutions to take on more risk, thus shifting the burden to the government. This, in turn, suggests that insurance carries with it the legitimate need to ensure that the insuring agency is not placed at undue risk.[11]

When deposit insurance is underpriced, the resulting subsidy also carries with it an inherent competitive advantage (just as burdensome regulations carry inherent disadvantages).[12] Unless all firms have the same set of subsidies and regulatory burdens, some will always be at a competitive advantage to others. This helps explain one of the reasons "competitive equity" has arisen as a potential criterion for new activity expansion.[13] Finally, subsidies arising from underpriced deposit insurance also create incentives for uninsured institutions to capture these subsidies; this explains why many non-banking firms have found the nonbank bank an attractive expansion opportunity. By forming nonbank banks, these firms are able to issue federally insured liabilities and potentially capture some of the subsidies associated with deposit insurance guarantees.

Over the long run, appropriate modifications in deposit insurance pricing to eliminate the subsidy in the existing flat-rate premium system will reduce the importance of risk in evaluating new banking activity expansion. Institutions that choose to expand their activities would be charged premiums in accordance with the risks posed to the insurance fund.

However, in the absence of revisions in the deposit-insurance pricing, the risks inherent in product expansion must be given careful consideration for three reasons: (1) Even if new activities are less risky, their combination with banking may facilitate greater risk taking by insured firms; (2) new activities, especially during the start-up period, may involve operations risk not fully understood by bankers as they enter the business or by the deposit insurance agencies in monitoring and assessing their risk exposure; and finally, (3) allowing nontraditional firms into the banking business increases the chance that the deposit insurance agencies will be exposed to uncontrolled affiliate risks and be required to rescue (especially under the existing set of failure-resolution policies) a wider and wider array of firms whose primary activities are essentially unrelated to the reasons that deposit insurance was put in place. This may result in an increase in government influence in the economy and certainly suggests the need for regulations or other governmental involvement to protect the insurance funds from undue risk. While desirable from the government's perspective such involvement may be costly and undesirable from the point of view of the affected business, especially if the economy is to function efficiently.

CRITERIA FOR NEW ACTIVITIES

As the provisions of the 1970 Amendments to the Bank Holding Company Act illustrate (see Benston, Eisenbeis, Horvitz, Kane, and Kaufman 1985), five considerations have most frequently been balanced in restricting the activities of insured institutions in the United States: (1) economic efficiency, (2) risk, (3) conflicts of interest, (4) concentration of power, and (5) competitive equity. It seems reasonable that these concerns should be examined for their continued importance today.

Economic Efficiency

It has already been suggested that the public has much to gain from activities that improve the efficiency of the financial system. Lower costs to consumers for financial services and lower production costs due to potential scale and scope economies translate into more efficient use of resources and potential reductions in the use of real resources in facilitating the exchange of real goods and services.[14] In addition, greater geographic and product diversification may result in increased safety and soundness and a more stable financial system. Therefore, efficiency considerations are the base against which other possible issues and concerns should be assessed. For this reason, decisions about new powers should give greater weight to activities that offer obvious synergies with existing activities—for example, those that offer potential scale and scope economies or that promise potentially to be risk reducing. However, management is in a better position than regulators to judge for a particular firm the possible advantages of entering an activity. One would presume that firms would not seek to enter markets or activities if they were expected to be unprofitable.

Risk

Because of moral hazard and the possible perverse incentives in mispriced deposit insurance, the insuring agency has a clear interest in limiting its potential risk exposure. The best way to do this is by properly assessing and pricing insurance (or by imposing risk-related capital requirements), by ensuring portfolio diversification, and by appropriate monitoring. Only when risk is not properly priced, or when the evaluation and monitoring of risk is difficult, should it become more important in new activity decisions. Even then, there are practical difficulties to the use of risk as a basis for decisions on the permissibility of new activities.

For example, from the perspective of the insurance agency, it is not the riskiness of the activity per se that is relevant but, rather, what happens to the total risk exposure of an institution when a new activity is added to its existing complement of activities. The risk exposure of the insurance fund may be increased or decreased, depending on the correlation of returns on the new activity with those already being engaged in and on whether the activity permits the organization to achieve a higher level of efficiency with a higher level of both risk and return. A negative correlation of returns of the activity with that of the insured firm can reduce the overall riskiness of the resulting firm, even though the variability of returns of the activity may be greater than the variability of returns of the firm before adding the activity (see Boyd, Hanweck, and Pithyachartyakul 1980; Meinster and Johnson 1979; and Litan 1985). Even in the case of activities that are negatively correlated with the returns of the insured entity, however, care must be exercised in concluding that the activity is risk reducing. If the activity is sufficiently large relative to the insured firm and has a greater variability of returns, then the risk-reducing benefits due to the negative correlation of returns may be swamped by the absolute variability of returns, thereby increasing the overall risk of the resulting entity. Alternatively, an activity whose returns are positive correlated with the returns of the insured entity may also be risk-reducing so long as the risks are not perfectly correlated, if a higher level of efficiency can be achieved. Most important, this analysis suggests that the risk concerns of particular activities are firm-specific and that it is not easy to generalize that certain activities generally should be permissible to banks while others not.

The firm-specific nature of activity risk only strengthens the point made earlier—that the prime considerations in deciding on new activities should be the ability of the FDIC or the other regulators to assess, price, and monitor risk. There is no evidence supporting limiting activities to financial activities, nor is there evidence suggesting that banks should not be permitted into commerce.

Conflicts of Interest

There are legitimate concerns to guard against potential conflicts of interest. Several different policy options have routinely been pursued to limit potential for conflicts of interest, including:

1. Outright prohibition of certain activities, such as the comingling of banking and investment banking;

2. Disclosure, as has been pursued in the securities industry and in reporting of insider transactions in banking organizations;
3. Regulation and limitations on permissible behavior, such as national bank requirements that commissions earned in the sale of credit life insurance accrue to the bank and not to the bank officer acting as an insurance agent;
4. Restrictions on exchange of information and personnel and requirements that certain activities be carried out in separate affiliates or departments, as in the establishment of the "Chinese Wall" in bank trust operations;
5. Promotion of competition; and
6. Imposition of penalties and remedies when abuses take place.

These options are not mutually exclusive, and each has proved effective as a means of limiting abuses and conflicts of interest. Most extreme, of course, have been outright prohibitions. In the case of securities activities, many are now arguing that outright prohibitions are too harsh, especially when a closer analysis also reveals that some of the concerns for abuses and conflicts of interest have proved not to have been supported by the evidence (see Flannery 1985 or J.P. Morgan 1984). Moreover, subsequent legislation and regulation have arguably eliminated or made the potential problems manageable.

As a rough guide, it is suggested that outright prohibition should be employed only if the potential conflicts are so great that the only way to control them would be to have a complete divorce between the credit granting and other activities. In such a case, no benefits or synergies would accrue to the consolidated firm, and shareholders could achieve the same diversification benefits in their own investment portfolio.

Concentration of Power

In general, the potential problems of concentration of power have been dealt with in two ways: (1) The comingling of banking and commerce (and to a lesser extent, between banking and investment banking) has been prohibited, and (2) the antitrust laws have been applied to banking and to the extension of powers to bank holding companies. In certain respects, these criteria have worked reasonably well. In particular, recent reviews of the experience under the Bank Holding Company Act suggest, for example, that there has not been undue concentration of resources in permissible nonbanking activities and banking concentration itself has not increased appreciably (see Savage 1985).

On the other hand, enforcement of the concentration of power criteria where the Federal Reserve has had discretionary authority has not been without problems. There is little guidance to be found in economic theory, in the empirical literature, or in the legislative and judicial deliberations to help the decisionmakers decide what types of combinations, what levels of concentration are dangerous or what increments of concentration are unacceptable (see Glassman and Eisenbeis 1978; Rhoades 1979; Glassman 1981; Rhoades and Rutz 1984; Rose 1978; Esty and Caves 1983). Even the legislative debate suggests several interpretations of what the exact fears were (see U.S. Congress 1969a, 1969b; U.S. Senate 1970).

The recent Treasury proposal to expand the array of activities for banking organizations deals with the concentration of power issues by restricting banking organizations to "financial activities." The Treasury has indicated a number of activities that would qualify as financial activities, including investment advice, leasing, extensions of credit, real estate development and brokerage, data processing, underwriting and dealing in revenue bonds, and sponsoring and managing an investment company. It has also proposed that the Federal Reserve would have the authority to define other activities, from time to time, as being permissible.

Redefining banking activities to include all financial activities has several potential advantages. First, it eliminates some of the contradictions that have evolved from selective regulation and exclusions under existing law. Second, it provides for evolution of powers as technology and financial markets change. Finally, it reduces regulatory avoidance activities by removing incentives for banking organizations to conduct certain activities in banks or subsidiaries that have differential powers.

On the other hand, to narrow the potential scope of banking activities with so little evidence of problems and abuses seems unduly restrictive. A more reasoned way would be to base new activity restrictions on concerns for protecting the risk exposure of the deposit insurance fund. Such a concern would suggest that the permissibility of particular activities should be based on the ability to assess, price, and monitor risk rather than on whether or not the activity is financial.

Competitive Equity

Competitive equity issues have arisen in the debate over expanding the powers of insured financial institutions primarily because of differential regulatory treatment of competitors and hidden subsidies associated with mispriced deposit insurance. Elimination of these two incentives for cross-subsidization should obviate the need for concern about competitive inequities associated with expansion of banking institutions' powers. Instead, policies to aggressively promote competition and to do away with protective regulation designed to restrict competition will let the efficient providers of services prosper and result in increased benefits to the public.

REVIEW OF FREQUENTLY MENTIONED NEW ACTIVITIES

The activities most frequently cited as attractive for banking organizations to enter can be conveniently divided into five categories: (1) securities activities including underwriting, brokerage, and mutual funds; (2) insurance, including underwriting of both general life insurance and property and casualty insurance and brokerage of property and casualty insurance; (3) electronic communications and data processing, including telecommunications and cable television; (4) real estate brokerage and development; and (5) miscellaneous other activities, including non-full payout leasing, management consulting, and travel agency activities (see Arthur Young & Co. 1983). In the cases of investment activities, insurance, and many of the miscellaneous activity categories (and to a lesser extent the electronic communications area, as well) banking organizations and bank holding companies have already engaged in many of these activities, either domestically or abroad. For example, general insurance activities, including underwriting, have long been permitted to national banks. The sole restriction has been that the activity may be carried only out in towns with population less than 5,000. In addition, several states, such as North Carolina, have long permitted state-chartered banks to engage in a full range of insurance activities, including general life insurance and non-credit-related property and casualty insurance. Similarly, the Garn–St Germain Act imposes differential limits on insurance activities of bank holding companies based on whether the company has greater or less than $50 million in resources. Such restrictions seem to be imposed more to protect the interests of the insurance industry than to address traditional concerns about concentration of resources, risk, or other abuses that might be involved. Certainly, too, the fact that U.S. banks may conduct abroad investment banking activities that are domestically prohibited suggests that the risks associated with such activities are of much less concern than other potential problems.[15]

Attractiveness of Particular Activities

Studies of the nature of the benefits associated with product expansion that might accrue and to whom—shareholders or customers— have been limited. Recently, Arthur Young & Company (1983) reviewed thirteen activities with regard to profitability, existing market structure, risk, and barriers to entry in an attempt to assess the attractiveness for entry by small, medium, and large banks. Only aggregated results are presented, and no attempt is made to identify or quantify the extent or nature of the sources of benefits flowing from the various activities. The study then attempted to evaluate the extent of synergies and potential scope economies that were associated with each activity, taking into account differences that may exist for different size banks.[16] Among the highest-ranked activities for all size banks were discount brokerage, real estate equity, insurance brokerage, and real estate brokerage. For large banks, additional attractive activities were securities brokerage, mutual funds and non-full payout leasing. Among the least attractive were telecommunications and insurance underwriting. A number of additional activities were ranked as unattractive for community banks, including data processing, futures brokerage, management consulting, mutual funds, and non-full payout leasing. Finally, the study attempted to combine the attractiveness of the markets with the ability of banks to enter. Among the most attractive activities for all size banks were real estate equity, insurance brokerage, and securities brokerage, while insurance underwriting, telecommunications, management consulting, travel agency, and insurance underwriting were among the least attractive. This study, however, did not consider some of the issues that are most likely to be of public policy concern, including risks to the insurance funds, potential for conflicts of interest, and concentration of resources.

Riskiness of New Activities

Relatively little work has been done on the riskiness of particular nonbanking activities presently being considered. Heggestad (1975) examined the riskiness of activities that were mentioned as potential laundry list candidates prior to passage of the 1970 amendments. By looking at the correlation of profits of banking with that of industry aggregate information, he attempted to identify activities that would reduce the variability of returns to the consolidated company. Wall and Eisenbeis (1984) updated Heggestad's results by applying the same methodology. They also looked at several activities presently under consideration and found that there were potential risk-reducing benefits for life insurance, thrift institutions (other than failing thrifts), and securities brokerage. These and other aggregate studies suggest that there are potential risk-reducing benefits from diversification; however, a number of recent studies suggest that the diversification benefits depend on many firm-specific aspects (Eisenmann 1976; Johnson and Meinster 1974; Meinster and Johnson 1979; Strover 1982). Therefore, activities that may be risk reducing for some firms may be risk increasing for others. This result suggests that it is difficult, and potentially misleading, to make judgments about risk based on industry aggregates and that case-by-case analysis is required in assessing the risk implications of activity expansion. Further support for this contention is found in work by Cole (1985), who attempted to evaluate the potential risk-reducing benefits of expansion by nonbanking firms into the commercial banking business by acquiring nonbank banks. Cole found that for his very small sample expansion into banking promised to reduce the variability of earnings for some firms and not for others. Even when risk was increased, however, the increases were not large. More important, it was not possible to generalize on the basis of industry classifications for either the acquiring or acquired firms—certain types of combinations were potentially better than others.

These risk studies are clearly limited because of the nature of the data, the small sample sizes, the difficulty in breaking out firms' specific considerations, and methodological problems as well. Despite these problems, however, the results do not suggest that risk associated with activity expansion is a major concern, especially for expansion into financially related activities. Moreover, to the extent that it is, then the permissibility of particular activities should be based on the ability of the insurance agencies to monitor, price, and assess risk in firm-specific cases rather than on the basis of generic risk characterizations of activity risk.

SUMMARY AND CONCLUSIONS

The review of the rationale for restricting banking activities suggests that the traditional concerns for economic efficiency, safety, soundness, concentration of power, and conflicts of interest continue to be valid. However, public policies to balance these concerns against economic efficiency objectives have at times resulted in distortions and have created perverse incentives because activity restrictions (and other constraints) have been imposed differentially and because deposit insurance has been mispriced.

Several policies could be implemented to rebalance the system: First, the repricing of deposit insurance, together with policies to promote competition, would create the flexibility to expand the permissible activities of banking organizations. Second, the analysis also suggests that activity risk is firm-specific. Thus, it is difficult to generalize that some activities should be permitted while others generally prohibited to banking organizations. In this respect, while little evidence exists to suggest that activities should be confined to those "closely related to banking," the need to protect the risk exposure of the insurance fund suggests that present provisions in the Bank Holding Company Act that provide that activities can be approved on a firm-by-firm basis should be continued. Finally, concerns about avoiding undue risks to the insurance funds, especially until deposit insurance mispricing has been corrected, imply that the main criteria for activity expansion should be related to the ability of the FDIC to assess, monitor, and price the risk implications on the total risk exposure of the firm.

NOTES TO CHAPTER 7

1. Subsequently, thrifts were granted expanded powers under the Depository Institutions and Regulatory Reform Act of 1980 and the Garn-St Germain Act of 1982, making them very similar to commercial banks.
2. For expression of the contrary view that such expansion represents an important threat to banking organizations, see Ford (1982).
3. For a discussion of some of the longer run implications of technological advancements in financial services, see Phillips (1985).
4. For discussions of the reasons for regulating banks, see Benston (1983a, 1983b), Di Clemente (1983), Corrigan (1982), and Golembe (1982).
5. National banks may only engage in those activities explicitly or implicitly granted to them under the act and under other federal banking laws (including the Federal Deposit Insurance Act, the Federal Reserve Act, and the Monetary Control Act). They are explicitly empowered to (1) accept deposits (the types of deposits are also determined by relevant statutory criteria), (2) lend money, (3) make mortgage loans, (4) act as a fiduciary, (5) discount and negotiate notes, bills of exchange, and other evidences of debt, and (6) in towns of under 5,000 in population, engage in general insurance and real estate brokerage activities. The act also prohibits national banks from carrying out certain functions, including becoming involved in lotteries, owning or lending on their own stock, and Glass-Steagall provisions on securities activities.

    The statute also contains an "incidental powers clause," which permits national banks "all such incidental powers as shall be necessary to carry out the business of banking." Because the statute did not define what was meant by the "business of banking," considerable litigation has arisen over interpretations issued by the Comptroller of the Currency. In particular, the First Circuit Court of Appeals rejected the Comptroller's claim that "incidental" powers were not tied to those expressly provided under the National Banking Act and therefore included any activity that was necessary, convenient, or useful to the general banking business. The courts rejected this argument and held that for an activity to qualify under the "incidental" powers provision, it must be "convenient and useful in connection with the performance of one of the bank's established activities pursuant to its express powers under the National Bank Act." This decision established that the essential criteria for new activities were their relationship to facilitating the carrying out of traditional banking activities and could not serve as a basis for authorization of nontraditional activities, which more than one Comptroller of the Currency had attempted in response to developments in the marketplace.

6. Banking organizations had long been involved in securities activities. National banks, however, were precluded from engaging in securities activities by the Comptroller of the Currency. As a consequence, they formed state-chartered affiliates and subsidiaries, which were permitted to engage in such activities. As recently as 1927 the McFadden Act expressly authorized national banks directly to engage in securities and investment banking functions.

7. Benston (1983a), for example, lists seven different kinds of regulations: (1) entry, (2) expansion, (3) contraction, including mergers, (4) prices paid for funds, (5) rates earned on loans, (6) supervision of management, and (7) customer relations.

8. In addition, deposit-rate and usury ceilings and tax policy have imposed to redirect credit flows to socially desirable purposes (primarily into housing). Federal Reserve reserve requirements and related regulations have been imposed, first to maintain the liquidity and safety of the banking system and more recently to facilitate the conduct of monetary policy. Recently, numerous consumer-oriented regulations have been imposed to ensure that banks treat customers in a fair and impartial manner.

9. It prohibited the ownership of nonbanking companies and required divestiture within two years. Certain nonbanking activities, however, were specifically permitted, and these included owing and managing bank holding company property, providing services to subsidiary banks, operating a safe deposit company, and liquidating property acquired by subsidiary banks. The only other activities permitted to bank holding companies besides the owning and managing of banks were those activities of a "financial or fiduciary, or insurance nature" that were "so closely related to the business of banking or of managing or controlling banks as to be a proper incident thereto" (section 4(c)(6) of the Bank Holding Company Act of 1956).

10. For example, see Villani (1984) for a discussion of new electronic mortgage search and origination systems that make it unnecessary for consumers to even enter a financial institution to consummate a mortgage with lenders nationwide.

11. For discussion of the incentives for excessive risk taking when deposit insurance is mispriced, see Buser, Chen, and Kane (1981), Kane (1985), or Karaken and Wallace (1978).

12. See Eisenbeis (1985). Proposals have been made to tax away or regulate away these subsidies. These are discussed in the next chapter. The analysis suggests that these methods also take away the benefits of engaging in the activities.

13. This point has direct relevance for assessing proposals to expand permissible banking powers within the bank holding company structure, which is not considered in this chapter. Unless holding companies operated as

mutual funds, if insurance is underpriced, competitive inequities will result. The real public policy issues may center on deciding which firms might be subsidized and on what basis, rather than ensuring competitive equity.

14. It is true that recent studies (see for example Humphrey 1985; Benston, Berger, Hanweck, and Humphrey 1983; Gilligan and Smirlock 1984; and Gilligan, Smirlock, and Marshall 1984) fail to find significant evidence of scale or scope economies, but these studies have not considered empirically the synergies possible with new computer technologies and new service offerings such as those provided by nontraditional suppliers of financial services.

15. A cynical comment might be that conflicts of interest are of much less concern when affecting foreign customers of U.S. banks than when involving domestic customers.

16. Among the factors considered were customer base transferability, distribution system complementarity, bank immage, product synergies, skill similarities, personnel policy similarities, risk, and defensive motivation for entry.

REFERENCES

Arthur Young & Company. 1983. "Assessment of Business Expansion Opportunities for Banking." Paper prepared for the American Bankers Association.

Benston, George C. 1983a. "The Regulation of Financial Services." In *Financial Services: The Changing Institutions and Government Policy*, edited by George G. Benston, pp. 28–63. Englewood Cliffs, N.J.: Prentice-Hall.

_____. 1983b. "Federal Regulation of Banking: Analysis and Policy Recommendations." *Journal of Bank Research* 14 (Winter): 216–44.

George G. Benston, Robert A. Eisenbeis, Paul M. Horvitz, Edward J. Kane, and George B. Kaufman. 1985. *Ensuring the Safety and Soundness of the U.S. Banking System.* Cambridge, Mass.: MIT Press.

Benston, George J., Allen Berger, Gerald A. Hanweck, and David B. Humphrey. 1983. "Economies of Scale and Scope in Banking." Washington, D.C.: Board of Governors of the Federal Reserve System.

Boyd, John H., Gerald Hanweck, Pipat Pithyachartyakul. 1980. "Bank Holding Company Diversification." Proceedings of a Conference on Bank Structure and Competition, Federal Reserve Bank of Chicago.

Buser, Stephen A., Andrew H. Chen, and Edward I. Kane. 1981. "Federal Deposit Insurance, Regulatory Policy, and Optimal Bank Capital." *Journal of Finance* 35: 1 (March): 51–60.

Cole, Rebel A. 1985. "Risk Implications of the Nonbank Bank." University of North Carolina, School of Business Administration. Mimeo.

Corrigan, E. Gerald. 1982. "Are Banks Special?" *Annual Report* of the Federal Reserve Bank of Minneapolis.

Di Clemente, John J. 1983. "What Is a Bank?" *Economic Perspectives* of the Federal Reserve Bank of Chicago 7:1 (January/February): 20–31.

Eisenmann, Peter C. 1976. "Diversification and the Congeneric Bank Holding Company." *Journal of Bank Research* 7 (Spring): 68–77.

Eisenbeis, Robert A. 1985. "Inflation and Regulation: Effects on Financial Institutions and Structure." In *Handbook of Banking Strategy*, edited by Richard C. Aspinwall and Robert A. Eisenbeis, pp. 65–123. New York: Wiley.

Esty, Daniel C., and Richard E. Caves. 1983. "Market Structure and Political Influence: New Data on Political Expenditures, Activity and Success." *Economic Inquiry* (January): 24–38.

Flannery, Mark J. 1985. "An Economic Evaluation of Bank Securities Activities before 1933." In *Deregulating Wall Street: Commercial Bank Penetration of the Corporate Securities Market*, edited by Ingo Walter. New York: Wiley.

_____. 1982. "Deposit Insurance Creates Need for Bank Regulation." *Business Review* of the Federal Reserve Bank of Philadelphia (January/February): 17–27.

Ford, William F. 1982. "Bankings New Competition: Myths and Realities." *Economic Review* of the Federal Reserve Bank of Atlanta 67: 1 (January): 4–11.

Gilligan, Thomas W., and Michael L. Smirlock. 1984. "An Empirical Study of Joint Production and Scale Economies in Commercial Banking." *Journal of Banking and Finance* 8: 67–77.

Gilligan, Thomas, Michael Smirlock, and William Marshall. 1984. "Scale and Scope Economies in the Multiproduct Banking Firm." *Journal of Monetary Economics* 13 (May): 393–405.

Glassman, Cynthia. 1981. "The Impact of Banks' Statewide Economic Power on Their Political Power: An Empirical Analysis." *Atlantic Economic Review* (July): 53–56.

Glassman, Cynthia, and Robert A. Eisenbeis. 1978. "Bank Holding Companies and Concentration of Banking and Financial Resources." In *The Bank Holding Company Movement to 1978: A Compendium*, pp. 209–261. Washington, D.C.: Board of Governors of the Federal Reserve System.

Golembe Associates, Inc. 1982. "Product Expansion by Bank Holding Companies." Washington, D.C.: Association of Bank Holding Companies.

Heggestad, Arnold A. 1975. "Riskiness of Investments in Nonbank Activities by Bank Holding Companies." *Journal of Economics and Business* (Spring): 219–23.

Humphrey, David B. 1985. "Costs and Scale Economies in Financial Intermediation." In *Handbook of Banking Strategy*, edited by Richard C. Aspinwall and Robert A. Eisenbeis, pp. 745–83. New York: Wiley.

J.P. Morgan & Co. 1984. "Rethinking Glass-Steagall: The Case for Allowing Bank Holding Company Subsidiaries to Underwrite and Deal in Corporate Securities." New York. December. Monograph.

Johnson, Rodney D., and David R. Meinster. 1974. "Bank Holding Companies Diversification Opportunities in Nonbanking Activities." *Eastern Economic Journal* (October): 316–23.

Kane, Edward J. 1985. *The Gathering Crisis in Federal Deposit Insurance.* Cambridge, Mass.: MIT Press.

Karaken, John H., and Neil Wallace. 1978. "Deposit Insurance and Bank Regulation: A Partial Equilibrium Exposition." *Journal of Business* 51 (July): 413–38.

Koch, Donald L. 1984. "The Emerging Financial Services Industry: Challenge and Innovation." *Economic Review* of the Federal Reserve bank of Atlanta 69: 4 (April): 25–30.

Litan, Robert E. 1985. "Measuring and Controlling the Risks of Financial Product Deregulation." Washington, D.C.: Brookings Institution, May.

Meinster, David R., and Rodney D. Johnson. 1979. "Bank Holding Company Diversification and the Risk of Capital Impairment." *Bell Economic Journal* 10: 2 (Autumn): 683–94.

Natter, Raymon. 1983. "Formation and Powers of National Banking Associations—A Legal Primer." Paper prepared by the American Law Division, Congressional Research Service, Library of Congress, for the House Committee on Banking, Finance, and Urban Affairs, 98th Cong., 1st Sess., May.

Phillips, Almarin. 1985. "Changing Technology and Future Financial Activity." In *Handbook for Banking Strategy*, edited by Richard C. Aspinwall and Robert A. Eisenbeis, pp. 125–48. New York: Wiley.

Rhoades, Stephen A. 1979. "The Economic and Socio-Political Issues Raised by Undue Concentration of Resources." *Issues in Bank Regulation* 2: 4 (Spring): 34–39.

_____. 1978, "The Effect of Bank Holding Companies on Competition." In *The Bank Holding Company Movement to 1978: A Compendium*, pp. 185–207. Washington, D.C.: Board of Governors of the Federal Reserve System.

Rhoades, Stephen A., and Gregory E. Boczar. 1977. "The Performance of Bank Holding Company Affiliated Finance Companies," *Staff Economic Studies* 90. Washington, D.C.: Board of Governors of the Federal Reserve System.

Rhoades, Stephen A., and Roger D. Rutz. 1983. "Economic Power and Political Influence: An Empirical Analysis of Bank Regulatory Decisions." *Atlantic Economic Journal* (July): 79–86.

Rose, John R. 1978. "Aggregate Concentration in Banking and Political Leverage: A Note." *Industrial Organization Review* 6, no. 3, pp. 193–97.

Savage, Donald R. 1985. "Depository Financial Institutions." In *Handbook for Banking Strategy*, edited by Richard C. Aspinwall and Robert A. Eisenbeis, pp. 177–202. New York: Wiley.

Strover, Roger D. 1982. "A Reexamination of Bank Holding Company Acquisitions." *Journal of Bank Research* 13 (Summer): 101–108.

U.S. Congress. 1969a. *Bank Holding Company Amendments* of the Committee on Banking, Housing, and Urban Affairs, 91st Cong., 1st Sess.

_____ . 1969b. Report to Accompany H.R. 6778, House Report 91–387, Committee on Banking, Housing, and Urban Affairs, 91st Cong., 1st Sess.

_____ . 1970. Report to Accompany H.R. 6778, House Report 91–387, Committee on Banking, Housing, and Urban Affairs, 91st Cong., 2d Sess.

U.S. Senate. 1970. *One Bank Holding Company Legislation of 1970*, 91st Cong., 2d Sess.

Villani, Kevin E. 1984. "Electrifying Trends in Housing Finance." *Secondary Markets* 1 (Winter): 25–32.

Wall, Larry D., and Robert A. Eisenbeis. 1984. "Risk Concentration in Deregulating Bank Activities." *Economic Review* of the Federal Reserve Bank of Atlanta 69: 5 (May): 6–19. "Bank Holding Company Nonbanking Activities and Risk," Paper presented at a Conference on Bank Structure and Competition, Federal Reserve Bank of Chicago, May.

FINAL REPORT AND RECOMMENDATIONS
(With Dissents Noted)

A. *Stability of the Financial System*

1. Unstable macropolicy can threaten the stability of the nation's financial system. Only the Federal Reserve can control bank reserves, a precipitous reduction in which would cause financial collapse.

   Hans Angermueller, Vice Chairman, and *Patrick Mulhern*, General Counsel, Citicorp.
   Should be clarified for accuracy by deleting "bank reserves" and inserting in lieu thereof "liquidity."

2. Deregulation of deposit interest rates has made it possible for banks to compete more effectively with each other and with other firms such as money market funds; but the combination of deregulation with entry of many suppliers of financial services into traditional banking markets has made some individual banks more vulnerable to failure.

   Lamar Smith, Senior Economist, U.S. Senate Banking Committee.
   Deregulation of deposit interest rates has made it possible for banks to compete more effectively with each other and other

---

Recommendations were accepted by majority vote of the participants. Dissents were offered in response to an opportunity provided those participants who strongly disagreed with the wording and/or substance of a particular recommendation.

firms such as money market funds; but liability deregulation combined with entry of many *new* suppliers of financial services into traditional banking markets has made some individual banks more vulnerable to failure.

Ted L. Spurlock, Vice President, J.C. Penney Co.
Change to: Deregulation of deposit interest rates has made it possible for banks to compete more effectively with each other and with other firms such as money market funds; but some individual banks, whose management is not able to respond successfully to the changes brought about by deregulation and entry of new suppliers of financial services into traditional banking markets, may be more vulnerable to failure.

3. **A lender of last resort with a well-defined policy is needed to reduce the threat of instability.**

Hans Angermueller, Vice Chairman, and *Patrick Mulhern*, General Counsel, Citicorp.
Delete "with a well defined policy." If such a policy is announced, it can lead to imprudent decisions by banks guaranteed to be supported and loss of depositor confidence in all others.

Joseph L. Bast, Executive Director, The Heartland Institute, Chicago.
Change to: While a lender of last resort is required by the banking system as it is currently organized, other forms of banking that do not require such a lender are possible and should be explored.

Sam Peltzman, Professor of Business Economics, Graduate School of Business, University of Chicago.
Delete A3.

4. **Some form of federal government deposit insurance is needed.**

Joseph L. Bast, Executive Director, The Heartland Institute, Chicago.
Change to: Private deposit insurance should replace current federal deposit insurance and, if this is not possible, the organization of deposit banking should be so changed as to make deposit insurance unnecessary.

Sam Peltzman, Professor of Business Economics, Graduate School of Business, University of Chicago.
Delete A4.

B. *Individual Bank Failure*

1. Any depository institution should be permitted to fail except where the result is likely to be the widespread failure of other depository institutions. Government policies with respect to both financial assistance to troubled depository institutions and insolvency resolution should be defined clearly, announced publicly, and modified only under exceptional circumstances.

    Hans Angermueller, Vice Chairman, and *Patrick Mulhern*, General Counsel, Citicorp.
    Delete second sentence. If such a policy is announced, it can lead to imprudent decisions by banks to be assisted and loss of depositor confidence in all others. Add to end of first sentence "or substantial disruption of the payments system."

    John F. Downey, Chief National Bank Examiner, Office of the Comptroller of the Currency.
    This is too simplistic and requires some definition of failure. I would recommend adding a third sentence: Policies should clearly define failure and the resultant impact on depositors, creditors, stockholders, and management.

    Robert A. Eisenbeis, Wachovia Professor of Banking, School of Business Administration, University of North Carolina.
    B1 is worded to rescue all large banks. I strongly disagree. Reword B1: No bank is too large to fail, but some may be too large to liquidate or merge quickly. In all instances uninsured creditors should incur losses.

    Allan H. Meltzer, John M. Olin Professor of Political Economy and Public Policy, Graduate School of Industrial Administration, Carnegie-Mellon University.
    Change to: Insolvent depository institutions should be permitted to fail. Government policies should prevent the spread of failures by functioning as lender of last resort to solvent institutions that are temporarily illiquid.

Robert S. Royer, Royer, Shacknai and Mehle.
Change to: Any depository institution should be permitted to fail.

C. *Deposit Insurance*

1. **Level premium federally provided deposit insurance enables depository institutions to accept more risks than they would if the insurance were properly priced.**

   George J. Benston, Professor of Accounting Economics and Finance; Director of the Center for Study of Financial Institutions and Securities Markets, Graduate School of Management, University of Rochester.
   Change to: Level premium federally provided deposit insurance gives incentives to depository institutions to accept more risks than they would if the insurance were properly priced.

   Stephen B. Bonner, Executive Vice President, Capital Holding Corporation.
   Change to: Level premium federally provided deposit insurance encourages depository institutions to accept more risks than they would if the insurance were properly priced.

2. **Risk related deposit guarantee premiums and/or capital ratio requirements are desirable and when feasible should be set using market-related measures.**

   William Poole, Professor of Economics, Brown University.
   Experience with the pricing of federal government services in general—and of flood, earthquake, and crop insurance in particular—does not inspire confidence that pricing of deposit insurance would in practice be effective in encouraging depository institutions to limit the riskiness of their asset and liability portfolios. Because the probable gain from attempting to price deposit insurance is minimal and the potential for mischief is great, I cannot support the recommendation for risk-related deposit insurance premiums. However, I strongly support the imposition of higher uniform capital requirement, in part because the market's cost of capital will thereby encourage them to follow prudent portfolio policies.

Robert S. Royer, Royer, Shacknai and Mehle.
Delete "when feasible."

3. **The scope of the deposit insurance system should be constrained.**

B. F. Backlund, President, Independent Bankers Association
   of America; President, Bartonville Bank, Peoria, Illinois.
Community bankers are going to have to insist on the
$100,000 deposit insurance as long as the large money center
banks are not allowed to fail.

Gary C. Gilbert, Chief Economist and Director of Regulatory
   Affairs, Bank Administration Institute.
The adoption of recommendations A3, B1, and C2 would
make it unnecessary to constrain the scope of deposit insurance. Existing or greater deposit insurance coverage would
promote greater deposit stability and, when combined with
these other recommendations and broader disclosure, would
still allow sufficient market discipline to prevail.

Kenneth A. Guenther, Executive Vice President, Independent
   Bankers Association of America.
This policy recommendation is totally unacceptable to the
Independent Bankers Association of America and should be
deleted.

Paul M. Horvitz, Judge James Elkins Professor of Banking
   and Finance, College of Business, University of Houston.
I have no objection to this except that I do not know what it
means. It should be changed so as to have some content or
dropped.

William B. O'Connell, President, United States League of Savings Institutions.
Recommendation C3 is rather vague but appears to be simply
unacceptable. Given recent events and the fragility of the
entire banking sector, we cannot support any effort to reduce
today's federal deposit insurance coverage. We suggest leaving
the coverage level as it is today.

D. *Disclosure and Accounting*

1. **Market value accounting should be encouraged.**

   Hans Angermueller, Vice Chairman, and *Patrick Mulhern*,
   General Counsel, Citicorp.
   Should delete in full as impractical.

   Thomas F. Keaveney, Partner, Head of the National Banking
   Practice, Peat, Marwick, Mitchell, & Company.
   Market value accounting should be encouraged for positions
   taken for trading profits and dealing profits. Market value
   accounting for investment positions should be discouraged as
   such accounting may result in wide swings in profits (reported
   and real). Such swings may unnecessarily undermine public
   confidence in the financial system.

   Barbara McNear, Senior Vice President, First National Bank
   of Chicago.
   Delete.

   Robert S. Royer, Royer, Shacknai and Mehle.
   Change to: Market value accounting should be used.

2. **Disclosure requirements to investors of all publicly traded**
   financial institutions should be administered by the Securities
   and Exchange Commission.

   Robert G. Dederick, Chief Economist, The Northern Trust Co.
   Change to: Since the premature disclosure of financial information can seriously impair policy alternatives open to financial institutions, disclosure requirements should be administered only by those regulators who have the responsibility for
   the safety and soundness of these institutions.

   John F. Downey, Chief National Bank Examiner, Office of
   the Comptroller of the Currency.
   Insert "minimum" before "Disclosure requirement." Other
   regulators should not be prohibited from imposing additional
   disclosure requirements.

   William B. O'Connell, President, United States League of Savings Institutions.
   Recommendation D2 is unnecessary. We suggest leaving to-

day's disclosure requirements and regulatory oversight responsibilities alone.

E. _Competition and Concentration_

1. Currently most sectors of the financial services industry are highly competitive and becoming more so. We see no need for additional antitrust statutes to cope with current and prospective acquisitions.

   B. F. Backlund, President, Independent Bankers Association of America; President, Bartonville Bank, Peoria, Illinois.
   I believe that in view of the expansion and concentrations that are taking place within the industry, the antitrust laws should be carefully reexamined as they affect financial institutions.

   Paul M. Horvitz, Judge James Elkins Professor of Banking and Finance, College of Business, University of Houston.
   Change to: But there is a need for more explicit guidelines as to the nature of market-extension (potential competition) mergers that are to be allowed.

   William B. O'Connell, President, United States League of Savings Institutions.
   Recommendation E1 is unacceptable. We believe that some limits such as a variation of those proposed in the recent House banking legislation are desirable. The largest financial institutions in this nation should not be allowed to merge at will.

   Lamar Smith, Senior Economist, U.S. Senate Banking Committee.
   Change to: Certain segments of the securities underwriting industry excepted, currently most sectors of the financial services industry are highly competitive and becoming more so. We see no need for additional antitrust statutes to cope with current and prospective acquisitions.

2. Antitrust standards and enforcement responsibility for financial institutions should be based on the same principles as those for nonfinancial firms.

Michael Mussa, William H. Abbot Professor of International Business, Graduate School of Business, University of Chicago.
I believe that standards for mergers and acquisitions of depository institutions may need to be somewhat different than for other types of businesses for a variety of important reasons.

William B. O'Connell, President, United States League of Savings Institutions.
Recommendation E2 is unacceptable. We believe that some limits such as a variation of those proposed in the recent House banking legislation are desirable. The largest financial institutions in this nation should not be allowed to merge at will.

F. *Powers of Financial Services Firms*

1. **Entry into the provision of all financial services should be open, provided that all firms are subject to common regulations for that activity.**

   Michael Mussa, William H. Abbott Professor of International Business, Graduate School of Business, University of Chicago.
   I believe that some restriction on the range of activities of various institutions providing financial services is necessary and desirable under current conditions and under conditions likely to prevail in the future.

   William B. O'Connell, President, United States League of Savings Institutions.
   We must strongly protest recommendation F1. We believe that both federally insured commercial banks and thrifts are special in nature. We oppose the mixing of commerce and industry with banking and support a so-called "thrift test" which is our proposed alternative position.

2. **All geographic constraints on firms providing financial services (including deposits) should be removed.**

B. F. Backlund, President, Independent Bankers Association
   of America; President, Bartonville Bank, Peoria, Illinois.
Removing all geographic restraints would accelerate the concentration of the financial industry. I do not think this is in
the public interest.

Eugene R. Croisant, Executive Vice President, Continental
   Illinois National Bank.
While the ultimate removal of geographic constraints on firms
providing financial services is desirable, practical problems
must be recognized. I recommend that the language in F2 be
changed to read as follows: Geographic constraints on firms
providing financial services should be removed in stages to
allow orderly transition and adequate opportunity for participating institutions to compete fairly.

Robert G. Dederick, Chief Economist, The Northern Trust Co.
Change to: All geographical constraints on firms providing
financial services (including deposits) should be removed
after a sufficient period of time has elapsed to allow local and
regional institutions the fullest opportunity to consolidate
their community positions and potentials before having to
confront interstate financial service concentrations seeking
comprehensive access into local markets.

Kenneth A. Guenther, Executive Vice President, Independent
   Bankers Association of America.
This policy recommendation is totally unacceptable to the
Independent Bankers Association of America and should be
deleted.

Michael Mussa, William H. Abbott Professor of International Business, Graduate School of Business, University of
   Chicago.
Geographic restraints on firms providing financial services
(including deposits) should be gradually relaxed and ultimately removed.

Barbara McNear, Senior Vice President, First National Bank
   of Chicago.
Substitution: Geographic constraints on firms providing financial services should be removed in an evolutionary manner to

maintain the stability of the banking system. A regional interstate banking approach will protect the stability of the banking system and will guard against the potential problem of
excessive concentration.

William B. O'Connell, President, United States League of Sav-
    ings Institutions.
We must strongly dissent on recommendation F2. We are
opposed to interstate banking as a trigger for nationwide
banking. Our alternative recommendation is opposition to
any trigger for nationwide interstate banking.

3. **Conflicts of interest should be dealt with through appropriate
    legislation and regulatory action; concerns about conflicts of
    interest should not restrict legislative and regulatory change.**

    Michael Mussa, William H. Abbott Professor of Interna-
        tional Business, Graduate School of Business, University of
        Chicago.
    Conflicts of interest should be dealt with through appropriate
    legislation and regulation; concerns about such conflicts
    should not necessarily impede other legislative or regulatory
    reforms.

    John E. McTavish, General Counsel, John Nuveen and
        Company.
    Change to: Conflicts of interest should be dealt with through
    appropriate legislation and regulatory action. Because of the
    multitude of relationships between a bank and its customers
    and because of the inherent leverage that a creditor possesses
    over his debtor any legislative or regulatory expansion of
    bank powers should address these conflicts.

    Robert S. Royer, Royer, Shacknai and Mehle.
    Change second clause to: concerns about conflicts of interest
    should restrict legislative and regulatory change.

4. **Issuance of federally insured deposit liabilities must be con-
    fined to separate legal entities whose activities are regulated
    by the insurer. Federal insurance should not be extended to
    other liabilities of affiliated entities or activities.**

George J. Benston, Professor of Accounting Economics and Finance, Director of the Center for Study of Financial Institutions and Securities Markets, Graduate School of Management, University of Rochester.
Dissent registered.

John F. Downey, Chief National Bank Examiner, Office of the Comptroller of the Currency.
I am strongly opposed to the phrase in the first sentence: "regulated by the insurer." This would replace OCC as prime regulator for national banks. I would accept the wording "federally regulated."

Robert A. Eisenbeis, Wachovia Professor of Banking, School of Banking, School of Business Administration, University of North Carolina.
I strongly disagree and wish to disassociate myself with F4. Change F4 to: with properly priced deposit insurance designed to price the risks to the insurance fund, there is no justification for restricting either the scope of banking agencies or where within the organization they are conducted.

John E. McTavish, General Counsel, John Nuveen and Company.
Add: The existing bank holding company structure does not adequately segregate deposit insurance from nonbank activities.

David Shute, Senior Vice President and General Counsel, Dean Witter Financial Services Group, Sears, Roebuck and Company.
An addition: It should be recognized that a pure legal separation may not be adequate to insulate a depository institution from liabilities of its nondepository affiliate. Thus, should a depository institution be held liable for the debts of an insolvent affiliate, there is an indirect exposure of the federal insurers. This underscores the necessity for stringent rules designed to perfect the legal separation of depository institutions and their affiliates, as well as the necessity for strict regulation to protect against conflicts of interest and other abuses.

LIST OF PARTICIPANTS

Robert Z. Aliber, Professor of International Economics and Finance Graduate School of Business, University of Chicago

Thomas Anderson, Chairman, Kemper Financial Services, Kemper Group

Hans Angermueller, Vice Chairman, Citicorp

B.F. Backlund, President, Independent Bankers Association of America, and President, Bartonville Bank, Peoria, Illinois

George J. Benston, Professor of Accounting, Economics and Finance; Director of the Center for the Study of Financial Institutions and Security Markets, Graduate School of Management, University of Rochester

Joseph L. Blast, Executive Director, The Heartland Institute, Chicago

Stephen B. Bonner, Executive Vice President, Capital Holding Corporation

Gene Bradley, Partner, Head of the Chicago Banking Practice, Peat, Marwick, Mitchell and Company

Richard Breeden, Deputy Counsel, Office of the Vice President of the United States

Edward E. Brennan, President and Chief Operating Officer, Sears, Roebuck and Company

Robert E. Brewer, Senior Vice President of Finance, K Mart Corporation

Dan Brumbaugh, Deputy Chief Economist, Federal Home Loan Bank Board

William Burke, Chairman, American Bar Association Committee on Commercial Financial Services

Charles Calomiris, Assistant Professor of Economics, Northwestern University

Kenneth Cone, Assistant Professor of Finance, Graduate School of Business, University of Chicago.

David E. Conner, Chairman and Chief Executive Officer, Commercial National Bank of Peoria

Eugene R. Croisant, Executive Vice President, Continental Illinois National Bank

George Daly, Dean, Graduate School of Business, University of Iowa

Robert G. Dederick, Executive Vice President and Senior Economist, The Northern Trust Company; former Undersecretary of Commerce

Bernard Del Bello, Assistant General Counsel, ITT Corporation

William Dolan, Partner; National Director of the Banking Industry Program, Arthur Andersen & Co.

John F. Downey, Chief National Bank Examiner, Office of the Comptroller of the Currency

Franklin R. Edwards, Professor and Director of the Center for the Study of Futures Markets, Graduate School of Business, Graduate School of Law, Columbia University

Robert A. Eisenbeis, Wachovia Professor of Banking, School of Business Administration, University of North Carolina

Meyer Eisenberg, Chairman, American Bar Association Committee on Development and Investment Services

Robert Evans, President, American Financial Services Association

Walter D. Fackler, Director of the Executive Program and Professor of Business Economics, Graduate School of Business, University of Chicago

Gary C. Gilbert, Chief Economist and Director of Regulatory Affairs, Bank Administration Institute

Steven Goldsmith, Executive Vice President, Integrated Resources

Larry Gorrell, Partner, Head of the Chicago Banking Practice, Arthur Andersen & Company

Stuart Greenbaum, Director of the Banking Research Center and Norman Strunk Distinguished Professor of Financial Management, J.C. Kellogg Graduate School of Management, Northwestern University

Alan Greenspan, Chairman and President, Townsend-Greenspan Company, Inc.; former Chairman of the President's Council of Economic Advisers

Kenneth A. Guenther, Executive Vice President, Independent Bankers Association of America

Alice Haemmerli, Vice President for Public Policy, Chase Manhattan Bank

Robert S. Hamada, Deputy Dean and Professor of Finance, Graduate School of Business, University of Chicago

William C. Harris, Commissioner, State of Illinois Commission on Bank and Trust Companies; former President of the Conference of State Bank Supervisors

Edward Harshfield, Executive Vice President and Chief Operating Officer, Household Finance Corporation

Charles Haywood, Professor, University of Kentucky and Consultant to the American Bankers Association

Stephen B. Herman, Vice President and General Counsel, Household Finance Corporation

Paul M. Horvitz, Judge James Elkins Professor of Banking and Finance, College of Business, University of Houston

Alfred Johnson, Senior Vice President and Economist, Investment Companies Institute

Jerry Jordan, Senior Vice President and Economist, First Interstate Bancorp.; former Member of the President's Council of Economic Advisers

Robert W. Kamphuis, Jr. Executive Director, Mid America Institute

Edward J. Kane, Reese Professor of Banking and Monetary Economics, Ohio State University

George G. Kaufman, John F. Smith, Jr. Professor of Finance and Economics, School of Business Administration, Loyola University of Chicago

Thomas F. Keaveney, Partner, Head of the National Banking Practice, Peat, Marwick, Mitchell and Company

Silas Keehn, President, Federal Reserve Bank of Chicago

Paul R. Knapp, Senior Vice President, Chief Financial and Administrative Office, Kemper Financial Services, Kemper Group

Philip Knox, Vice President and General Counsel, Sears, Roebuck, and Company

Roger C. Kormendi, Associate Professor of Economics, Graduate School of Business Administration, University of Michigan; Institute Director, Mid America Institute

Gerald J. Levy, Vice Chairman, United States League of Savings Institutions; President, Guaranty Savings and Loan Association of Milwaukee, Wisconsin

Charles Lotter, Legislative General Attorney, J.C. Penney Co.

Joseph E. Luecke, Chairman and Chief Executive Officer, Kemper Group

Charles L. Marinaccio, Commissioner, Securities and Exchange Commission

Barbara McNear, Senior Vice President, First National Bank of Chicago

John McTavish, General Counsel, John Nuveen and Company

Allan H. Meltzer, John M. Olin Professor of Political Economy and Public Policy, Graduate School of Industrial Administration, Carnegie-Mellon University

Patrick Mulhern, General Counsel, Citicorp

Michael Mussa, William H. Abbott Professor of International Business, Graduate School of Business, University of Chicago

William B. O'Connell, President, United States League of Savings Institutions

James Pearce, Vice President and Economist, The Federal Reserve Bank of Dallas

Sam Peltzman, Professor of Business Economics, Graduate School of Business, University of Chicago

William Poole, Professor of Economics, Brown University; former Member of the President's Council of Economic Advisers

Theodore Roberts, President, The Talman Home Federal Savings and Loan Association of Illinois; former President of the Federal Reserve Bank of St. Louis

Richard N. Rosett, Dean of the Faculty of Arts and Sciences and Professor of Economics, Washington University

Robert S. Royer, Partner, Royer, Shacknai and Mehle

Karl Scheld, Senior Vice President and Director of Economic Research, Federal Reserve Bank of Chicago

John D. Seymour, Executive Director, Illinois Task Force on Financial Services

Michael Shepherd, Deputy Assistant Attorney General, United States Department of Justice

David Shute, Senior Vice President and General Counsel, Dean Witter Financial Services Group, Sears, Roebuck and Company

David Silver, President, Investment Companies Institute

Leonard S. Simon, Chairman and Chief Executive Officer, Rochester Community Savings Bank

Lamar Smith, Senior Economist, United States Senate Banking Committee

Irvine Sprague, Director, Federal Deposit Insurance Corporation

Ted L. Spurlock, Vice President, J.C. Penney and Company

Edward R. Telling, Chairman and Chief Executive Officer, Sears, Roebuck and Company

Robert E.L. Walker, Chairman, American Bar Association Committee on Banking Law; Partner, Holland and Knight

J.W. Henry Watson, Assistant Professor, Committee on Public Policy Studies, University of Chicago

Gilbert R. Whitaker, Dean, Graduate School of Business Administration, University of Michigan

Kenneth Wright, Senior Vice President and Economist, American Council of Life Insurance

INDEX

Information, 1; costs, 174; and deposit insurance, 109–110; and technological advances, 147, 148–149
Insider transactions, 178
Insurance, selling of by banks, 125, 140, 171, 178, 180–181, 182; *see also* Deposit insurance
Insurance companies, 10, 33, 114–115, 125
Interest rates, 1, 39, 119–120; ceilings, 42, 59, 62–63, 73, 124, 137, 142–143; and demand deposits, 20, 29, 59, 134, 143 n. 2; and deregulation, 191–192; and failure, 54–56, 72; and money market mutual funds, 142–143; and thrift institutions, 12, 55, 59, 72, 121, 130, 135–136, 142
International Monetary Fund, 131, 133
Investment advice, 179
Investment bankers, 11, 68, 171, 177
Iowa, 22

Jackson, Adnrew, 6
Jaffee, Dwight, 31–32
Johnson, Rodney D., 177, 182
J.P. Morgan, 178
Junk bonds, 56

Kane, Edward J., xi, 55, 62, 97–120, 175
Kansas, 22
Kaufman George C., x–xi, 49–75, 87, 175
Keaveny, Thomas F., 196
Keefe, Harry, 102
Knickerbocker Trust Co., 16
Knoxville, Tenn., 53, 71
Koch, Donald L., 169

Land developers, loans to, 90, 92
Large numbers, law of, 152–153
Latin America, loans to, 90–91
Law, John, 5
Lawrence, C., 156
Leasing activities of banks, 179, 180, 181
Lender of last resort, xi, 88, 192; and central banks, 83, 87, 88, 95; and concentration of banking, 153; and Federal Reserve, 16–17, 87, 94, 116, 172–173

Liquidity, 59–60, 73, 83
Litan, Robert E., 177
Local market concentration, 162
Lombard Street (Bagehot), 81–82
Long-term, fixed interest instruments, 136, 137
Lotteries, 184 n. 5

McCall, Alan S., 55
McFadden Act, 20, 185 n. 6
McFadden-Pepper Act, 7
McNear, Barbara, 196, 199–200
McTavish, John E., 200, 201
Maisel, Sherman J., 50
Malfeasance, 52
Management: and accounting procedures, 101–102; and conflict of interest, 151–152; and failure, 52, 93; liability, 102; removal of, 3, 72, 106
Management consulting services, 181
Martin requirements, 31
Marine National Bank, 16
Market-value accounting, xi, 89–91, 132–134, 196; and deposit insurance, 101–105, 136, 137
Marshall, W., 156
Maryland thrifts, 71, 85, 86, 88–89, 158
Mayer, Thomas, 34
Meinster, David R., 177, 182
Meltzer, Allan, xi, 32, 79–95, 193
Mergers, 150, 156, 157, 158–161, 198; forced, 23
Merrill Lynch, 115
Mexican debt, 93, 94, 115
Michigan, 13–14
Michigan National, 54
Miller, Merton H., 139
Miller, Randall J., 25
Mississippi, 22
Mobile home industry, 54
Modified payout, 107–108
Monetary Control Act, 174, 184
Money market mutual funds, 29, 63, 92–93, 122; drafts on, 173; and housing funds, 33; and insurance, 115; and interest rates, 142–143
Money supply, 25–27; and failures, 16, 20, 70–75; and Federal Reserve, 3, 8, 25–27, 41, 70, 131; and government monopoly, 4

Moral risk, 136–137, 174, 176
Morgan, J.P., 16
Mortgage bankers, 9, 12
Mulhern, Patrick, 192, 196
Municipal bonds, 27
Mussa, Michael, xi–xii, 121–143, 198, 199, 200
Mutual building and loan societies, 28
Mutual savings banks, 2–3, 28, 43–44 n. 13; *see also* Thrift institutions
Mortgages, 30–34, 40, 134; adjustable rate, 59, 60, 121, 137; and bank notes, 13–14; costs, 33; and discrimination, 34, 38–39; electronic search systems, 185 n. 10; holders, 44 n. 17; and mutual savings banks, 28, 44 n. 17; valuation, 103
Mutual savings banks, 18, 20, 106; and mortgages, 28, 44 n. 17

National Banking Act, 5, 22, 172, 184 n. 5
National banks, 5, 6–7, 14, 71; activity limitations, 184 n. 5, 185 n. 6; and insurance sales, 178, 180
National Commission on Consumer Finance, 37
National Credit Union Administration (NCUA), 2–3
National Credit Union Share Insurance Fund (NCUSIF), 22
National Currency Act, 5
Natter, Raymon, 173
Nebraska, 22
Nejezchler, Lynn, 54, 71
New York City, 9, 16, 125, 131, 144 n. 7
New York Clearing House, 14, 16
New York state; branch banking, 9, 58; deposit guarantees, 22, 44 n. 15; free banking, 13, 14
New York Stock Exchange, 16, 124
Nonbank banks, 122, 149, 171, 182, 185 n. 9; and deposit insurance, 175, 201
Non-full payout leasing, 180, 181
Noninsured deposits. *See* Uninsured deposits
North Carolina, 180
Northern Trust, 54
NOW accounts, 25, 155, 173

O'Connell, William B., 195, 196–197, 198, 200
Ohio, 22; thrift institutions, 43 n. 11, 85, 86, 88–89, 93, 99
Ohio Deposit Guaranty, 99
Oil industry loans, 54, 61, 90
Oklahoma, 22
Operations risk, 57–58, 73
Oregon, 54

Panic of 1873, 16, 28
Panic of 1893, 16
Panics, 16, 28, 70, 79–85, 94
Peach, Nelson W., 57
Peltzman, Sam, 192
Penn Square Bank, 17, 53–54, 130
Pension funds, 9, 10
Peterson, Richard L., 37, 52, 64
Philippines, 115
Pithyachartyakul, Pipat, 177
Politics, 145, 153–155; and deposit insurance, 97, 98, 105, 114, 117–120
Poole, William, 194
Posner, Richard A., 139
Private deposit insurance, xi, 3, 25, 100; and federal deposit insurance, 114–115
Production efficiencies, 125
Prudential Insurance, 122
Public Bank of Detroit, 54
Purchase and assumption transactions, 130
Pyle, David H., 113

Real-bills doctrine, 10
Real estate activities of banks, 171, 180, 181
Real estate investment trust (REIT), 57
Real Estate Settlement Procedures Act, 35
Recessions, 17, 79
Redlining, 34, 35, 36, 38
Regulation B., 35, 38
Regulation Q, 12, 29, 30, 33, 59, 63, 68, 169
Regulation Z, 35
Regulatory risk, 58–59, 60, 73
Repossession, restrictions on, 36
Reserves, 3, 119; and certificates of deposit, 174; and demand deposits,

ABOUT THE EDITORS

George G. Kaufman is the John F. Smith, Jr. Professor of Finance and Economics at the School of Business Administration, Loyola University of Chicago. He received his B.A. from Oberlin College, M.A. from the University of Michigan, and Ph.D. in economics from the University of Iowa. He was a research fellow, economist, and senior economist at the Federal Reserve Bank of Chicago from 1959 to 1970 and has been a consultant to the Bank since 1981. From 1970 to 1980 he was the John B. Rogers Professor of Banking and Finance and director of the Center for Capital Market Research in the College of Business Administration at the University of Oregon. He has been a visiting professor at the University of Southern California, Stanford University, and the University of California at Berkeley, and a visiting scholar at the Federal Reserve Bank of San Francisco and the Office of the Comptroller of the Currency. Professor Kaufman also served as Deputy to the Assistant Secretary for Economic Policy of the U.S. Treasury in 1976.

Professor Kaufman's teaching and research interests are in financial economics, institutions, and markets and in monetary policy. He has published extensively in the *American Economic Review, Journal of Finance, Journal of Financial and Quantitative Research*, and other professional journals. Professor Kaufman is the author of *Money, the Financial System and the Economy* (3rd ed.) and *The U.S. Financial System: Money, Markets, and Institutions* (3rd ed.) and co-editor of *Innovations in Bond Portfolio Management: Dura-*

tion Analysis and Immunization (1983). He has served on the board of directors of the American Finance Association, as president of the Western Finance Association and the Midwest Finance Association. He is presently on the editorial boards of four professional journals— *Journal of Financial and Quantitative Analysis; Journal of Money, Credit and Banking; Journal of Bank Research;* and *Journal of Financial Research.* He has served as a consultant to numerous government agencies and private firms, including the Federal Home Loan Bank Board and American Bankers Association. In 1982 Professor Kaufman was elected a trustee of the Teachers Insurance Annuity Association and College Retirement Equity Fund (TIAA-CREF), the largest private pension fund in the country.

Professor Kaufman is a research fellow with the Mid America Institute and the coordinator for the institute's project area on financial institutions and markets. He served as academic coordinator for the symposium.

Roger C. Kormendi, Associate Professor Economics at the Graduate School of Business Administration of the University of Michigan, received his B.A. in economics from the University of Virginia and Ph.D. in economics from the University of California, Los Angeles. He was an Assistant Professor and Associate Professor of Economics at the Graduate School of Business of the University of Chicago from 1976 through 1985, and was also on the faculty of the University of Chicago's Committee on Public Policy Studies, 1984–85. Since 1984 he has been the Institute Director and Director of Research of the Mid America Institute for Public Policy Studies.

Professor Kormendi's research interests are in the areas of macroeconomics monetary and fiscal policy and financial economics. He has published on a variety of topics in the *American Economic Review*, the *Journal of Political Economy*, the *Journal of Monetary Economics*, the *Journal of Law and Economics*, and other scholarly journals. He is the co-author with Michael Mussa of *The Taxation of Municipal Bonds: An Economic Appraisal.* His current research projects involve the issues of government deficits, the balance of trade, foreign aid, monetary instability, and the economics of defense mobilization. He is currently a research consultant to the World Bank and the Institute for Defense Analysis. He served as Assistant Editor of *Economic Inquiry*, has been a consultant to government agencies and private firms, and has testified several times before committees of both the U.S. Senate and the House of Representatives.

ABOUT THE CONTRIBUTORS

George J. Benston is Professor of Accounting, Economics, and Finance and Director of the Center for Study of Financial Institutions and Securities Markets at the Graduate School of Management, The University of Rochester. He is a member of the editorial Boards of *Journal of Finance, Journal of Bank Research, Journal of Money, Credit and Banking, Journal of Accounting and Public Policy.* His Ph.D. is from the University of Chicago. He also has an M.B.A. from New York University and a B.A. from Queens College and is a C.P.A. He has served as a consultant to the Federal Reserve Board, The National Commission on Consumer Finance, The Commission on Financial Structure and Regulation (Hunt Commission), The Federal Home Loan Bank Board, The Comptroller of the Currency, The Banking and Currency Committee of the U.S. House of Representatives, the American Bankers Association, and several private organizations, banks, and other corporations. Professor Benston is the author of over sixty-five scholarly articles, monographs, and books. His books and monographs include *Corporate Financial Disclosure in UK and the USA; Financial Services: The Changing Institutions and Government Policy;* and *Contemporary Cost Accounting and Control* (the latter two as editor); *Conglomerate Mergers: Causes, Consequences and Remedies; Investors' Use of Published Financial Accounting Data: A Review of Evidence from Research; Savings Bank-*

ing and the Public Interest; Bank Examination; Federal Reserve Membership: Consequences, Costs, Benefits, and Alternatives; An Empirical Study of Mortgage Redlining; and *An Analysis of Causes of Savings and Loan Failures.*

Franklin R. Edwards is Director of the Center for the Study of Futures Markets at Columbia University. He holds a Ph.D. from Harvard University and a J.D. degree from the New York University Law School. He has been a member of the faculty of the Columbia Business School since 1966 and also has served the school as vice-dean responsible for faculty and academic affairs as well as the institution's strategic planning.

Professor Edwards teaches the regulation of financial markets and institutions at both the Columbia Business School and the Columbia Law School. He also teaches courses dealing with the economics of financial markets and with government/business relations. Professor Edwards has published more than forty articles in these areas, is a frequent speaker before university and business groups, and has testified several times before congressional committees on proposed legislation.

Within the last few years he organized two major conferences: one on financial regulation, sponsored by the Columbia University Law School's Center for the Study of Law and Economics, and one on the regulation of futures markets, sponsored by the Center for the Study of Futures Markets. The first of these resulted in the book *Issues in Financial Regulation*, and the second was published as the second issue of *Journal of Futures Markets* (Summer 1981). He recently published two articles in *Journal of Futures Markets* dealing with the regulation of futures markets.

Prior to joining Columbia University, Professor Edwards worked at the Federal Reserve Board and at the Office of the Comptroller of the Currency in Washington, D.C. He is an active consultant to a number of regulatory agencies in Washington and to financial institutions and law firms.

Robert A. Eisenbeis is the Wachovia Professor of Banking at the School of Business Administration, University of North Carolina at Chapel Hill. He did his undergraduate work at Brown University and holds his M.A. and Ph.D. in economics from the University of

ABOUT THE CONTRIBUTORS 221

Wisconsin, where his major field was money and banking and minor fields were math and econometrics. He has served as a financial economist at the Federal Reserve Board specializing in banking mergers and acquisitions. He was Assistant Director of Research at the FDIC and was responsible for basic research, policy analysis, and review of proposed bank mergers. Dr. Eisenbeis returned to the Federal Reserve Board in 1976 where he became Senior Deputy Associate Director in the Division of Research and Statistics and served as the senior officer in charge of basic research on banking market structure and performance and analysis of proposed bank holding company acquisitions, mergers, and new holding company activities.

Dr. Eisenbeis has authored more than forty articles in professional economics, finance, and statistics journals. He has co-authored four books, and a fifth is in progress. Most recently he co-edited a book on banking strategy. Much of Dr. Eisenbeis's professional work has been devoted to problems in banking and finance with particular emphasis on the application of classification procedures to such problems as loan review, bond evaluation, and problem bank identification. He has served as a consultant to numerous agencies and firms, including the American Bankers Association.

He presently serves on the editorial advisory boards of three professional journals—*Journal of Bank Research, Journal of Banking and Finance, Journal of Economics and Business*—and has served in the past on the editorial boards of three other journals—*Issues in Bank Regulation, Journal of Financial and Quantitative Analysis*, and *Journal of Financial Research.*

Edward J. Kane is the Reese Professor of Banking and Monetary Economics at Ohio State University. He received his B.S. degree from Georgetown University and his Ph.D. from Massachusetts Institute of Technology. He has taught at Boston College, Princeton University, and Iowa State University and held visiting professorships at Istanbul University and Simon Fraser University. He has served as consultant for the Federal Deposit Insurance Corporation, the Federal Home Loan Bank Board, the Department of Housing and Urban Development, various components of the Federal Reserve System, the American Bankers Association and the Joint Economic Committee and Office of Technology Assessment of the U.S. Congress.

Professor Kane is a past president of the American Finance Association and a former Guggenheim fellow. In 1981 he won an Ohio State University Alumni Award for Distinguished Teaching. He has published widely in professional journals and serves currently on six editorial boards. Professor Kane writes occasional columns for *The American Banker* and is a research associate of the National Bureau of Economic Research. His most recent book is *The Gathering Crisis in Federal Deposit Insurance*. He is a trustee and member of the Finance Committee of Teachers Insurance Annuity Association (TIAA-CREF).

Allan H. Meltzer is the John M. Olin Professor of Political Economy and Public Policy at Carnegie-Mellon University. He has been a visiting Professor at Harvard, University of Chicago, University of Rochester, the Yugoslav Institute for Economic Research, the Austrian Institute for Advanced Study, the Getulio Vargas Foundation in Rio de Janeiro, and the City University, London. His reputation in the field of money and capital markets has brought frequent assignments with congressional committees and as a consultant to the President's Cabinet, the President's Council of Economic Advisers, the U.S. Treasury Department, the Board of Governors of the Federal Reserve System, and foreign governments and central banks.

Dr. Meltzer's writings have appeared in numerous journals, including the business press here and abroad. He has served on the editorial boards of many professional journals. His career includes experience as a self-employed businessman, management adviser, corporate director, and consultant to banks and financial institutions.

Professor Meltzer is a founder and co-chairman of the Shadow Open Market Committee. The members of the committee are economists from banks, business, and academic institutions organized to issue policy statements about current events to government agencies and to the public.

In 1983 Professor Meltzer received a medal for distinguished professional achievement from the University of California, Los Angeles.

Michael L. Mussa is the William H. Abbott Professor of International Business at the Graduate School of Business, University of Chicago. He received his B.A. degree from UCLA and his M.A. and Ph.D. in economics from the University of Chicago. He has served on the faculty of the Department of Economics at the University of

Rochester and also as a visiting faculty member of the Graduate Center of the City University of New York, the London School of Economics, and the Graduate Institute of International Studies in Geneva, Switzerland. In 1986 Professor Mussa was appointed a member of the President's Council of Economic Advisers. In 1981 he received the Prix Mondial Nessim Habif from the University of Geneva for his research in international economics.

Professor Mussa's main areas of research are international trade and finance, macroeconomics and monetary economics, and municipal finance. His publications include *A Study in Macroeconomics; Taxation of Municipal Bonds* (with Roger Kormendi); and numerous articles in *Journal of Political Economy, Journal of Monetary Economics, Journal of Money, Credit, and Banking, Journal of International Economics*, and other scholarly journals. In addition to research and teaching, Professor Mussa serves as an editor of the *Journal of Business*, as a member of the Business Forecast Panel for the Graduate School of Business, and as a consultant to the World Bank.

DATE DUE